Swell

A WATERBIOGRAPHY

JENNY LANDRETH

B L O O M S B U R Y
LONDON · OXFORD · NEW YORK · NEW DELHI · SYDNEY

Bloomsbury Sport
An imprint of Bloomsbury Publishing Plc

50 Bedford Square   1385 Broadway
London   New York
WC1B 3DP   NY 10018
UK   USA

www.bloomsbury.com

BLOOMSBURY and the Diana logo are trademarks of Bloomsbury Publishing Plc

First published 2017
This paperback edition first published 2018

British Library Cataloguing-in-Publication Data
A catalogue record for this book is available from the British Library.

Library of Congress Cataloguing-in-Publication data has been applied for.

ISBN: PB: 978-1-4729-3896-1
ePub: 978-1-4729-3897-8

2 4 6 8 10 9 7 5 3

Typeset in Minion by Deanta Global Publishing Services, Chennai, India
Printed and bound in Great Britain by CPI Group (UK) Ltd, Croydon CR0 4YY

MIX
Paper from
responsible sources
FSC® C013604

To find out more about our authors and books visit www.bloomsbury.com.
Here you will find extracts, author interviews, details of forthcoming
events and the option to sign up for our newsletters.

Contents

ABOUT THE AUTHOR

Jenny Landreth is a script editor and writer. She has written two guide books, on the great trees of London and on the best places to swim in the capital. Jenny has written for all sorts of publications, and was the main contributor to the *Guardian*'s weekly swimming blog, covering everything from pool rules, to swimming with children, and where to swim in New York. She lives in London. @jennylandreth

Introduction

The history of swimming is jam-packed with great photos of people in bizarre get-ups or extraordinary locations. But there is one photo I particularly love, of a group of ordinary-looking women leaping into an ordinary-looking lake – judging from their costumes it probably dates from the late 1920s. One of the women is star-jumping off a high board into the water; she is clearly happy and physically confident, exuding a sense of abandon. Our lives are very differently circumscribed – in every respect I have it much better than she did. We have, after all, come a long way. But still, I want to be her.

This is the story of how she and women like her got to jump into that lake and how I (eventually) did too. The story of how both of us became swimmers. How we came from having no rights to (almost) full parity, and how swimming can be a barometer for women's equality. How women had to fight for what we now take for granted and how the 'swimming suffragettes' – the women who did that fighting, did things first, who broke conventions and broke moulds, who achieved success against the odds – helped us. The doors for today's swimmers did not open by accident or benevolence, and this is the story of the women who forced these doors open.

The famous quote about Ginger Rogers – that she did everything Fred Astaire did only backwards and in high heels – feels very appropriate here. This is the story of the swimming world's equivalents of Ginger Rogers, and an opportunity to say thank you. Thank you for being so amazing, and for paving the way for the rest of us. But not everyone can be a Ginger Rogers, tap-dancing to Tesco in a glamorous outfit. That way social devastation lies. So this is not just a story about the famous women. This book features lots of ordinary people too. We all have our own story to tell about how we learned to swim (or not), our relationship with water, the people who encouraged us and the places we came to cherish or loathe. I'm inordinately pleased with myself for coining the word 'waterbiography' and I hereby grant you the right to use it freely. Because we all have a waterbiography, whether we're ordinary or not. This book is mine. I hope it encourages you to delve into your own watery past and put your story together.

There are a few themes in this book: class, equality and struggle; perhaps the most constant is the snack theme.

This book might make you hungry, so keep food handy while you read. And some of the inequities might make you rage; if that's the case, I highly recommend going for a swim.

*

Author's note: I'm not a big fan of cute terms for the lady version of things. Some words have dropped from use more readily than others but it still requires constant vigilance for the eager feminist. I find it hard not to use the term 'actress' for instance, but happily chucked the word 'comedienne' in the bin. It feels like it belongs to a different era, to Marti Caine. I also disdain the practice of marketing perfectly normal things differently to women – comedian Bridget Christie has a brilliant routine about Bic biros 'for her', about how women's hands are too delicate for your average man biro. I have an ironic pack of them on my desk but haven't found the strength to rip the plastic open yet.

So why have I called some women in my book 'Miss'? I've called myself Ms for a good thirty years and to my knowledge it has rendered no man impotent with rage. But historical reports invariably identify women via their marital status, using 'Miss' or 'Mrs', and when I'm referring to those reports, I do the same. I think it's preferable to use 'Miss' rather than to simply use women's surnames, and I've resisted that where possible, because it sounds rude and should be the preserve of public schools and Parliament. I have found that since I started using Miss and Mrs I've taken to wearing a pinny and curtsying whenever a man comes into my home. It just feels right.

Chapter 1

My Waterbiography (Part I)

I can't remember not being able to read, though as I was not some kind of infant genius, there was definitely a time. Once you know how to read, it's almost impossible to put yourself back in your own tiny shoes to when words were incomprehensible. You can recreate some of the feeling by visiting a country where their letters don't look like your letters and you've forgotten that phones can translate or that guidebooks are still a thing. But even then it's fleeting, and you know you can always point at pictures, that your thoughts continue to appear in recognisable forms and that sentences end with full stops. Once it's there, it's there.

But I *can* remember not being able to swim. I can recall the gush of panic at being out of my depth with no ability to save myself and, more prosaically, standing by the side of a pool staring at the water thinking 'That's not for me'. And while I now can swim, it's a skill that doesn't have quite the same sticking power as reading. Some years and lots of swimming miles later, I can still get to that same place of panic. Like one minute the skill was there, the next … gone. And then the particular wave will break, the moment will pass, I'll shove that feeling away and carry on. I can do it, after all.

I can remember not being able to swim, and I can remember learning, and who taught me. It was a two-step process, and the first step was taken at Sparkhill Baths in Birmingham in about 1969 when I was eight. The teacher was my Aunty Mary, my father's sister, a woman of indeterminate old age whose chin wobbled when she tried to suppress a laugh. Nobody thought we 'should' learn to swim, there was no compunction, sports were not a thing our family did. We were more arts 'n' crafts. My mum certainly couldn't swim and it remains a terrifying thought to her, though occasionally I've seen her try to get into the spirit and puff vertically across a pool in the hop-jump style of a nervous bird. Apparently my dad could swim, but he's not around to ask and none of his four daughters have any memories of him either taking us to the pool or joining us in the bitter sea on holidays (though there is one photo of him in shorts). I asked my mum once if Dad could swim and she said, 'Yes, your father was an amazing swimmer, he swam for the school.' But the information went no deeper than that, she had nothing else to add; my parents are of that generation that didn't divulge, and he'd have put 'being a good swimmer' in the same category as 'rescuing prisoners of war in Burma' – personal information one shouldn't discuss.

I think my father never took us swimming because he just didn't get involved, a parenting technique I applaud. I am from the days before parental input was invented. We weren't hoiked around from lesson to lesson all weekend; if you wanted to learn a language, you borrowed a book in that language from the library and read it; if you wanted to go horse riding, you'd go and catch a horse and ride it yourself. (Given that I'm talking about the urban Midlands, that should have been really hard but actually I did do that, and so can ride.) An adult wouldn't have done something because a child was interested in it; a child would have done something because an adult was interested in it. Fortunately for us, Aunty Mary liked to swim so we were taken along. She did us in batches, the older two first – I'm second in line – then the Little Ones, at her local pool.

Aunty Mary was a spinster from the days when that was a word; she was that family essential from all good 1950s domestic novels: the quirky aunt. She took us girls off in pairs to her tiny terraced house for funny sleepovers in funny beds. She had interesting collections in old boxes, little dolls that could break (oops), pyjama cases in the shape of dogs that she'd named (Pongo and Patch) and a funny sliding plastic door to her spare room that concertinaed back on itself. We wished we had concertinaed plastic doors instead of the boring wooden ones. She had time to make excellent hot chocolate. She also made miniature gardens in biscuit tins, using shiny foil milk-bottle tops for ponds and bits of gravel for vast rockeries. She was inventive, available and inquisitive. Mostly, with her wobbly chin and spinster status she seemed a bit odd, which in turn fascinated and slightly scared us. What Aunty Mary did was simple: she stepped into the space outside my mum's comfort zone, and took us to the pool.

I was marched to Sparkhill with a costume rolled in a towel under my arm. No fancy swimming bag for me, no shower gel, goggles, nothing other than the absolute necessities. We had what we needed and no more. The clothes I wore as a child were usually function over form and managed to be simultaneously too tight and shapeless. For swimming we had what were essentially thick cotton bags with small elasticated holes for our legs that left harsh red rings on our thighs. A fanciful band of shirring at the top may have looked decorative but that too left its mark – a stinging indented pattern across my chest. There was no similarity between adult and children's costumes; bikinis were certainly not an option, they were for remote, glamorous people in magazines. New things were rare – I'd have one new dress a year, from the Ladybird shop, with wooden ladybirds for buttons. They were treasured dresses; expensive. But at least, as second and largest child in a line of four, I was in the top tier so I got things first-hand. We had a lot of stuff handmade by my mum's friend – dresses all in the same pattern but different colours. Drip-dry nylon was exciting; I favoured this early nylon heavily, along with the colour orange, and tried to combine the two as much as possible. Orange nylon hot pants. An orange nylon bell-sleeved flared-leg pyjama suit with a long zip right down the front, which left a thick pinch mark on my skin when I lay on it. Sliding electrically between my orange nylon sheets in my orange nylon pyjama suit at night, I sparked like a distant fire.

At Sparkhill, the only real instruction we got from Aunty Mary was 'get in the water'. This wasn't delivered in a nurturing way, we got no gentle handling, there was no notion we might be frightened – and neither would we have thought to express that aloud to an adult. We were just expected to get in with no fuss. I remember being in the chilly water, under an echoing high ceiling. It would have definitely been gloomy; light bulbs were much dimmer then and only switched on if absolutely necessary. If you could see your feet on the bottom of the pool you didn't need the light on, it would have been extravagance when you had serviceable eyes. This was a time when economy was king, when to eat a whole Mars bar would have been a crazy dream; when we got one, which was extremely rare, we had to cut it into four.

I remember big brick-shaped tiles, white ones and black ones in lines. I remember playing with Aunty Mary and her bobbing round us, making fun games out of nothing.

Trying to run in the water, how it made your legs heavy and slow like a film at the wrong speed so you'd slow your voice down too, make it round and boomy. I remember shivering like a loon afterwards, dressing in wooden cubicles, trying to roll thick dry socks up thick damp legs. I remember talc. I remember Aunty Mary's swimming costume, so faded the lines of stitching looked bright; it had a skirt that floated out, and independent conical breast moulds that would dent if you pushed them (I never pushed them). I remember that we didn't get our hair wet, just the stringy ends. I don't remember it being a 'lesson', having structure. I don't know what I learned beyond 'get in the water'; probably not a thing.

The second part of the process was school swimming lessons in Wyndley Baths, Sutton Coldfield, in the early seventies, and this is where I can remember staggering across my first width, though God knows what stroke you'd call it. If that was doggy-paddle, the doggy would have drowned well before it reached its stick. My primary school was a convent and we were too busy singing charmingly at funerals to be taken swimming by the nuns; the only thing I can positively remember being taught there is that you shouldn't wear lipstick because it makes your own lip colour fade. Pale-lipped Sister Godrick told me that. Swimming at a convent would have necessitated stripping off at least a top layer which would have caused major problems for the nuns. (There would have been hysterical clutching of rosary beads if they'd known about other games we played. Girls in their final year, to mark a burgeoning independence, got their own cloakroom with a door that shut. We used the privacy mostly for mock séances, kneeling on the cold concrete under a huddle of gaberdine coats, a group of earnest eleven-year-olds in a Catholic school trying to contact the dead. The privacy of the cloakroom was also important for the keen monitoring of everyone's budding breast development. Well, I wasn't monitoring, I was in a vest till I was fifteen, but other more bosomy girls were. For this purpose, they invented a game – where 'game' means minor psychological bullying – where you had to hoik your shirt up, put your hands behind your head and walk towards the wall. If your nipples hit first, that was good. If your nose hit first, that was bad. Having a big nose and not a sign of breast, I always lost. I haven't tried it lately so can't offer a progress report.)

My secondary school was still Catholic but not a nunnery, and they did take us swimming; I remember the vicious whistle-pipping of our PE teacher, Mrs Hassle, the kind of nominative determinism a writer would shy from making up – too obvious. I was always the child 'least likely to' for Mrs Hassle, the child whose whole body sagged at the mention of doing any kind of exercise. I must have been a depressing prospect for her, but she was a depressing prospect for me too, so in that sense at least we were equal.

I was twelve by the time I swam that first width. By today's standards, that is too late. Not just very late, positively too late. These days, if you don't have your children entered for their Masters in swimming by the time they're seven, really, what has your nanny been doing? Some of the mad-eyed dangerous boys in my class – Jerry and Eamonn, I'm looking at you – could already swim so they went to the deep end, something I looked at with a mix of envy and fear. I was still at the stage of having to put my face in and blow bubbles. Still dry-haired. I just wasn't sporty, had no sense of my physical self. I suspect I knew even at twelve that I'd spend the next thirty years reading and smoking so there wasn't much point being good at something like this.

We were taken to Wyndley, a shiny new pool, a homage to glass and dark wood that sang modernity to us, sang about the future, was brightly lit! We must have taken messages of profligacy and extravagance from all that light: the sense that it would never run out; we could have all the electricity we wanted, when we wanted, whether we needed it or not. Fritter it away, we did. The pool's design included a filter system (I didn't know it was this at the time) which constantly pushed water down gutters that were pleasingly round-edged and white-tiled. The water slopped down in a continuous cycle to somewhere far far away in the building's mysterious bowels. The gutters were a major source of temptation and worry. The fear was being trapped, or losing something down there – a thin friend, maybe. Boys would shove their arms in as far as they could to see if they'd get dragged down until Mrs Hassle pipped her whistle to get their attention. I was in the rubbish group, and our challenge: a width. It was a huge distance, a width. We set off, a thrash of spindly uncoordinated arms hitting the water so hard it stung, backs arched, heads and bums up, a series of little U-shaped bodies bobbling across. Halfway, that desperate feeling that you're going to put your legs down despite yourself – overcome. Then a stretched hand, fingers feeling the cold tiles of the other side. Done it! Swum a width! First badge!

I didn't progress much further than that for years. I got more competent at swimming distances, I could maybe manage two or three widths, but I still swum in a U-shape and I still didn't get my hair wet. As a teenager, my exposure to the pool increased massively when I got a Saturday job in the cafe at Wyndley. I'd worked as soon as I was legally able in school holidays, we never had money and I liked having money, just a bit of it for sweets (I probably mean cigarettes) and cheesecloth shirts from Tammy's. The cafe was a great environment even for a sulky teenage girl: lifeguards made handsome by dint of their potential to actually guard life (one of them drove a budgie-yellow Porsche, which only now makes me think, how the hell did he afford that on his wages? And why did he choose such a dreadful colour?), and rough rude kids you could be difficult to. Swimming? Don't be ridiculous. I was sixteen, and, having been educated at a Catholic school, certainly didn't have the physical confidence to get my body out and put it in public in a costume. I was much happier in my cafe overalls. When I look at my body now, how little I care what people see or think, I wish I'd known then how lovely young people are. I did own a bikini from when I went on holiday for a week with Rosemary Lowe to the Scilly Isles. Just the one bikini – we would never have had choice. A photo exists of me in this bikini, and my arms are so tightly crossed you can palpably feel the tension; my gritted teeth are the giveaway. I loved this bikini – cotton, blue-and-white thin stripes, a little cord halter neck – but I wasn't happy in it. God no, embarrassing.

Then, in a twist of irony (synchronicity?) that would only become apparent years later when I got completely obsessed with outdoor cold-water swimming, I got a summer job running the cafe at Wyndley's sister pool, a lido beside Keeper's Pool in Sutton Park. Like I didn't appreciate how lovely the young are simply by dint of their youth, neither did I realise how much I should treasure this place. It was a purpose-built pool and it sat beside a murky lake with a diving platform which was almost exclusively used by the kind of boys (Jerry and Eamonn) who would spin the cars on fairground rides. The lido was small and shallow and splashy; the key feature of the place, for the youth of Sutton at least, was a grassy bank for sunbathing which we did with great alacrity and absolutely no sun cream, which hadn't been invented. Did anyone swim seriously in those days? I can't remember, or I wasn't looking. My youth rendered real swimmers invisible, in the way that age renders me invisible *from* real swimmers now.

I did get in the lido a couple of times, or at least sat on the edge and splashed my feet. And I braved the lake once, because I remember picking at the skin infection it gave me, in bored moments during my O-level exams. But mostly I slouched in a glorified shed, serving the kind of unhealthy crap I moan massively about in lido cafes now. Burgers with fried onions bought in pre-chopped. Hot dogs in brine, left on a slow-rolling heat all day, which I dragged out of the water with tongs and plopped onto cotton-wool bread. The little broken bits of hot dog, the knobbies floating at the bottom of the pan, I sold off cheap to the scamps and scoundrels of Sutton who were many and various. Crisps, sweets, hot Ribena, hot chocolate. A jug of filter coffee bubbled thickly away for the sophisticated kind of guy who drove round in, say, a budgie-yellow Porsche. Hot Bovril doled out one spoon per cup, except for the biker I quite liked who wanted it strong, Two Spoons Gary. And me, leaning out the hatch in my overalls, a teen constructed almost entirely from sarcasm, watching young people have fun in the pool and thinking, 'God. How shallow. You won't catch me doing that shit.'

Hundreds of years pass in a flash, and now you would certainly catch me doing that shit. Now I love swimming, love it so much that I go on swimming holidays. I prefer outdoor cold water, but anything will do, I'm really not fussy. I'm still not exactly a good swimmer but I will get my hair wet. And call it the spirit of nostalgia, or call it a peculiar kind of genealogy, but when I started to think about how I learned to swim, I wanted to return to the sites of my formative experiences. Where other people trace their family trees, or write their autobiographies in the vague hope that their children might be interested one day, I decided to revisit these three first pools. I started to write my waterbiography.

Or, at least, I tried to, only Sparkhill Baths was closed in 2009 following an 'asbestos incident'. I don't like people taking the piss out of the Brummie accent, but 'asbestos incident' really lends itself. There was a campaign and plenty of local newspaper headlines calling for the council to restore the pool for this bit of the inner city. But costs only ever go up, and the private sector waits eagerly at the door. The council decided to demolish the historic 1930s building and replace it with a shiny new facility built with some private investment. I hate the phrase 'private investment'. I looked at pictures of the building online and it's a box and it could be anywhere. I wasn't even sure it was in the same place. It's a bit of history, totally gone. I knew I'd have more luck at Wyndley, though, because my mum still lives just round the corner.

It was a rainy day when I headed up there, and externally, nothing had changed. Wyndley was opened in 1970, and if I say it's the largest centre of its kind in Birmingham, we already hit a problem. People in Sutton Coldfield do not say they are in Birmingham, even though they are. They are in a Royal Town which is separate, meaning better; this was decreed by a king, and you can do what you like to postcodes, it's still not Birmingham. Wyndley is a big brick square on a sloping site, the huge walls of glass are the defining feature inside and out. The building was refurbished after another 'asbestos incident' (it was obviously a popular Midlands building material) and the first tragic thing I noticed inside – no cafe. Where it once was, there's now a space with two large vending machines. Christ, that depressed me. In a country where obesity is rife and where generic shit is inescapable, this little cafe, home to delicious home-fried mass-produced burgers and hand-boiled frankfurters, gone. The fact that somebody might have talked to you, even just to say 'Sugar?' – gone. Of course, it is much more 'cost-effective' to get a bag of crisps out of a machine and train the managers to fill the shelves when they run out. I hate the phrase 'cost-effective' almost as much as 'private investment'. I was left wondering if Sutton was trying to delete my history. I made a bet with myself that if I went to the shopping precinct, the duvet shop where I had my other casual job will have gone too. I checked. It had.

(A historic note about the duvet shop. It's hard to imagine a time before duvets, but it exists. We used to have sheets and blankets on our beds, before duvets arrived in Britain in the late seventies. This was a time when the word 'tog' meant nothing to us, nothing at all. Duvets were terribly exotic and extremely desirable to the more forward-thinking Sutton Coldfielder, like me. I longed for one. The shop also sold towels, so even now, not only do I know the difference between a bath sheet and a bath towel, I can still do a complex sales pitch explaining the virtues of different togs for different seasons.)

In Wyndley, I changed and put my clothes in a plastic basket which I handed in through a big hatch to a lifeguard, who put it on a shelf and handed me a rubber wristband. I remember timed entry on busy days, the constant fuzzy announcements – 'All green wristbands get out of the water. ALL. GREEN ...' Today it's still the same funny old system it ever was, and I like it – it's more personal than lockers, an opportunity for eye contact with someone. I wonder when they'll get something more cost-effective. I went through to the pool, which existed in my memory as an Olympian field of water, stretching as far as the eye can see ...

... to find it's not that at all. The pool is the standard 25m with a deep diving area to one side, but still it's a great space. So much glass means that there are no walls to clutter up with posters and signs and warnings and adverts. It's clean and light, the view of trees a welcome untidy touch in a highly regulated environment. The seventies design features – the dark colour of the wood, the concrete diving boards – have accidentally remained contemporary, it looks almost fashionably Scandinavian. Today there's a boom across the pool so you can't swim a long length. Instead I swim across into the diving area which used to feel so terrifying I could get palpitations just looking at it as a child. It's rather glorious; a view opens up underwater of legs and space and deepening blue that's very pleasing. Swimming across that deep section, I get an image in my mind, an aerial shot, a hard-working body ploughing across a vast blue ocean. As the camera pulls back, the body becomes smaller and smaller until all you can see is sea.

After my swim, I collect my basket and ask the lifeguard if the boom is ever lowered so you can swim right down, like in the old days. 'No,' he says, 'but it would be great. Why do you ask?' I tell him I love swimming long lengths and he sighs 'me too'. We discuss how it's a disgrace that Birmingham has no fifty-metre pool and he tells me a bit about his own swimming life: swimming for the county, training all over the place. And I tell him about my local pool, the ninety-metre Tooting Lido, so we chat about outdoor swimming, how he did his first open-water swim last summer and how much he loved it. It's just a moment, just a conversation. It simply feels good, two swimmers coming to this mutual passion from entirely different directions – he young and competitive, me slow but sure. The hare and the tortoise, if either could swim.

My final pool of the trio is at Keeper's, in Sutton Park, which begins just behind the Wyndley complex. I love Sutton Park, it's the best park in the country, but I don't live there. I wouldn't fit in Sutton Coldfield, not least because of the Royal Town mentality. My mum's friend once said that she'd like to vote Lib Dem, but the Sutton candidate had a beard, and 'if he knew Sutton people, he'd know we would never vote for someone with a beard'. I neither have a beard nor am I standing for election, but that's a fairly unambiguous message. Sutton people are proud of the park and rightly so, it's nearly two and a half thousand acres, plenty big enough to get lost in, and I've managed to do that more times than not. It's a great place for running, wildlife, trees, ponds, walking, and at one point in my life, not swimming. The council website describes it as 'delivering a sense of wilderness within an urban environment' which is a good attempt to destroy the magic of the place. I went off, through this cherished spot in a landlocked city, in search of Keeper's Pool.

I found Keeper's Pool – it's one of seven lakes in the park. But of the lido that used to be beside it, there was not a trace. It is gone, completely. My little cafe shack, gone. Even the lake's diving platform has gone. The bank we used to sunbathe on is still a bank but without the context. In a park that prides itself on being 'untouched', one particular bit of history has been utterly erased. First opened in 1887, the lido was a victim of arson in 2003 and 2004, and so demolished and the site re-landscaped. Here for over a hundred years, then done and dusted, like it never happened. I felt personally affronted. Every time I visit the park now with my children, we walk past the spot where the lido used to be and they say, 'Do tell us Mum, did something else used to be here?' So sarcastic. If I lived in Sutton, I'd campaign for a lido in the park, but given the animosity towards people with beards, I can barely bring myself to think how people who like to swim outdoors would fare.

My waterbiography has not had an auspicious start. Two out of three places, gone, even if in one of them I barely got in the water. I certainly hadn't learned to swim in any meaningful way in any of them, hadn't progressed beyond the anxious scrabbling and bobbing. And here I am, a keen swimmer with a waterbiography that moves way beyond that hopeless beginning. Because now, I've swum all over the place. Hot, cold, outdoor, indoor, new, old, beautiful, ugly. I've swum in glacial lakes, and pools with CCTV in the changing rooms and signs in the showers that shout 'NO SHAVING NO SPITTING'. My life of swimming has mostly happened in public pools, as they are what I prefer. 'Wild' swimming has its attractions, but seems to have an inbuilt conundrum. Here's a lovely unspoilt place, says Person A. YOU'VE ATTRACTED ATTENTION TO OUR LOVELY UNSPOILT PLACE, yells Person B. Well, I'm Person C – I like a nice splash-about in a river as much as the next person, but I don't always want to pull up my camper van beside a freezing tarn and call out 'hurry up with your oatcake, Jonty, there's a super spot here'. Sometimes, I can't be bothered getting wet and weedy. Mostly, I want showers and I want lifeguards. I think most of us are Person C, the fearful ninnies who feel better when there's someone watching over us (not staring, that's weird). Or at least, we're ninnies most of the time, we may go a little 'wild' on our holidays, in the sea (and probably call it just plain swimming), but mostly, when it's scary we stay within our depth, and quite often don't want to get our hair wet.

This was my start, and I owe a debt of gratitude to Aunty Mary for getting me in in the first place. But who got *her* in? When she was a child, in the second decade of the twentieth century, most women didn't swim, particularly not those from her lower-middle-class background. Even by the 1960s she was unusual. But something must have drawn her to it, told her it was possible. As I stand at the edge of a thriving London lido, dressed in a relatively meagre scrap of Lycra in the first quarter of the twenty-first century, there's a whole line of women behind me who kept going, kept getting in, kept breaking the taboos of what women could and couldn't do. Made it possible for me to be here. If it wasn't for this bunch of formidable women, my swimming foremothers, I wouldn't have been in any pool. I'd like to know who they are; I'd like to thank them. But to be able to tell the full story of how I am allowed to be a swimmer at all, we need to go much further back.

Chapter 2

The Great Outdoors

If the tide is out on certain beaches in Britain, you have to traipse through a lot of mud to be able to swim in clear water. As with these beaches, so with history. To find women in the history of swimming in Britain, you have to traipse through a lot of mud. The tide was out for a very long time. That in itself isn't anything new; history is almost always about men. What is amazing, looking at the amount of restrictions and myths and baggage we carry from down the muddy years, is that we ever got in the water at all.

People have been flinging themselves across bodies of water in all sorts of higgledy-piggledy fashions since forever, but the consensus is that the Romans officially brought swimming to Britain. Women had their fun in Roman bathing houses – the posh ones would have cavorted separately from the men in their own space, and the less posh would have been there for various man-servicing duties. Caesar was considered to be a great swimmer, and Roman soldiers were required to learn to swim in their armour, an essential skill if you're going to be conquering islands like Britain, not just shaped by water but drenched in it. When you think what a fuss we make nowadays if the cut of our swimsuit isn't exactly to our taste, you realise what formidable athletes these guys must have been. They would have looked on Iron Man competitions with scorn – 'Yeah. I'll do that before breakfast. Then what?' But apart from those few posh lady cavorters who probably never even took their feet off the bottom of the Roman bath, there are no women in this part of the story. We do start to appear further along the timeline, but only in a passive role as sexual protagonists. Viking soldiers developed a cleansing ritual called Haagdyve, where they would get in the sea around Shetland and the Orkneys and wash themselves, a thing that came about because women rejected them if they were dirty. In some senses, not much has changed; there aren't many men who'd get into those freezing waters today without some sort of promise at the end of it.

There's a great chunk of time when women only appear in the swimming story as mythological creatures, and you have to wonder why mermaids were invented. They have been responsible for luring innocent men to their watery deaths since Homer wrote *The Odyssey*, and are an idea that continued right to the end of the nineteenth century. Considering the pace at which the world was industrialising and developing at that point, you'd have thought the notion of mermaids might have bitten the dust earlier, but the persistence of imagination is an admirable thing, and mermaids were a very useful invention. A socialist analysis of mermaids, if such a thing were to exist, might suggest they were a tool of the bosses invented to avoid health and safety complaints, because when men were out at sea for months on end, dehydrated and malnourished, hallucinations were a common result. If a man chucked himself overboard thinking a beautiful siren was calling to him, was that a result of his mental state, of understandable human frailty brought on by terrible working conditions? No, it was a watery witchy woman wot done it. A feminist analysis might say that men invented mermaids to allow them to shift responsibility for their behaviour onto women. Sexy women are too powerful! Men cannot resist! Even the most benign version – the poor innocent drowning woman that some man heroically wishes to save – doesn't cover itself with glory. Women are either sexy and evil, or frail and needing protection. And they manage all of this without even having vaginas! Funny how it worked out that marriage to a human man always saved them. I apologise if I've spoiled a perfectly decent Disney film so early in the book. It won't happen again.

Men kept flinging themselves into water with no discernible skill, making it up as they went along, until near the end of the sixteenth century with the publication of the first swimming book in this country. *De Arte Natandi* was written in 1587 by Sir Everard Digby (a name that is too perfectly pompous even for sitcom), and he wrote in Latin to give it the air of Proper Science. Translated into English in 1595 by Christopher Middleton, it was published at a time when philosophers were keen to bring order to the universe, to rank things – God was superior to man, and man was superior to the animals, and as some of the 'best' animals highest up the chain of command could swim, man needed to be better than them. Swimming ability had other advantages, the book said. As well as underlining men's superiority, it also enabled them to escape from danger, and it had health benefits. The book is illustrated with woodcuts of a rather endearing roundly man figure, frog-legging across a flat stream with his hands often crossed protectively over his bits.

It's not really surprising that women weren't joining in. As well as matters patriarchal and being evil sex mermaids, for us water had another, different set of connotations and potential dangers. Our relationship to it could best be described as 'risky'. Trial by water was generally accepted as an unofficial way of weeding out witches. In 1597, around the same time as that first swimming book, James VI of Scotland published his book *Daemonologie*. In it, he decreed that water had magical powers given by God. He said, 'God hath appointed that the water shall refuse to receive them in her bosom that have shaken off the sacred water of baptism and wilfully refused the benefit thereof.' Basically, he was rubber-stamping the idea of dunking disobedient women. For the next two hundred years (and add another fifty years for rural areas where ideas took longer to shift), water was punishment for a particular kind of woman. I would almost certainly have been that 'particular kind of woman' – and if you've ever found a stray hair on your chin, one of those ones that come from nowhere and grow inches in a day, so would you. A small mole on your arm? Own a cat? DROWN THE WITCH. The first recorded case of a 'swimming' was in 1615, one Mary Sutton of Bedford, who unfortunately floated. The last official case was in 1809; there was a woman sentenced in 1817 but she survived because the water level was too low, and unofficially, there were instances in rural Britain as late as 1864. Mermaids and witches, on they persist. The idea that a woman might, in that climate, fancy nipping down to the river to bathe was unlikely. The possibility that you might be reported as a witch as you dandled along would be enough to frighten off even the most determined of us.

But there were two types of women in history. The first kind (definitely the witchy type) was solid. Wrapped in layers of old boiled wool of indeterminate sludgy colour, or fabrics woven from stalky vegetable matter, she would have sunk to the bottom of a horrid lake like a boulder, probably giving off a noxious gas as she mouldered down there. But not all women were witch material. There was another, more delicate kind of woman – let's call her a 'lady' – and she was equally unsuited to water. Prone to fluttering hysteria and flights of nervous fancy, she was much more decorative. Primped and fancied-up, she would have floated on the top of a pretty babbling brook, fizzing and popping like a gilded prawn cracker. She might have paraded at spas as they became fashionable but would have rarely chosen to get in and get wet. The very thought! If she did get in, it would have been as a coy object to be spied upon salaciously. She was the kind of woman who inspired art and poetry. Poetry like 'The Swimming Lady, Or, A Wanton Discovery', written by Pepys in the 1680s. In what is essentially a piece of early porn, Pepys tantalisingly describes her stripping off slowly, thinking she's not seen. Each part of her body is slowly revealed until she can wait no longer, and 'Into a fluent stream she leapt'. At that point,

> Each Fish did wish him self a man,
> about her all were drawn,
> And at the sight of her began
> to spread about their Spawn:

(Shall we just take a moment to appreciate that charming image? He carries on …)

> She turn'd to swim upon her back
> and so displaid her Banner,
> If *love* had then in Heaven been,
> he would have dropt upon her.

Turns out, there's a young man watching, with poor impulse control. He, and who can blame him, leaps in and pulls her to shore, where he 'covered her agen'. While she lies crying (which is understandable, this being sexual assault) he fortunately agrees to marry her. Delightful, isn't it? So on the one hand, women were being drowned as witches, and on the other they were unwitting participants in the male gaze, and more. And frankly, if my only swimming options had been witch or sexy lady to be peeped upon, I too would have stayed home and stayed dry.

Over the late 1600s into the 1700s, we still had our heels stuck in the mud, but were starting to glimpse some of the clear water in the distance. Our inland spa towns, originally built around their water sources in Roman times, began to attract wealthy visitors corralled in opulent buildings especially created for the purpose. There were women among their number! And it wasn't just immersion in water that became popular, the temperature of the water was relevant too. Talk about 'working with what you've got' – cold water became known as a cure-all for diseases internal and external, and we were fortunate to have plenty of cold water, so people began to flock to the coast. There's a certain democratisation in the sea since it's free for everyone, so while spas were for the elite, sea bathing gained in popularity across all classes. Women weren't excluded, but we were siphoned off to separate parts of the beach because the sights on offer presented us with 'moral dangers'. There was no such thing as a swimming costume at that point, so men mostly swam and frolicked nude and women needed to be protected from such distressing sights. (In that sense, I think we may have come full circle. There are occasions now when I see some of the teeny half-thongs men wear, the whole lot waxed and all the bits slung to one side in what looks like a bright Lycra condom, that I definitely feel I need protecting from.) This is where it gets a bit 'shutting the stable door': even though women were segregated onto a separate area of the beach, they were required to be modest; it wasn't 'proper' for a woman to be seen in her bathing attire, what was essentially a flannel nightie. I don't know who was supposed to be seeing it, but presumably they never knew (cf. that Pepys poem) who might be lying in the dunes trying to get a flash of skin. To us now, wearing a flannel nightie in the water would seem massively restrictive (and if you ever tried for your life-saving badge while wearing your pyjamas, you might empathise), but then, given the many layers of metal and bone and petticoat and undergarment and silk and wool that women were required to layer themselves in for normal day wear, it must have felt enormously freeing.

By the late 1700s, we started to clear the mud and paddle in the shallows of the water itself, because at last there are accounts of brave pioneer women getting into the sea. In November 1782, novelist Fanny Burney describes her adventures: 'We rose at six o'clock in the morn and by the pale blink o' the moon went to the seaside where we had bespoken the bathing-woman to be ready for us, and into the ocean we plunged. It was cold but pleasant. I have bathed so often as to lose my dread of the operation.' Fundamental human experience really doesn't change, however many the years, and those last two sentences will have resonance for any cold-water swimmer today, for whom cold is more than pleasant, it's desirable. It's enlivening, and exhilarating and somehow essential and maybe it's written in your DNA but you don't know that until you know it. And the notion that it might be addictive is certainly one that will chime. Swimming in cold water is ridiculous, it seems unfathomable, it's maybe even a form of madness, and yet here we are, doing it. And then doing it again the next day, willing the temperatures to drop.

The bathing-woman Fanny Burney refers to would have been a woman in charge of a newfangled 'bathing machine', a kind of glorified garden shed on wheels, invented by a Quaker to help preserve a woman's modesty. In this hut, our plucky novelist would have changed into her flannel slip before some hardy working woman, known as a dipper, yoked a horse to the shed, pulled her to the shoreline and gently (or perhaps otherwise) persuaded her into the water. In that simple image lies a whole world of class and privilege. Two women, one a pale and fragile creature, a woman of words and ideas, undressing out of her silks and fineries in a shed, her delicate bones rattling as the cranky wheels grind down the beach; the other a necessarily solid woman built of hard physical graft, toiling away to get this contraption across the pebbles. One woman in service to the modesty and decorum of the other. Before I start a class war, some small consolation might be found in the fact that some of these dippers were celebrated figures in their towns. Mary

Wheatland, immortalised on postcards as 'The Bognor Mermaid', a title which holds less glamour than its inventor might have hoped, ran the machines to the east of the pier on that beach from 1849 until her retirement, aged seventy-one, in 1906. Brighton's most famous was Martha Gunn, described as a 'large, sturdy woman' who dipped from 1750 to 1814 when she retired from ill health. After sixty-four years of hoiking posh women down the pebbles in a shed, Martha earned the ultimate Brighton accolade of having a pub named after her. Still there, it's now a gastropub. It's unclear whether that's what Martha would have wanted.

The most luxurious of these bathing machines had canopies that extended from their roofs almost down into the water, so you could be immersed and nobody would catch a glimpse of you at all. And if you displayed any reluctance, your dipper might well have given you a good old shove into the water. Very relaxing. And don't forget: Fanny Burney was doing this in November. At this point in history, the sea-bathing season was in the worst possible months, because the colder the water, the more medicinal the effect. On a hot summer's day, even the grey chop of the North Sea can be hard to resist, but in the middle of November? Remarkably easy to stay on dry land. It's still a challenge despite all our fleeces and thermal layering and socks and hand warmers and flasks of tea for afterwards. Having some beefy woman prepared to push you in might be really good incentive to get a move on. Fortunately, and eminently sensibly, the bathing season shifted at the start of the nineteenth century to when the temperatures were warmest.

It is compulsory if you're writing any kind of history of women to include Jane Austen, and like Fanny Burney, Austen was a keen sea bather too. She wrote to her sister of the delights of getting in the water at Lyme Regis in 1804, and 'staying in rather too long'. It would have been one of the few activities an unmarried woman was allowed to indulge in, and almost for that reason alone, however cold the water, it certainly beats needlepoint. Austen gave Mrs Bennet a line in *Pride and Prejudice* that 'a little sea-bathing would set me up for ever' to underline the health benefits, which would have been Austen's official reason for enjoying the water, but it also put distance between Mrs Bennet's view of coastal trips, and that of Austen's younger characters. Their enjoyment of places like Brighton and Weymouth leaned less towards the therapeutic and more towards the 'morally lax' seductions and temptations. Ah, the young. Nothing changes.

For every famous lady novelist recounting her adventures, there would have been a merry band of ordinary working women and girls who maybe could and would get in the water. Women who worked in harbours and fishing villages, or who were raised by rivers or on the coast. Girls who might have joined their brothers frolicking in the waves on a hot day. These were not women whose whole lives revolved around leisure, they were not the ones discussed in fine literature and draped across lithographs. But they're a reminder that the pleasures of being immersed in water have never been something that only belongs to one class.

'By 1800 men and women were bathing together in the sea in some cases,' reports Christopher Love in *A Social History of Swimming*. 'Although there were already trends towards segregation of the sexes in bathing,' he goes on, 'there was also an acceptance of mixed bathing in some areas and social circles.' By the middle of that century, though, those social circles were very limited, bohemian even, and segregated swimming was the norm. These were Victorian times after all, and we know that in those repressed days even the sight of a nicely turned table leg might send men into a giddy lustful spin, let alone the thought of being in the same bit of sea as an actual living woman. The queen herself may have been gaily bathing twice a day on her holidays for pleasure, but in other respects her time was marked by moralistic prudery. Yes, our very own Queen Victoria took to the sea at the Isle of Wight in July 1847. Encouraged by Prince Albert who was a fan, Queen Victoria had a rather fancy bathing machine parked at their private beach at Osborne House. From within it, she'd emerge in billowing robes and a perky sea cap, remaining under the canopy until only her head was visible above the water. That was as much about privacy as modesty – the whole of the Western Empire might have collapsed in shock and disgust if a picture had been taken of the queen 'undressed'. She wasn't the first royal to swim, but she was the first royal woman and the first to do it for pleasure not just health. 'I thought it delightful,' she is reported as saying, 'till I put my head under water when I thought I should be stifled.' It marks the birth of an enduring image still guaranteed to enrage lane swimmers in any modern pool: the woman swimming breaststroke with her head up, in a decorated swim cap, probably chatting.

Because mixed bathing roused a red-faced blustering concern, by the 1860s all sorts of by-laws were in place in coastal resorts to stem this source of potential outrage. By-laws like this one, from Suffolk: 'A person of the female sex shall not, while bathing, approach within one hundred yards a place at which any person of the male sex, above the age of twelve years, may be set down for the purpose of bathing.' By-laws that led to situations like one reported in Hastings, where a male swimmer was required to stand some distance from his own wife, vainly shouting directions to her while she tried to master the basics of swimming. You can picture the scene: a man standing way up the beach, bellowing fruitlessly to a woman in the water, 'Move your arms. YOUR ARMS.'

The *Guardian*, obviously approving of these by-laws, reported in the summer of 1864 that 'prudery apart, the present mode of bathing at those places can scarcely be described as decent'. It's a nice touch, to suggest it's not prudery. It's prudery. 'It is the sort of thing which on the banks of the Thames or other rivers, wherever these banks are peopled, is magisterially prohibited as "indecent bathing"! Now it is not obvious why, if prohibited in our rivers, it should be permitted on our coasts.'

Outside the rigorous policing of behaviour on beaches, as Britain became increasingly industrialised, other things started to change. The working class started to 'holiday' (in itself, another new invention) at the seaside as rail travel became cheaper. There was commercial entertainment provided at these places, and exercise became popular; women were encouraged towards the gentler sports of croquet, tennis and some kind of gymnastic, ribbon-flinging exercise known as calisthenics, perhaps a kind of early Pilates. And sea bathing became quite the thing for women – bathing, as distinct from swimming, which was still a manly preserve; only a small number of women were learning to swim, but more were getting in the water.

Spurred on by the example set by the queen, women were given their own areas to bathe in modern resorts around the country; usually they had at least one Ladies' Bathing Pond, but the bigger resorts offered a selection, some cold, some temptingly 'tepid'. And one newspaper writer was quick to offer tips on how 'the fair sex' should approach bathing. Don't get in on your first day at the seaside, he advised, you need time for your system to adjust to all that 'unwonted ozone'. Two hours after breakfast, ladies should 'undress as quickly as possible and enter the water boldly'. That remains good advice; how many of us have spent a good half-hour, water up to our blue-mottled thighs, waiting for the 'right' wave, rising on tiptoes or giving a little jump to avoid waves splashing our bellies? The writer knew that hair would be an issue, and urged ladies to '[take] care to wet the top of the head even if, in deference to luxurious tresses, a regular "duck" is not effected'. Oh how I love the phrase 'luxurious tresses'. It makes me think of Cheryl [insert current surname here] off the shampoo ads. The article goes on: 'Take a succession of brisk dips immersing the body right up to the chin, and then retire to the machine, having spent under five minutes in the water.' Five minutes? Five minutes! It takes me longer than that just to get *in*. But after that humungous effort, the paper decrees that if your teeth are chattering and you have 'a blue appearance around the mouth and nails', you've got to drink a strong brandy while you dress. There are no concurrent newspaper reports of hypothermic women with big hair and blue lips staggering around the beaches of Britain necking brandy, but it's an image I shall cherish.

Of course, then as now, not all women were put off from swimming by worrying about their hair, as illustrated by the activities of one Mrs Cecil Samuda. *The Gentlewoman's Book of Sport* (published in 1892) included various chapters written by experts in each particular field, and alongside a heavy emphasis on various types of fishing (trout, salmon, bass and tarpon each got a chapter) and the expected inclusion of tennis, archery, skating and so on, Mrs Samuda wrote a chapter on swimming, recounting her own experiences with the stated aim of enthusing other women. And apart from the couple of stories she recounts where she was required to use her prodigious life-saving skills – in my limited experience, I've never found that stories about people nearly drowning are the ones to trot out if you're hoping to encourage others to plunge in – Mrs Samuda was clearly a formidable swimmer, and a blast. As was her sister. She records an event where this sister, aged just sixteen, as a result of a bet agreed to swim a quarter of a mile in the sea 'not only wearing all the undergarments of a lady including corsets, but also attired in a heavy Fishwife serge dress [which sounds exactly the type of thing sold in the Toast catalogue for £350], boots, hat and gloves, and carrying in one hand a huge scarlet Turkey twill umbrella opened [nice touch], and in the other a large bouquet of somewhat gaudy flowers, presented to her for the occasion'. What a fabulous picture of an inspiring young woman. And, of course, both her hands being full, the young woman would have been required to swim this quarter of a mile using only her legs. If you've ever done drills in a pool holding a float and just kicking, you'll know what a prodigious feat that was. I can barely manage 50 metres on a good day. She arrived on the beach 'amidst the cheers of an admiring crowd'.

Mrs Samuda fondly recalls the end-of-summer-holiday water gala that she and a group of young fellow swimmers of both sexes put on. The programme, for the week of 6–11 September 1890, looks fun. A week of races short and long, on your back, on your front, one-handed, legs only, then some diving and floating, and all culminating in a grand 'Water Carnival' which sounds brilliant and in need of reviving. The main event would be a swim from the middle of a lake to shore, with a slight difference in that the competitors were to be dressed in 'any old clothes which they could collect', a list which included boots, hats and parasols. Then on to the showing-off bit, where the competitors 'are at liberty to exhibit as many water-feats as they choose' such as, Mrs Samuda suggested, 'writing a letter, placing it in an envelope, addressing it and returning with it safely to shore'. Writing a letter in the middle of a lake may not sound like the biggest draw in terms of spectator excitement, but Mrs Samuda assures us that it's 'most amusing', and it's certainly odd. Other water feats she lists include 'Catherine Wheels in the water' 'undressing under water' and 'smoking under water', a trick that it's fair to say has completely fallen out of favour today.

To complete the image you may have of Mrs Samuda, her preferred swimming get-up deserves a mention. 'I most strongly recommend scarlet Turkey twill for bathing dresses,' she says. 'It is delightfully light, holding no water, it takes a long time to fade or wear out and is most picturesque in appearance. We have all ours made with knickerbockers and a short skirt, a good deal trimmed with white cotton braid; we also wear scarlet thread stockings, for decency's sake, and scarlet waterproof caps.' It's worth thinking about Mrs Samuda wearing this lot puffing away on a cigarette underwater next time you're looking for a swimming hero.

Recounting her swimming adventures on the Isle of Wight, Mrs Samuda talks of stepping out of the bathing machine, and these bulwarks of respectability had become a regular sight at the biggest resorts in the late nineteenth century. But they cost money to keep and use, and so excluded anyone but the wealthy and the growing middle class. And the rise of 'the family' meant that men and women wanted to bathe together, with their children. Families were put off by segregated bathing, and families meant cash for burgeoning holiday resorts. Thirty years after the moral blustering and imposition of strict segregation by-laws on the beaches, the pendulum of moral outrage began to swing in the other direction. Society was becoming mobile and freer. It was a clash between the old repressive ways, the province of the middle and upper classes, and the changing social mores. As 'the family' rose, so inexorably did mixed sea bathing. By 1899, the first resorts were announcing their conversion, with the glamorous destination of Bexhill being one of the first places to officially allow it. And 'mixed bathing will be permitted at Yarmouth and Gorleston during the coming season', the newspapers announced in April of that year. 'Hitherto the corporation has voted against this form of amusement.'

By 1901, legal segregation by sex had ended on British beaches. It had taken a hundred years for us to go from starting to mix, to being segregated, then swimming together again. Mixed bathing had been in fashion, out of fashion, legislated against, and then finally legalised. The bathing machine, that constant and lurking reminder of the horrors of impropriety, had never been compulsory anyway, and now also fell out of fashion. John K. Walton talks in

The British Seaside of how in 1912 'mixed and "macintosh" bathing [on beaches] were spreading even among the ostensibly respectable'. A telling use of 'even' there – being in mixed company still marked you out as belonging distinctly below stairs, though it was permitted. (And 'macintosh bathing' isn't the perverts' charter its name might suggest. It meant going to the beach in your cossie, with a mac over the top. We've all done it. It came about because the compulsory changing facilities on beaches were costly and limited.) One of the most vocal opponents to mixed bathing was a Tonbridge councillor, Mr Donald Clark, who raved that 'by making girls look like wet Scotch terriers, mixed bathing stops more marriages than any other cause'. Mr Clark's specificity of dog breed is very impressive, and it was maybe that attention to detail that encouraged the *Daily Mail* to employ him to rove the coast of Britain over the summer, looking for offence. It's interesting to see that it's the same paper now as it ever was.

Mr Clark may have been a frothing prude but those making our laws, whose cogs normally grind exceedingly slowly, were relaxing about new freedoms. A Home Office memorandum of 1922 referred to 'old fashioned plans of allocating particular parts of the beach to a particular sex'. And in a particularly enlightened class-conscious comment, a Mr Veale in the Ministry of Health informed a colleague that his department didn't look favourably on restrictive by-laws as being 'likely to interfere with bathing by the poorer classes … as distinct from visitors who can afford to pay'.

Things were moving in favour of mixed bathing from up high. And with mixed bathing came the opportunity for women to really learn how to swim properly, because men (who'd been afforded the opportunity and encouragement to learn) could teach them.

Exactly how that worked is illustrated by a request from the ladies of the Berwick Amateur Swimming Club, in the spring of 1913. They asked the council if they could be allowed to share their pond with men three mornings a week, so the men could teach them to swim properly. Much to everyone's annoyance, the request was turned down. 'The arrangement really would have inflicted a hardship on nobody,' reported the local paper. 'Poor Berwick.' And while it's charming that the ladies of the Berwick Amateur Swimming Club couldn't actually swim, that their enthusiasm and ambition were clearly mismatched with their ability, they weren't alone. There was a downside to the increase in women bathing, which is easy to spot if you look at any local newspaper of the time. In between startling news stories like 'TEN YEARS FOR STEALING TROUSERS', or 'STORMY WEATHER WAS GENERAL IN FRANCE YESTERDAY', or, a personal favourite, 'DISAPPOINTMENT AT BIRMINGHAM', there's one repeated headline: WOMAN DROWNED. WOMAN DROWNED. WOMAN DROWNED. We may well have got out of the mud and into the clear waters. But it was clearly time that women learned to swim in them.

Chapter 3

Going Indoors

While one swimming battle was being fought on the beaches, there was another going on indoors. Both were about gaining access for women swimmers. But it was no good having access if you couldn't actually swim.

The idea that women should learn to swim had started to take root in the middle of the nineteenth century, when the physical fitness of girls and young women came onto the agenda. It was a time when people were in thrall to science, and the medical and scientific community, almost exclusively male, were coming up with all sorts of theories about women that seemed to lead to the same conclusion: you can't fight nature. And nature definitely said women were lesser. Definitely. The science men said so. Physically, a woman's biology was her destiny, and we were almost entirely defined by our reproductive capabilities. But they also developed the idea that women's inferiority wasn't just in our bodies, it was also down to difference in men's and women's brains. They didn't conjure this notion of a sexed brain out of the blue, they weren't actively making things up that would denigrate women, they were simply working with what they had – we might call it confirmation bias. From it, they decreed that we simply, indisputably, were the weaker sex, in both brain and body. You can almost imagine the faux-distraught throwing up of hands, the casual shrugs – 'we'd love to be equal, ladies, but nature'. The theories they presented about the state of womanhood, beautifully presented in obfuscating scientific terms, were magically, coincidentally, about preserving male dominance in all areas, including sport. Isn't it funny how that happens? Society went along with it, because society generally likes order, and things which disrupt that sense of order are threatening, unnatural. The male scientists and doctors were on hand to preserve that status quo, to pickle it in embalming fluid.

These establishment theories were not spontaneous, they didn't arise out of nowhere; they came about in response to social developments, like the (gasp in horror) education of women. And the first female voices to counter that status quo were pretty conservative. They didn't go in all guns blazing; instead, they suggested that young women definitely needed to be fit … to be better prepared for the physical toll of pregnancy and childbirth. It wasn't about anything as grandiose as equality of the sexes, or fitness because that's better for a healthy society, or ridiculous modern notions of personal happiness, or even to stop us drowning in great numbers. It was so we could become 'more perfect vessels' for motherhood. Elizabeth Blackwell, the first woman on the British Medical Register, thought that improving the human race was women's sacred duty – but recommended exercise because 'energetic and active bodies are ... expressions of a sovereign nature'. I take this to mean that she approved of women being healthy as long as this was in the pursuit of a higher calling – motherhood.

A number of sports were deemed suitable for this righteous task. Walking – yes. Fencing – yes, but 'nothing violent to deplete the jaded system'. Cycling – when bikes were first introduced, it was mooted that no woman should take up such a thing without first consulting her 'medical man'. But within twenty years that opinion had changed and cycling was seen as the saviour of women, particularly 'middle-aged spinsters passing through a period of mental fermentation and physical irritability of varying degree'. (Oh God. So bleak. A country beset by hordes of furious cycling spinsters, mentally fermenting away.) Golf – yes, but only putting. Tennis – yes, but in doubles and only serve underhand. Archery – why not, just be careful where you're pointing that arrow, ladies. Horse riding – yes, saddle me up. Swimming – yes, a big yes, as long as it wasn't done aggressively and, of course, the costume was modest. As Patricia Vertinsky says in *The Eternally Wounded Woman* (possibly the best title ever filed under 'Feminism', and the perfect book to be seen reading on public transport if you want people to keep a distance), 'with its educative effects of cultivating the willpower, its predicted possibilities of increasing fertility, the opportunity for developing muscular strength and endurance, and the added bonus of cleanliness, recreational swimming epitomized medically appropriate sportive exercise for the modern woman'. What Vertinsky means, in laywoman's terms, is that swimming is good for your brain, your body, your standards of hygiene … oh, and your womb. Everything is judged on what it does to women's wombs.

Three women doctors played an important public role in countering the dominant male view, women who promoted exercise generally and swimming particularly for women and girls. The first was Elizabeth Garrett Anderson who, in the 1860s into the 1870s, was vocal about the value of swimming not just for health but also for the 'development of strength and grace'. (Those two necessarily went hand in hand. You didn't want to suggest that women might turn into some ghastly facsimile of a man.) Walking, gymnastics, a bit of delightful waltzing and a few rounds of croquet were on her agenda, but swimming got top billing from her. *The Times* reported in 1870 that 'she said so strongly did she think swimming necessary that she had practised for many years to acquire facility in that art'.

Next to make a splash was Mrs Frances E. Hoggan MD, the first woman to be registered as a doctor in Wales.

On 21 April 1879, she read her paper 'Swimming and Its Relation to the Health of Women' to the Women's Union Swimming Club, an audience that surely would have been very partial to her message. Hoggan's paper was full of the general benefits of swimming, and questioned why that benefit should be restricted to men, particularly when it was women who would physically and mentally benefit most from it. Why did women particularly need to swim? Mrs Hoggan showed how they were constantly restrained by expectation and experience. Swimming encourages 'lungs which in ordinary life breathe but feebly'. It allows movement of the hip joint 'which otherwise is seldom moved with any degree of freedom'. It eases backache caused by 'the languid movements which are often encouraged in girls as being more graceful'. And, referring to the corsets women were forced to wear, it helps with 'the injurious practice of encasing in steel'. You imagine these poor middle-class women – panting for breath, stiff, practically motionless, in permanent pain – and they sound like goldfish taken out of the tank and left to flap around feebly on the side. I can't help feeling that maybe, as we're not goldfish, it's not water these women were wanting, but a massive dose of liberation.

Despite her achievements as a doctor, Mrs Hoggan's views on the capabilities of her own sex hadn't moved far from that of her male colleagues. Her paper went on to outline the specific advantages for women and the list is not exactly complimentary. Women's voluntary muscles are naturally weaker. We have inferior chest capacity and bad posture, our nervous systems have less stable equilibrium, our want of exercise causes internal congestions. Basically, we're in a terrible state. My God, we needed to swim.

Mrs Samuda, she of the underwater smoking in a scarlet Turkey twill bathing dress, was equally down on the frailties of women. Some of them, she decreed, simply should not learn to swim at all, the 'naturally delicate girls suffering from "anaemia" or any sort of palpitations of the heart … it is just so much time wasted'. (The quote marks around anaemia suggests she simply doesn't believe in it, like any rational person might talk about 'homeopathy' now.) 'They derive little pleasure or benefit from the practice,' she said, 'while they are a constant source of annoyance and anxiety to their friends.' Having been a massive fan of Mrs Samuda earlier in our story, I'm going off her a bit at this point. She sounds too like Mrs Hassle, my PE teacher; I can entirely imagine her pipping an aggressive whistle and yelling at me as I struggled along. 'Oh, for goodness' sake, Landreth. KEEP UP.'

The third woman was Dr Elizabeth Sloan Chesser. A Glaswegian by birth and a keen follower of suffrage causes, Sloan Chesser 'belonged to that brave band of women who at the end of the century flouted conventional opinion by insisting on the right of women to higher education and to follow a career', the *Glasgow Herald* reported in her obituary. Like Hoggan, she followed the dominant idea that women were disadvantaged because of their sex but still, it's hard to read her proclamations as woman-friendly. Again, her motive was creating a better, stronger race of mothers; for her, a woman's health was 'more precious than knowledge', which seems to contradict the *Herald*'s kindly view. Sloan Chesser was keen to warn of the dangers of over-exercise, because a woman obsessed with sport would not be fully prepared for the obligations of married life. Our first duty was to be fit to undertake domestic duties effectively and, again, swimming was top of her list of 'allowable' sports. The idea that I might swim in order to be fit for my domestic duties is almost enough to put me off swimming entirely. But in Sloan Chesser's time, the start of the twentieth century, women didn't have the luxury of being so contrary.

The second half of Mrs Hoggan's speech in 1879 laid out where the main battleground for women's rights to swim was: indoor pools. The Victorians loved to build, because they could, and the fact that more people were swimming in the sea (especially the middle classes) led to an increase in support for public baths. Many of the first pools were privately built and owned, but the 1846 Baths and Washhouses Act enabled local authorities to raise or borrow money to build public pools open to all. ('All' meaning 'all men', at this juncture.) In 1865, there were fifty public baths in England. Twenty years later, that number had doubled, and by 1901 they'd doubled again. (Scotland had to wait a bit longer for their boom, under different legislation.) Two different propositions arose with this boom. The first was that women should get some limited access to pools that were otherwise designated for men.

The second was that pools were built specifically for the use of women. Both things took some time and persuasion to actually come about.

One of the first pools to admit women into a space exclusively intended for men was Marylebone Baths in central London, in 1858. The move came about because of the energy and determination of women who lived in the area, and one woman in particular, novelist Elizabeth Eiloart, who joins our roster of swimming foremothers to whom we owe a debt. As well as writing novels with snappy titles like *Ernie Elton, the Lazy Boy* and *Tom Dunstone's Troubles, and How He Got Over Them*, Elizabeth Eiloart edited *The Englishwoman's Journal*, which in turn was connected to the Ladies National Association for the Diffusion of Sanitary Knowledge, or LNADSK as it was never known. LNADSK may have been upper-class women educating working-class ones, but their intentions seem solid. They published various invigorating pamphlets around the health of mothers, the benefits of fresh air, and one called 'Why Do Women Not Swim', where they encouraged women to stop being passive. 'So you, dear reader, when you swim, do not go about like a floating coffin, but be cheerful, enjoy yourself.' The thought of Victorian women lying immobile on the water in all their garb, like gloomy wooden boxes bumping into each other, made me smile. Swimming was something Elizabeth Eiloart felt strongly enough about to lead the campaign to open Marylebone Baths to women. She took it to the all-male committee who controlled the

Baths, and who were fiercely opposed to the plan. They were eventually persuaded by the indefatigable Mrs Eiloart to graciously allow women access one day a week, for a trial period. That's a theme that's already becoming familiar – the men in charge, resolutely and bombastically clinging on to the way things are. The women's journal *Work and Leisure* reviewed the day the pool was 'thrown open to the feminine public', and they were ecstatic in their praise. 'And oh!' they exclaimed, 'what a delight for the dwellers in city confines, just passing from the hot and dusty streets, to leap into this clear flood and feel that sense of exhilaration which free exercise in the water always bestows.' As well as extolling the physical freedoms that swimming allows, the review talks about the bonds of female friendship. 'This expanse of ambient fluid buoying up the frame, with space for the free play of every limb, and with pleased friends and companions around, sharing and heightening the enjoyment.' Their enthusiasm is infectious, but 'ambient fluid' might sound a touch too womby for us to lose ourselves totally in the image.

(If the idea of the 'free play of limbs' sounded morally deviant to the repressed Victorian middle-class woman, they would have been reassured by the steep entrance fee of 8d. Working-class women would not have been able to afford that, and it was deliberate; 8d was 'quite sufficient to keep it select'. Sexual politics can sometimes feel like a sledgehammer in comparison to the subtle and sly knife of class politics.)

Elizabeth Eiloart's success was motivation for women in other places to campaign for similar rights. Women were dependent on men to grant them access; it was a constant struggle, and they didn't relinquish their power easily. But male opposition couldn't match the determination by individuals and groups of women to get equal swimming rights. Women like Eiloart were essentially frontline swimming suffragettes – the first ones bold enough and angry enough and with the vision (and time) to take up the fight, to realise that the ballot box was not the only struggle. They demonstrated what the female body was capable of, the space women could take in the public arena, and how the lot of women could be improved. Maybe suffragists is a more accurate description, as they weren't employing direct-action tactics but instead campaigned via the more polite and entirely middle-class methods of meetings, letter-writing and discussion.

Twenty years after Marylebone Baths let women in on a Wednesday – a precious one day in one pool in one city – the number of pools were in boom times, but women's access remained limited. Women had access to the men's baths at certain times of the day, or nothing. 'Certain times of the day' invariably meant during working hours, which would least inconvenience men, and completely exclude working women from the equation. Restriction by class wasn't just aimed at women. Working-class men were only allowed into second- and third-class pools, via a scaled entrance fee. If you've ever been repeatedly dive-bombed in the pool by exuberant boys, you might decide that some exclusions sound like a very good idea. In Manchester, noisy boys were shunted into a boys-only Penny Bath, so-called because that's how much it cost to get in – but it was short-lived because boys would beg outside for that penny. Every aspect of that story illustrates how annoying small boys can be.

Mrs Hoggan concluded her 1879 speech to the Women's Union Swimming Club with vigorous insistence that the right to swim should be extended to all women. 'Wherever there is a public swimming bath for the use of men there ought, in common justice to girls and women, be one for their use too.' Just because women had been a bit slow on the uptake wasn't reason enough to absolve the men with wallets of their responsibility to all parts of the community, Hoggan said. Her final cry was rallying, if a little wordy. 'Just as we have asserted the principle that girls as well as boys are to be educated so … public provision as is made for healthy recreation and exercise shall have reference to the needs of women as well as men … It will not be long before swimming, by common consent, takes prominent and recognized place.' Such a fervent call: surely the crowd would have responded with a mass air punch. Or at least the educated Victorian woman's version of the air punch. Maybe the vigorous flapping of a pamphlet.

Things were shifting, slowly. As the Victorian building boom continued, their design got fancy, with Turkish baths, plunge pools and showers, all things to attract the ladies, apparently. And architects started, on a small scale, to add separate pools for women. In 1862, Brighton got their first Ladies' Bath – though this was more in the 'getting clean' tradition than actual swimming. Opened in 1871, Stockport's magnificent (and privately owned) Victoria Baths offered a total of six separate pools, three of which were for women – one cold pool, and a first- and second-class 'tepid' option. 'Tepid' let punters know that the water was heated, but it's surely the least attractive word for advertising that fact. In 1874, Paddington Baths offered three pools for men, and one for women. The plans, as reproduced in the book *Great Lengths*, show how many complex design machinations were required to keep men and women apart, and how many services were duplicated 'purely to ensure', the book says, 'that bathers of different sexes (and the staff who serviced them) were kept apart'. In 1877, a (private) complex was built on the King's Road, Chelsea, with one of the three pools specifically for women. The Cornwallis Baths in Liverpool had a ladies' pool that had originally been designated as the men's third-class pool – please yell WOMEN ARE NOT THIRD-CLASS MEN at this point. By 1888, Hampstead Baths on Finchley Road was Britain's first public baths to offer first- and second-class pools for women. Hornsey Road and Kentish Town did the same in the following decade – London was leading the way. By 1898, there was a grand total of fourteen public baths with women-only pools, and although that sounds like great strides from nothing, the statistics show that men outnumbered women swimmers by ten to one. It's not surprising; women had fourteen pools between them in the whole country, and the rest of the time they were still begging for leftovers.

Where women did get space, somehow it was decreed that they didn't need as much as men. They were teeny tiny delicate things, they really only needed a souped-up jam jar. In Ashton-under-Lyne, the ladies' pool opened in 1870 was one-ninth the area of the men's. In the pools at Paddington, the space for ladies was one-fifth of the three men's pools combined. In the Lambeth Public Baths opened in 1897, the two men's pools were both larger than the women's. The order of size was straightforward: first-class men, then second-class men, then women. Maybe we just genetically weren't as splashy, taking us back to the early scientific notions of lady brains. Or maybe it's in our cultural DNA, to be socially minded. I've been in pools where one man chooses to butterfly up one lane and the rest of us end up politely backwashed into the drain, and have sometimes envied that complete lack of concern for anyone else.

Despite their restricted access, feeble brains and tiny fragile bodies, women took to swimming with verve, and the end of the nineteenth century saw a significant event for British swimming – for international swimming, even. 15 August 1892, Townhead Baths in Glasgow: the first ever women's championship in a British pool. The event was written up in the *Glasgow Herald* and they describe a building packed to the 'utmost rafters', a quadrille band playing dance music through the evening, and a display of graceful 'ornamental swimming' by Messrs John Cunningham and Joe Milne that was 'much appreciated'. (Men did all the diving and synchronised swimming displays at this point in history. It was only when women began doing it that it was downgraded as a sport.) There was only one race for women – the 200 yards freestyle – but nonetheless, the paper declares it to be the principal item. And why not? This was the first ever, after all! The entrants were Miss Emma Dobbie, Miss Jane Dobbie, Miss Mary Livingstone, Miss Maggie Roy and Miss Jessie McMillan. The paper records the race: 'All got away to a good start and Miss E. Dobbie at once shot to the front … Miss Dobbie held a decisive lead until the 150 yards was reached, where she was challenged by Miss Livingstone, who made a gallant spurt … but the leader had a bit to spare and responded gamely to the call.' Miss Emma Dobbie won, with a time of 4 minutes 24 seconds. She became the first woman to win a British swimming championship – an achievement worth remembering.

In an ugly display of my competitive urge, I timed myself swimming 200 metres freestyle to see how I compared to Miss Dobbie. I thought that the thirty (and the rest) years I have on her might balance out the advantages my streamlined costume confers on me, compared to her cumbersome outfit with all its resultant drag. I did it in a 50m pool which confers disadvantage in having fewer push-offs, and obviously 200 metres is further than 200 yards. My time was 4 minutes 22 seconds. I beat her! Sisterly solidarity be damned, I felt momentarily like a champion.

Then I realised I was swimming front crawl in goggles, and she'd have almost certainly been doing a slower stroke, without. And then I thought I'd find out the contemporary record. At the time of writing, the current world record for a woman over this course is held by Federica Pellegrini, who can swim it in 1:52:98. To mix my sporting metaphors, that certainly kicks my four-plus minutes into touch. I am duly humbled.

It was a few years (1901) before the first 'official' women's competition was organised by the ASA (Amateur Swimming Association). In it, women swam 100 yards (as opposed to the men's mile) and the winner got a vase (the men got a cup). Vases are useful, women are supposed to like vases. But cups are grand. They get displayed proudly on a shelf without anyone sticking flowers in them.

One of the regular swimming entertainments of the time that women could more easily partake in was 'plunging' competitions. In the Long Plunge, participants would dive in and glide, face down, as far as possible in one minute without breathing or taking a stroke, and this was exactly the kind of thing that a more refined lady could enjoy without the indignity of breaking into a sweat. This form of entertainment has been revived at my home pool, Tooting Lido, by the very active South London Swimming Club, who keep this unheated lido open for members out of season (October to April) and run events through the year. A new plunge record was set there by Hilary Jennings in 2016 – a whopping 66 feet, 4 inches.

Taking the opportunity to quiz a living expert, I ask Hilary what makes a good plunge. 'I think it's mostly physiological (I'm very buoyant) and the water temperature and busyness of the pool [seems to] make a difference to general distances,' she says. 'If it's colder you are higher in the water and lots of splashing swimmers can send people into the wall, cause them to turn turtle or [in one recent case] do a complete U-turn and end up back where they started.' And if you're thinking of trying a plunge yourself, she offers some tips, which might not be what you'd expect: 'The most tricky thing is trying not to laugh or worry how big your bum looks as you float past the spectators.' (Did worrying about the size of their bum affect the plunging women of the nineteenth century? Let's hope not. My own tip is: never worry how big your bum looks, it'll always be fine.) And Hilary offers some valuable insight into the type of preparation a plunging expert undertakes. 'Generally my preparation involves a lot of lying in plunge position, on the sofa, on my bed, et cetera ... it's a tough sport at which to excel.' If you're interested in instituting your own plunge competition, that sounds like the kind of training most of us could manage.

If all or any of this sounds frivolous and inconsequential, it isn't. Every race and plunge and event and pool was a brick in the building of a movement. Each one contributed in some tiny way to a thesis – which is that there is a direct correlation between sport and the emancipation of women. Historian Eric Hobsbawm explains what that means in practice for women at the start of the twentieth century. He uses tennis as his example but it's equally applicable to swimming. 'Almost for the first time sport provided respectable women … with a recognized public role as individual human beings, separate from their function as wives, daughters, marriage-partners or other appendages of males inside and outside the family.' Hobsbawm uses the term 'respectable' to describe the women who gained from this small emancipation. So again, we can see the class distinction that's rumbled through the story so far. The public role that sport gave (middle-class, respectable) women was not just as participants, forming friendships and spending time in relative freedom with other women in the water. It was also as teachers; the fact that women could only be taught to swim in indoor pools by other women meant they were able to forge good careers. In the Royal York Baths in Regent's Park in 1866, the ladies were taught by Mrs Woodbridge, the wife of a noted local professor. Miss Humphrey was the swimming mistress at Paddington Baths, and Emily Parker (sister of the swimmer Harry Parker) was teaching by fifteen years of age. That's a sobering thought if you've ever watched a modern fifteen-year-old struggle to get off the sofa to fetch another bowl of cereal. Often, teaching was but one part of these women's swimming lives – Fanny Easton was a teacher for twenty years from 1881 as well as appearing in various swimming 'entertainments', assisted by her pupils. Then there were swimming family dynasties; Alfred Ward, a London swimming master, brought his whole troupe of children into the profession; by 1891 his daughters Florence and Maud (at the ripe ages of seventeen and thirteen) were 'professional swimmers' and another daughter, Minnie, had joined the famous Beckwith troupe. At fourteen, Agnes Beckwith was running classes for girls in London schools alongside her other swimming achievements. And when the ASA created a professional teaching qualification in 1902, certificate number 15 was the first one given to a woman, a Miss Muriel Austin, aged twenty-three, of Richmond.

Access for women had grown so far beyond the initial one day a week in one London pool that by 1912 the ASA were pushing for more baths that could be used by both sexes at the same time. Just as the argument for mixed bathing had arisen on beaches, it became the issue indoors too (and with the same moral objections). It's no good having one set of freedoms in one area, and a different set entirely somewhere else. It wasn't a black-and-white issue, with public opinion in favour, and old-git bureaucracy against; there were plenty of members of the public who really objected to mixed bathing and some men who might otherwise be described as patrician who were in favour of it. Despite the naysayers, it was introduced in bigger cities (London, Birmingham, Manchester) with some considerable commercial success, which may explain why some bureaucrats were in favour. Follow the money.

There are always going to be curmudgeons who resist change. Curmudgeons like Mrs Grundy. In 1912, the

Oldham Baths Committee resolved not to consider the question of mixed bathing in the public baths. The gavel bangs. No! Won't even talk about it! Away with your filthy modern ideas! According to local press a Mr Frith, who had proposed the notion, crossly laid blame for its failure at the feet of Mrs Grundy. 'He thought,' the paper said, 'the sooner she was put in the baths and drowned the better.' I was quite keen on the progressive nature of Mr Frith until he started threatening to drown Mrs Grundy, and now I'm wondering why he was so damn keen to get in a pool with mixed bathing in the first place. But in the same way that Tonbridge's Mr Donald Clark had harrumphed about women in the sea looking like wet Scottish terriers, responses to the idea of mixed bathing indoors showed how dangerous people like Mrs Grundy thought it was. The temptations! It could only possibly be allowed with strict regulations about dressing and undressing, and rules about what side of the pool different sexes were allowed to get out on. Even the idea of family bathing wasn't innocent – because families might accidentally mix! It's as if people's sense of morality was so flimsy and ill-constructed that it could collapse at the slightest whiff. As if being in an enclosed body of water with human beings to whom you're not married might tip you into some kind of uncontrollable sexual rampage.

We don't know if Mr Frith succeeded in drowning Mrs Grundy, but we do know that people like her couldn't stem the tide of mixed bathing indoors. And by 1918, we know that tens of thousands of women were swimming. We were resolutely into clear water, looking back to shore at the mud we'd traipsed through. We know it, because someone did a survey, and who doesn't love a survey?

Agnes Campbell's 'Report on Public Baths and Wash-houses in the UK' is a weighty tome, and it details how the numbers of pools and swimmers rose across the country from 1901 to 1914. In London, tickets issued went from 3.2 million in 1905 to 4.5 million in 1914. In Bradford in the same period, numbers went from 62,000 to over 212,000, and in Burnley they doubled from 81,000 to over 164,000. (Obviously those stats include repeat business.) By 1914, the ratio of men to women was highest in London; in Birmingham it was 23:100, 10:100 in Liverpool and 18:100 in Bristol. In Scotland, the ratios were highest in Dunfermline, and in Dublin and Belfast they were extremely low. In what now feels obvious, they were lower in 'shipping centres where men's industries dominate', Campbell writes, and higher 'where there are a good many women living at home under conditions in which they are free to use the Baths during the day time'. Yet again, it's a class issue.

While the ratios of men to women in some places might make encouraging reading, the way Campbell states the bald facts about inequality between the sexes does not. She believed that swimming was a 'wholesome recreation' for young people, that 'boys and girls should be actors rather than spectators', but saw a lack of parity very clearly. She also makes a financial point. 'Although girls have less money at their disposal,' she writes, 'and the provision made for them is inferior, they are usually asked to pay equal or in several cases higher fees than men or boys and they have to meet additional expense in the matter of costume and caps.' Put simply, it is not fair. Campbell attempts to justify these additional costs by saying that 'from the point of view of the management, a ladies bath gives more trouble than a man's'. The required dressing rooms are more elaborate, hair-drying facilities are required, and 'the water is more quickly fouled by nap from the costume, and by stray hairs'. There's no doubt that clumps of stray hairs in the water are annoying, whosever head they fall from. But it's still not fair. Despite it, let's take heed of those positive ratios and what they tell us. They clearly show a massive swing. Women were definitely starting to swim.

Chapter 4

Exceptional Women (Part I)

If you found the analogy of the last two chapters, that of trudging through mud to get to clear waters, to be a boggy, depressing one, this chapter will perk you right up. Because this one is about the swimming suffragettes who boinged right over that mud as if they were wearing springy trampoline shoes. They were the first wave: women who got in regardless and performed extraordinary feats, feats that would be impressive enough now but at the time were just plain tremendous. Not only were they exceptional in their own right, they also acted as inspirational role models, so they're crucial to the story of how I, and every other woman swimmer of the twenty-first century, ended up with the freedoms we have.

At the end of the nineteenth century, it's unlikely that many working-class women would have read *The Gentlewoman's Book of Sport*, where Mrs Samuda extolled the virtues of swimming. It's equally unlikely that medical pronouncements from the likes of Mrs Hoggan in 1879 or Mrs Sloan Chesser a couple of decades later would have had much immediate impact on anyone other than a select bunch of educated middle-class women. The burgeoning women's rights movements might have reached a small number of working women, but most had lives far removed from the 'niceties' of voting. The notion of swimming, in a world constrained by lack of choice and lack of opportunity wrapped up in lack of time and money, must have seemed like it came from some fanciful, unattainable, far-off land. It's suggested that middle-class women were put off using public pools initially, because their origins as places to do laundry and have a wash meant they were associated with the health and welfare of the working class. If that leads to a momentary dip in your sympathy towards these middle-class women, please remember it is possible to have empathy for one set of people while acknowledging how much tougher it was for another. It was very sludgy at the bottom of this particular hierarchy of oppression, and the situation for working-class women was far more pernicious; they were excluded in just about every practical way possible. And if their consciousness wasn't raised by changing medical pronouncements or the gradual shift in the perception of women's abilities among an educated elite, how did things ever change?

It took role models. As we know, sport was dominated by men, and when middle-class women did participate, there was a double concern – either the women would become masculinised, or the sport would become feminised. The issues around femininity weren't applicable to working-class women, as there was no expectation on them to be feminine. You can't work in my factory for 11 hours a day and be treated like a fine lady. I can't pay you a pittance for slaving over my grate and then declare that you're not physically capable of the sheer hard grind of it all. You can't feed your increasing family on a tiny shrinking budget and still be in the very pink of delicate lady fitness. In fact, we actively require you, this one class of women, *not* to be concerned by all the restrictions we put on this other class, not to be constrained by appearing 'feminine' or 'ladylike' because that might stop you working. Whichever way you turn, it's not a great set of controls. But for a very small number of women, sport in general and swimming in particular provided a way out, an alternative destiny. There were female boxers, a ladies' cricket team and a small group of professional women swimmers. These sportswomen couldn't alter the hard facts of poverty and lives lived around hard domestic labour, but they could show what women were capable of. It was the original 'this girl can' and perhaps no girl could better than Agnes Beckwith.

25 August 1875. A historic day in the British swimming calendar: Captain Matthew Webb becomes the first man ever to swim the English Channel, in a time of 21 hours

and 45 minutes. It was an outstanding achievement, and Webb gained national and international fame and a career as a professional swimmer. Of course, no one ever achieves a Channel swim alone and Webb was no exception; one of his key swimming coaches was a man called Frederick Beckwith.

Professor Frederick Beckwith was a central figure in the Victorian world of natation – and there's two words to deal with here before we can move on with the tale. Firstly, 'professor'. Beckwith wasn't a professor in the academic understanding of the word but it was commonly used among the small cadre of Victorian men who were experts or champions and who wanted to capitalise on that in an entrepreneurial way, usually by becoming swimming tutors. 'Professor' signalled their availability to the wider world, and left no doubt in anyone's mind of their status at the top of their game. Who better to trust, if you're betting on a swimming race, than the 'professor' who organised it? Then there's 'natation'. It's from the Latin for swimming, and doesn't it just give it an air of science and grandeur? I'm not walking, I'm perambulating. I'm not speed-walking, I'm practising pedestrianism. I'm not a swimmer, I'm a natationist. Just saying it and suddenly my whole demeanour has changed – my chin is up, my manner rather superior, I'm definitely well educated.

Beckwith was one of the best swimmers of his day, Champion of England no less, and using the capital that inferred on him, he ran a small fiefdom as swimming master at Lambeth Baths for over twenty years. But he had more to advertise than just the tutoring. He turned his ability into a whole entrepreneurial career. Sport-as-entertainment was big business in Victorian Britain, and Beckwith was master of promotion not just of himself but of the whole sport. (It wasn't entirely self-serving; he also founded the National Philanthropic Swimming Society in 1859, to promote swimming among the working classes.) He ran aquatic events in baths, theatres and aquaria across the country, and his whole family were involved, including his children, even as babies. One might say his daughter Agnes Beckwith was born to it.

By the time she was four years old, in 1865, Agnes was making regular appearances in swimming displays as one of the 'Beckwith Frogs'. Dressed in 'fleshings and drawers', they'd dart around in glass tanks, showing off their underwater skills. Her older sister Jessie was the first real crowd-drawer but Agnes increasingly became central to the troupe. The Beckwith Frogs performed in carnivals, competitions and galas, and by the time she was nine Agnes was performing with her brother Willie as 'Les Enfants Poissons' in a Parisian aquarium. Nine years old, performing underwater in Paris in 1870. It's an almost unbelievable life she was living, exceptional for the times.

Three weeks after Captain Webb made his first Channel crossing, Agnes was to undertake her first major endurance swim. Beckwith heard rumour that another professor, London champion Harry Parker, was planning a swim for his swimming-teacher sister Emily, then fourteen, in the Thames. Emily was six months older than Agnes and 'stout in the build', against Agnes's more 'slight, diminutive' figure. (These things were clearly important, though we have no idea what size Captain Webb wore.) Beckwith was determined to be the first, the publicity was crucial to his standing, so on 1 September 1875, Agnes dived off a boat at London Bridge and swam five miles down the Thames to Greenwich. Wearing 'a tight bathing costume of rose-pink llama trimmed with lace, her long flaxen hair neatly bound by a ribbon', Agnes, in a combination of side- and breaststroke, completed the swim in fractionally under one hour eight minutes. This is an incredible time – we must assume that the flow of the river pushed her along. 'For a powerful man the feat may not be an over difficult one', the papers reported, 'but it is a test of endurance for a slight young girl like the present performer.' The crowds agreed – they lined the banks, and she blew kisses as she went. Boats and vessels of all sorts bobbed around her, the whole river busily following her journey, coming in to take a closer look at this marvellous girl. On her arrival at Greenwich, a band played 'See the Conquering Hero Comes'.

A week later, and Agnes's achievement was bettered by Emily, who swam seven miles from London Bridge to Blackwall in just over an hour and a half, and, as with Agnes, thousands of people gathered to watch. 'The river was alive with small craft,' the papers reported, 'the decks and rigging of all the vessels within sight were covered with clusters of eager on-lookers.' Then, 'amid much cheering, the young swimmer plunged quietly into the Thames'. To almost constant cheers, the sound of river pistols and even the firing of a small cannon, her way ahead kept as clear as possible by the river police, Emily swam a vigorous breaststroke down the river, appearing to 'rather relish the excitement'. It sounds like a carnival, but not everyone shared that almost palpable enthusiasm. Feathers were ruffled. It sullied the achievements of Captain Webb, people thought. Girls disporting themselves in public in this way was very poor taste. It degraded swimming as an activity. It was an advertising ruse (and yes, that one does have a ring of truth to it). One London journal declared that 'man can no more claim the water as his exclusive domain as he can the land'. It's hard to tell whether they think this a good thing or bad.

Agnes, having been the first to complete the amazing feat, was of great commercial value to her dad. After she swam three-quarters of a mile in the Tyne in May 1876, a forty-minute cold-water ordeal, Beckwith was able to advertise her as 'Heroine of the Thames and Tyne', and she was much in demand as a swimming teacher at Lambeth Baths. Some of the press were keen that she should just stick to teaching, the proper vocation for a woman. But her biggest challenge was ahead. In July 1878, now the ripe old age of seventeen, Agnes undertook a twenty-mile swim, from Westminster Bridge to Richmond and back. Again, the crowds gathered in their thousands to follow this 'youthful water sprite' dressed in a 'closely fitting amber suit adorned with white lace, a jaunty straw hat and fluttering blue ribbons' on her journey. Reading the reports, I could feel myself screech to a halt on 'jaunty straw hat'. Of all the feats of imagination these swims are requiring of us, maybe the hardest to comprehend is that one might undertake to swim twenty miles of the Thames in a jaunty straw hat. Nonetheless, Agnes did, 'gliding prettily along' for 6 hours 25 minutes, getting out of the water to rapturous greetings. Still in jaunty straw hat we presume, though no one would blame her if she'd ditched the wretched thing before she'd even got to Lambeth Bridge.

Born one hundred years after Agnes, my own experience of swimming in the Thames was somewhat different. Precisely no people lined the banks to cheer me on, my outfit had no lace trim and my head gear was entirely functional. And of course, I wouldn't be allowed to swim where she did in such a casual fashion – by-laws introduced in 2012 mean you can only get in from Putney Bridge to beyond the Thames Barrier with prior consent from the Port of London Authority, who control river activity. The question remains as to why you'd want to – the tidal pull of the river is very strong, it's bitingly cold, it's a crowded waterway full of boats small and enormous, moving at speed. You could be squished in a second. If that doesn't deter you, maybe the millions of cubic metres of raw sewage that finds its way into the Thames every year when heavy rainfall overwhelms our sewage system will. My Thames swims, which include a particularly charming kilometre from Hammersmith to Chiswick Pier that required changing into my costume on the pavement outside a pub and then dandling gaily along past glorious gardens on a beautiful summer's evening, were all tightly managed according to tide, and featured no sewage. Agnes would not have been so fortunate. This was Victorian London; Bazalgette's sewerage system might have been newly installed but people still chucked anything and everything into the water. If Agnes didn't encounter at least three dead dogs, a few random bloated limbs and quite a lot of poo, I'll eat a jaunty straw hat.

Agnes was now the nineteenth-century equivalent of a superstar, 'the greatest lady swimmer in the world', trumpeted the Royal Aquarium, where she did frequent ornamental and scientific displays. In May 1880 she did a thirty-hour swim there, taking her meals in the water, and in September the same year, swam one hundred hours over six days. Having kept going from 6 a.m. to 11 p.m. on two days and 6 a.m. to 10.30 p.m. on the next four, people were still keen to criticise. She took rests overnight! they screeched. Imagine what a tragic lot of trolling eggs they would have been on Twitter.

Agnes Beckwith was not, as far as we know, a suffragette. But she was certainly a swimming suffragette. To all intents and purposes she was simply a good and dutiful player in her father's circus. But by playing that role in the way she did, she paved the way for women to participate in swimming in their tens of thousands, and to make their entrance into the

Olympics in 1912. Agnes had a life well lived, for more than just herself.

Agnes was the greatest, but others were great. Some were acclaimed speed or distance swimmers, like Laura Saigeman, Lily Smith, Theresa Johnson and Eileen Lee. On 9 September 1875, Brighton's Harriet Elphinstone-Dick swam with Helen Saigeman from Rottingdean to Brighton; the *Brighton Gazette* declared that 'These young ladies have accomplished the greatest swimming feat of the present day, with the exception of Captain Webb's Channel trip'. (Elphinstone-Dick then moved to Melbourne and opened the city's first women-only gym.) Others were acclaimed at the more 'ornamental and fancy' end of things, and swimming extravaganzas featured all sort of 'female natationists', like Florrie Tilton, Nellie Sylvia, Alice Sinclair, Minnie Johnson and Annie Luker. It's a strong roll call of Victorian names (though Annie Luker was born Hagar Anne, which has yet to get its resurgence in popularity. Not many girl babies get called Hagar these days). Like Agnes Beckwith, Annie Luker was born into a swimming family, as her father was also a professor involved in training Captain Webb. As well as being a swimming teacher, again like Agnes, in 1892 Annie set off to swim from Kew to Greenwich with the express aim of establishing herself as 'female champion of the world'. After sixteen miles of swimming and no refreshment, she gave up. To undertake a swim of that distance is one thing – but no refreshment? Unthinkable! One of the joys of training for a long swim is surely the breaks a person might take to shovel down a great big wodge of peanut-butter flapjack or home-made fudge. However, Annie turned her swimming skills to other financial advantage by becoming 'Lady Champion Diver of the World'. From January 1894 for eight years, twice a day, she'd plunge 90 feet into a small tank at the Royal Aquarium. Talking to the *Penny Illustrated* paper in 1902, she describes how she inherited her abilities from her father, taking to the water 'as naturally as a duck does'. 'I was the first and only lady to dive from Blackfriars Bridge into the Thames at low water,' she says, a feat that would have been as ridiculously dangerous as it was scary, yet she felt no nerves.

Her diving may have been a high point of the Aquarium's schedule, but she shared billing with all sorts of speciality acts. Contortionists, acrobats, conjurors, a lady who swallowed electric light bulbs 'with apparent ease', 'fancy and ornamental swimmers' and various musical turns. It was the Variety Show of its day, twice a day, every day. Among the acts on offer, Mr Fred Neeri's 'Legmania' sounds particularly appealing, with the enduring lure of a set of manic legs, as does Mr Baker's Gambling Pig. 'This pig will play anyone at nap,' one paper reported. 'Though it is not quite certain of beating you it probably will … The pig played quite correctly and was small and pink.' Oh, the understated poetry of early newspaper reports. 'Another pig played "The Last Rose of Summer" with only one mistake,' the report continued, though is not explicit as to how or what the pig played on. 'They are worth seeing, especially the one that is good at nap.' However much a person loves a swimming display, it's almost impossible not to be distracted by a card-playing pig.

Most of the early swimming stories come together via newspaper reports and the work of niche historical biographers. But for Annette Kellerman, we can go direct to source. Written in 1918, her book *How To Swim* starts with a chapter entitled 'The Story of My Swim to Fame and Fortune', which gives a pretty clear hint of her trajectory to the heights of the swimming firmament. She's not being hyperbolic – Kellerman became one of the highest paid Hollywood stars in the world, on a reputation made in Britain. Born in Australia in 1887, she started swimming at her father's insistence when it was recommended as a way of coping with her leg condition – she had rickets and wore steel braces on her 'weak and ill-formed legs' – and very quickly she 'caught the mermaid fever'. Her skills took her to many race meetings for both speed and distance, but in 1905 she decided to further her fortunes and come to England – thanks to women like Agnes Beckwith, it had become a place where she could really make her mark. Kellerman needed to find a way to make people take notice, so she swam the Thames from Putney Bridge to Blackwall. Like you do. 'I shall never forget that swim through the flotsam and jetsam of London,' she wrote, 'dodging tugs and swallowing what seemed like pints of oil from the greasy surface of the water.' But it worked – she clearly cut something of an attractive figure because people did take notice; exactly as she'd planned, she started to draw crowds. Her first big European race was the seven-mile 'Swim Through Paris', undertaken by her and seventeen men. There were only four finishers and she was one of them, declaring it 'the most thrilling race I was ever in'.

Then Kellerman decided to attempt the Channel. Nobody had succeeded since Webb, and no woman had ever tried – she was the first. That takes some chutzpah, and it seems Kellerman had that in spades. On 24 August 1905 at 2 a.m., the crew assembled. 'The pores of my skin had been rubbed full of porpoise oil' – yes, this really happened, actual porpoise oil – 'and my goggles glued on.' Goggles were a relatively new invention in this country, and they looked more like clunky great motorbike goggles than anything we might recognise today. Kellerman advocated the use of bear grease to seal her goggles, though how she discovered that brings all sorts of images to mind. All in all, hers would have been horribly cumbersome and she'd have smelt like a zoo. The Channel rules then were as now: you are not allowed to touch the boat or other people, even when you're being fed. The men who'd tried it mostly swam naked but Annette was required to wear a 'tiny bathing suit'. Even that chafed – 'my flesh under the arms was raw and hurt fearfully' – and would have made every move increasingly painful; a saltwater chafe is a very particular kind of wincing persistent sting that catches on every movement, and swimmers now use Vaseline to try and avoid it. Her swim was unsuccessful, and though she had two more attempts, she was not to become the first woman across the Channel. But what she had done was help turn Channel swimming into an event. 'I had the endurance but not the brute strength,' she said in explanation. 'I think no woman has this combination; that's why I say that none of my sex will ever accomplish that particular stunt.' There's that chutzpah again, this time misplaced. Her message seemed to be 'if I can't do it, no one can' – not exactly the rich seam of sisterhood we might hope for from our sporting inspirations. She was, as we know, to be proved wrong.

Kellerman used her fame to embark on a North American vaudeville tour, and eventually, having established herself as a 'Diving Venus', was tempted into Hollywood and a well-documented life in front of the camera. In her autobiographical chapter of *How To Swim*, alongside tales of the glamour and glitz of a showbiz life and the hullabaloo of fame and fortune, Kellerman talks about what 'this glorious human experience' of swimming meant to her. First she shows that she too can be distracted by a pig. 'My father told me that all animals swam except the monkey and the pig. And I didn't want to stay on their level. The pig, he said, always cut its throat in the water … Some day I am going to buy a pig and try it.' Thankfully there's no evidence she undertook this particular experiment, but we do know that she really should have questioned the tales her father told her a little more rigorously.

'Swimming is a pleasure and a benefit, a clean, cool, beautiful cheap thing we all from cats to kings can enjoy,' she goes on. 'The man who has not given himself completely to the sun and wind and cold sting of the waves will never know all meanings of life.' And then in a few quiet words she finds her poetry. 'The water always teaches me a new story,' she writes, a sentence that rings round my head, a simple idea perfectly expressed, a swimmer's truth.

Kellerman and Beckwith both benefited from parental support and encouragement, however financially motivated Beckwith's may have been. For Hilda James the reverse was true – her swimming career was angrily disrupted by her mother. It started, and might have ended, with religion.

Born in Liverpool in 1904, Hilda James's family's strict religious rules (as Jehovah's Witnesses) meant that she was let off RE classes in her Church of England school, and rather than do extra maths she chose to spend that free time in Garston Swimming Baths; so far so good – her mother knitted her a costume. It was there, aged eleven, that she won her first certificate, and from that, her swimming went from strength to strength. By the age of thirteen she was swimming an hour every evening, and had joined a club. Six months later when she had to quit school to fulfil family duties (the curse of the young woman, to be slotted into a caring role), Liverpool City Council gave her a complimentary one-year swimming contract, which meant she didn't have to pay club fees and be a burden on a stretched family budget. Hilda was clearly talented, she started to travel and compete, with her ma's grudging approval. By the time she was fifteen she was training at 6 a.m. every morning and for three hours every night, and was winning amateur championships. In

March 1919 (aged fifteen, let's not forget), the ASA gave her a certificate 'for honorary services rendered to the ASA in demonstrating the correct methods of swimming'. She had a leading coach in William 'Bill' Howcroft, a man who was to play a pivotal role in the battle against her mother's disapproval, which seemed to come and go like the tides. Hilda began performing at galas, and developed what sounds like an early comedy routine to win round her audience, doing silly water tricks like swimming feet first, diving like a duck, doing 'The Crab' where she'd swim sideways along the pool with her hands clacking above her head like pincers. Admittedly, it's no Gambling Pig, but it brought the fun of swimming entertainments into a serious competitive arena.

At sixteen, Hilda James did her first Olympic Trials in Southport doing the Ladies' Backstroke. Now called Old English Backstroke, it involves using both arms at the same time and a kind of breaststroke frog kick to your legs, as opposed to the single arm and flutter kick that we'd use in backstroke now. It requires quite a lot of room, throwing your arms around like that. I call it the Margolyes, having seen the wonderful actress Miriam Margolyes do it in a rather fabulous and stately way up and down the pool in the old Clapham Baths. Hilda was selected for the English Olympic team, and in 1920 went to Antwerp. The city had been badly bombed in the First World War, and the Stade Nautique was not the glamorous location we've come to expect from Olympic venues. Instead, the Olympians were given a cold and dirty roped-off canal basin to compete in.

It might be your very version of swimming hell, but Hilda and her three teammates, Connie Jeans, Grace McKenzie and Charlotte Radcliffe, won a silver medal for the 4x100m relay. But it was what Hilda learned there that changed the face of British sport. Races at the time were generally swum with a stroke called the Trudgeon, a name which doesn't conjure up visions of streamlined speed. It's a kind of head-up/overarm/scissor-kick/side stroke, one I have tried to replicate in a pool but it's very anti-instinctive if you've learned how to do front crawl; it makes you feel like you need a lovely flowery swim cap and a lady pal swimming alongside you discussing the youth of today. The Americans were using a new stroke though, called the 'American crawl' and Hilda decided she wanted to learn it – they were smashing records, after all. So she was taught by fellow Olympian Ethelda Bleibtrey in that stinking canal basin, and brought the skill home. She was the first woman to swim crawl in Britain – she changed what we now do as a matter of course in the water.

With her new stroke, Hilda started smashing records everywhere she went; she became known in the press as 'The English Comet'. Invited to compete in the US by the Women's Swimming Association, headed by the formidable Charlotte Epstein with whom she'd forged a friendship in Antwerp, she went on to gain international stardom. This is where her coach came in, in a pastoral capacity. There's no way Hilda's mother would have allowed her to travel to the US alone, so Bill Howcroft's wife agreed to act as a chaperone, and her mother was forced to relent. While she was there, she did speed races and had her first experiences of open-water swimming races, which would have been a shock for a competitor used to the boundaries and calm of a pool. The press loved the eighteen-year-old. 'Man! What a gal!' they declared, in what's almost a parody of an American newspaper headline. But man, what a gal indeed.

Matters came to a head with her mother as the 1924 Olympics approached. The only way Mrs James was going to allow her daughter to attend was if she could personally chaperone her. But there was no budget for that. And if Mrs James wasn't going to the Olympics for free, Hilda wasn't going at all. Now, I've made some pretty dreadful decisions as a parent, but this? This is not a parenting style I admire. Hilda was left off the Olympic team for '24, which could have been disastrous and must surely have been a bitter disappointment. Fortunately, her strong character meant her swimming life didn't end here. She still raced, she did further international tours, and she was still a major 'swimming celebrity', still 'The English Comet'. And in 1925, Hilda James emancipated herself, rebelling completely against her mother by becoming a star on the Cunard cruise line as their resident 'swimming instructress'. Given the family grief she'd faced to get where she was, the image of this fascinating, characterful woman roaring round the English countryside in the 1920s on the motorbike she bought with her wages is a particularly enduring and enjoyable one.

Agnes Nicks was a London office worker who really wanted to break the standing cold-water record. In August

1928, she attempted to swim from Teddington to Waterloo
Bridge, only giving up after six and a half hours. On Boxing
Day of that year, a photo exists of Agnes up to her neck in
water looking sombrely at the camera – and no wonder.
'In water registering thirty-six degrees,' the caption reads,
'Miss Agnes Nicks, the young London endurance swimmer,
swam from Tottenham Bridge to London Bridge in the river
on Boxing Day. Six other girls refused to enter the water
because of the wintery conditions.' Thirty-six degrees is just
above freezing; to be in that water for more than minutes
takes a particular kind of bloody-minded stamina, plenty
of acclimatisation and an ability to disregard all the self-
preservation signals your body is giving off. It's completely
inadvisable unless you really know what you're doing, and
are practised. Agnes obviously had stamina in bundles.
Even though I too am addicted to cold-water swimming,
I'm much more likely to be one of the 'six other girls' on a
swim of that length and in those temperatures, and am full
of admiration for the guts and determination this would
have taken our 'London typist'. The following summer the
papers report that she successfully swam from Teddington
Lock to Waterloo and back, spending thirteen hours in the
water and gaining a new freshwater record for Britain and
for herself. There's something prosaic and unblinking in her
gaze yet she obviously had a core of strength and self-belief.
A woman who went on and on until she got it done, and
then the next morning got up and went to the office, as if
nothing had happened.

Four women, each playing a part in the early days of this story of women's swimming. Each one exceptional in their way – some loudly, and others with no fuss at all. Agnes Beckwith as a role model particularly for young and working-class women without any material advantage. Annette Kellerman for her chutzpah and glamour. Hilda James for changing how we swim. And Agnes Nicks for representing an understated kind of heroine who just quietly does what she wants, outside the normal expectations for women of her class. All of them forging their own path, breaking new ground. Feminism is often measured in waves, and that seems very appropriate in this context; these women were the first wave of a feminism in action. It's with Agnes Nicks's story that I find a particular layer of kinship, because of the cold. But there's something in all of them I admire, and something each of them gave to our swimming story that's made it what it is. It's here I wish that there was a swimming equivalent of the term cyclists use, saying '*chapeau*' as they doff their caps to each other in respect. Because I'd like to doff my swimming cap to these women. *Chapeau*, women. *Chapeau*.

Chapter 5

The Clubbable Woman

It's usually only men who are described as 'clubbable', and before I knew what that actually meant I agreed with it. Lots of them are, especially the ones on the internet. But in its meaning of 'suitable for membership of a club by account of being popular or sociable', there are plenty of women who are eminently clubbable too. The rise of ladies' swimming clubs at the turn of the twentieth century is great proof of that. Women were clearly keen to associate with each other, to form social groups outside of the normal restrictions on their lives, and, yes, to get swimming.

It'll be no surprise to read that men's swimming clubs came first, and two of the earliest were at Eton College in the 1820s. Of course, they couldn't have called it something normal like 'The Eton Swimming Club'. That would have been far too easy for ordinary people to understand. No, Eton had the Philolutic Society which is an annoyingly obfuscating way of saying 'lovers of bathing', and a subsection of that, an elite within the elite, the Psychrolutic Society, or 'lovers of cold water'. It's how I should introduce myself now – 'My name is Jenny, and I'm a psychrolutist' – if I want to keep people guessing.

Through the second half of the nineteenth century men's clubs were proliferating, establishing the idea of organised swimming. The rise in the number of clubs relates directly to the rise in indoor swimming facilities, as they moved from being exclusive private places to being public, and accessible to the middle and respectable lower classes. The London Swim Club was founded in 1859, and by 1879 there were sixteen clubs across London alone. Where there was access to outdoor swimming, clubs sprung up there too, and a few tried to be progressive, like the Jersey Swimming Club whose minutes in 1868 show that they were considering admitting women. It took them a mere nine years to act on that consideration and build a women's changing shed, but then some old geezer must have had a conniption at these female upstarts because in 1885 club rules were amended to state that no woman was eligible to hold office in the club. It's on record that the Jersey women had to contend with voyeurs – peeping Toms as they were more innocuously known then, the scamps – who lounged around their changing facilities at high tide, hoping for a glimpse of something untoward like a bit of flesh. High tides do have a habit of bringing in the rubbish. So even in the exceptions, women were barely tolerated (and peeped upon) rather than having their own spaces, something that sounds familiar in the context of this story so far. And yet feats like those achieved by Agnes Beckwith were being celebrated in the popular press; she'd promoted the idea of swimming, the press capitalised on that, and, in turn, inspired young women were racing to join or form clubs and be like Agnes. It may be one of the few times that tabloids have had a positive impact on women's lives.

With the influence of women like Agnes, and the slow rise in the number of pools allowing women in, more women's clubs formed, specifically to help them learn to swim. Clubs like Kingston Ladies, which was formed in 1898 and is still going strong (though they started in the River Thames and only moved indoors when a specific pool was built), and the Glasgow Naiads, the first ladies' swim club affiliated to the Scottish Amateur Swimming Association in 1900. The Perseverance Ladies' Club – such a great name – were clearly a bolshie lot and had the radical idea of performing in front of a mixed audience, only to be thwarted by the ASA who rejected the proposal. At the time, 1901, only women's fathers were allowed to watch, though this was later relaxed to include husbands. There were clubs like the Ladies' Tadpole Swim Club, which began at Kensington Baths in 1892. Built in 1888, these baths followed a familiar format, with three pools for men and one for women. They were demolished in 1985, and, according to English Heritage, the site was subsequently used for a car park. I'll understand if that sentence makes you want to throw things. The Kensington Lady Tadpoles wore fetching suits of a navy twill, with a scarlet sailor collar and trimmings, which sound marvellous and not at all suitable for swimming. Some women's clubs had members who achieved great things, like the 'psychrolutic' Agnes Nicks who was a member of Highgate's Excelsior Club, and Olympian Bella Moore, a member of Scotland's Premier Club. Other familiar names pop up – on a 1903 poster advertising an event for the Women's Swim Club of the Borough Polytechnic Institute, one of the judges is listed as Mrs Fawcett. There's no more detail than that. So is this *our* Mrs Millicent Fawcett, famous suffragist? The dates fit, the academic setting fits, we've already encountered her sister Elizabeth Garrett Anderson promoting the health benefits of swimming, and we know there were other sporty suffragettes. In the 1913 *Suffrage Annual and Women's Who's Who*, of the 650 entries, nineteen were swimmers, including one Emily Wilding Davison (thirty-two were golfers, but that's someone else's book). Mrs Fawcett being a judge is one of those entirely missable details that you catch by chance and they give you pause. You stop, you look again, you start to build a scene from one tiny bit of texturing detail and you hope, you want it to be her. I want it to be her, I'm not sure why.

The history of specific swim clubs is eminently accessible in local libraries and archives. In my own searches, a poster came to hand, the kind of thing one describes as 'charming' and 'delightful' in plummy tones, while serving tea to a vicar. An A4-sized sheet of paper, browned by time and a little nibbled maybe by mice, it's a simple illustrated piece that looks like the hobby work of a young woman. The page has a small watercolour brown boat painted at the top, and hand-drawn line illustrations round the side – shells, a pixie figure adding notes to a book, a reclining figure in the bottom corner. With the words arrayed around the watercolour boat, it declares itself to be a 'List of Ladies Wishing to Found a Ladies Swimming Club for Brighton'. Beneath that announcement, the centre of the page is taken up with signatures, mostly written in pencil that's faded and so hard to read. On the left, a list of thirteen names, and some of them can be just about made out. Louise Muspratt. Rosa Potts. Violet Heisch. On the right, with a pencilled note in small script that these are 'promised for next year', another list of signatures. Gladys Beatrice Samuel. Helene Gengoult, Maudie Gibbs. (I have an abiding affection for old British names. There's something deeply satisfying about a 'Maudie Gibbs' or a 'Rosa Potts', and they're best enjoyed by being spoken out loud. I watched a documentary once about Marks & Spencer which featured two women called Olive Crisp and Betty Marriage. Those two names have stuck with me over quite a few years, they somehow represent everything that is great in a name. Singly they are strong – Olive Crisp. Betty Marriage. But in combination with each other, they are the perfect double act. They are ineffably real and solid names, such ordinary words, boring almost, there's nothing fanciful or fluffed up. It's not just that they're 'of their time'. It's that ... a writer wouldn't make them up, they would sound too unbelievably prosaic. They're the best names. Give me a Betty Marriage or an Olive Crisp over a Rupert Ponsonby Smythe any day of the week.)

That list of women on the left-hand side of the poster achieved what they set out to achieve – on 2 December 1891, thirteen women met at 25 Old Steine for the inaugural meeting of the Brighton Ladies' Swim Club. Their meetings are meticulously recorded from the off, in a set of hardback books the colour of accountancy. The minutes are mostly charming and benign and maybe, if I'm honest, a tad tedious. There's a polite tone that pervades, because Ladies *are* polite, and the formal language of proposing and seconding, recorded in pages of slender, slanted writing that makes an undemanding mark on each page, keeps them on the straight and narrow. That first meeting starts with the important business of what they'd wear. 'Proposed by Miss Brignall seconded by Miss Styer that the Bathing Costumes should be red with the Brighton Arms embroidered on the left breast, caps optional, carried.' At the second meeting, a month later, they'd had a little think and elaborated on those plans. 'Proposed by Miss A. Muspratt and seconded by Miss Brignall that the Bathing Costumes be red and trimmed with black with the Brighton Arms embroidered in black on the left breast. Carried.' The costumes were to be red, that was decided. Now they could get on with the serious business of swimming.

By 1914, the *Swimming Magazine* was rammed with details about different ladies' swimming clubs – Sarnian, City of London, Gloucester, Exeter, Thistle (Aberdeen), Windsor, Dartford Premier Club, Swansea Ladies – from right across the country. By the time we hit 1918, Agnes Campbell says in her report that 'it is usual in small places to find two or three clubs for men and boys, and one for ladies', but in cities the numbers were more significant. In Manchester that year, there were 134 clubs for men and 30 for women, and in Liverpool, 75 for men and 63 for women.

There's something about women's clubs, though. Something about women gathering together, the community of women, which people just cannot let lie. The very idea seems to unleash a heap of resentments and belittlements which, when you check them against reality, are entirely baffling. Sometimes it's an apparently harmless scorn, the idea that women's clubs are really just an excuse to gossip (about men, of course) and drink sweet fizzy wine (for reference, see all assumptions about women's book groups, ever). I say 'apparently harmless' because it's pernicious rubbish that feeds into a horribly undermining narrative around what women do, how frivolous and shallow we always are, even down to how we speak (hysterically, shrilly). And it doesn't always stop at a mild bit of scorn, it can be full-blown rage – I've seen grown men get utterly furious about the idea of a women-only space, as if being excluded from something might literally kill them. As if this particular kind of 'community' is threatening the very fabric of society. If I could do graphs, I'd put one here. The X axis would be 'Groups of women from 1900 to the present day' and the Y axis would be 'Fury'. The plotted points would bob along the bottom in a nice straight line to start with, get a bit lively around the time when the suffragettes made everyone terribly cross, and then go rocketing off into orbit somewhere around the time of Greenham Common, never to come back down again.

But actually, the value of congregating with people with similar aims and experiences is well understood; plenty of men get it either instinctively or when a light is shone on their own preferences. (For reference, see all anecdotes about men going to football with a group of mates, ever.) And strict segregation was definitely a plus point in women's desire to congregate. In the pool there was little danger of them coming into accidental contact with men … except sometimes they did, which is when unrest ensued. The women of Brighton in 1892 wanted to circumvent any 'issues' by proposing that 'the members of the club who cannot swim should if possible be taught by a swimming mistress'. They wanted to remain a women-only group, I get it. (I also get the idea of joining a club for an activity that you couldn't yet do. It's a badge of intent, of acknowledging 'these are my people'.) When a Mr Eagle was appointed to tutor the Croydon Ladies' team, established in 1891, he was required to get special dispensation from the Baths Committee before being allowed in. Derbyshire's Belper Ladies' Swimming Club, formed in June 1910, had all sorts of bother around the matter of men, as the records of their meetings show. Like the Brighton ladies, the matters they dealt with were mostly polite and moderate – who would occupy what position on the committee, what they'd wear (again) and what the rules would be. The minutes show how they planned the events for their first gala, and again their aims were humble, as the Belper ladies were not yet 'confident in their proficiency', and a little 'shy at displaying their abilities', bless them. They proposed the gala include a couple of short races, a Long Plunge, and a few 'fun' events for the end of the evening. Swimming underwater, a candle race, a stocking race and a blindfold race. A blindfold race sounds innocuous enough, you might think ... unless you've actually tried swimming blindfold. I've been made to do it as some kind of 'trust' exercise, and it's horrible. Even in the safe, enclosed environment of a small pool surrounded by friends, it was very discombobulating and unpleasant. Don't try it. It is not innocuous at all. Belper ladies may have been shy, but they were made of stronger stuff than me when it comes to swimming blindfold.

And then the sticky issue of who would teach them raises its head. In March 1913, it was proposed 'that we ask Mr and Mrs Stapleton to give instruction' and 'that we ask both Mr and Mrs Stapleton to go in the water with us, if Mr Stapleton will not go in, to instruct us from the side'. Come on, Mr Stapleton, show us what you're made of, get in the water! Trying to be sympathetic to Mr Stapleton, I ponder whether it made the poor fellow anxious, the thought of being in the same water as women he wasn't married to? Or did Mr Stapleton have dreams of being an amazing teacher with a clutch of women natationists looking up to him forever in his debt, but was doomed by social mores that demanded his feet remained dry? So little information and so much conjecture from a simple set of records; on the one hand, I've conjured a quivering and ineffectual Mr Stapleton, and on the other, a thwarted superhero. This is what happens as you search the sparse lines in these books, you extrapolate, fill in the blanks, the minutiae becomes the mystery.

The issue of Mr Stapleton dragged on and more than a year later an answer appears – the Urban District Council didn't want to allow Mr Stapleton in the baths at all. Not anywhere. Mr Stapleton, what *have* you done to earn this reputation? By June of 1914, the ladies went to the council asking them to change their mind, with no luck. The minutes record that they 'held to their decision not to allow Mr Stapleton or any other gentleman to be our instructor'. So it wasn't Mr Stapleton that was at fault, it was any man at all. Meanwhile, the council gave permission for Mr Patrick, the Baths Superintendent, to wander in and out of the room willy-nilly! The ladies wanted Mr Stapleton

IN, and Mr Patrick OUT. The council said they would speak to Mr Patrick, and resolved to try and find a female professional to teach them (what about Mrs Stapleton? Had she retired to her chamber in despair by this point?) but in the meantime, without a proper instructor and Mr Patrick freely wandering, the club membership dwindled. It's one tiny story in one tiny club in a small town, but it's revealing. Everything the women wanted, they had to negotiate with men who weren't inclined to give it. There were very few women teachers, but how could women learn to swim if men couldn't teach them?

Part of the records for the Stafford Ladies' Swim Club (SLSC) is a minute book from March 1960 to 1981, a hardback maroon exercise book with a neat label on the front, and my heart beat a little faster as I turned the cover. Would it contain a similarly small story from which I'd build? What glimpses of life would I get? What intrigue and drama?

The SLSC was founded in 1901, met at the town's Royal Brine Baths until they were closed and the club moved to the town's new leisure centre in 1974 – and there you are, public-pool history in one sentence. The Brine Baths had opened at the end of the nineteenth century when salt water was seen as a cure-all, and Stafford brine, piped in from salt works in the town, was considered to be particularly superior, better than the Dead Sea even. Municipal pride is such a wonderful thing; our salt water is better than your salt water, and does anybody want to start a fight? Early photos of the SLSC show a large bunch of capable, confident women; a 1928 postcard of their first life-saving team has seven swimmers in formless singlets, their arms crossed and their faces set in intense, determined looks. The postcard is signed on the back 'Mum x'. I wonder who 'Mum' is. A swimmer? A life-saver? She's sent the postcard to her child – why? Is she saying 'Look, it's me!' or 'Look, it's you!'? Is that her, sitting in the centre of the pic in a voluminous gymslip, in charge of the team?

The SLSC minutes are mostly, as in Belper and Brighton, concerned with small purchases (stopwatches, cards, gifts for ailing committee members) and elections to office. We learn that there are a lot of vice presidents in this club. That the same names come over and again: Mrs C. Pitt. Mrs I. Slinn. Mrs L. Voce. Reading any set of records that cover a period of time, you become attached to and intrigued by the names you see repeated over the years. You start to look out for them, you want them to still be there, and you wonder where they went, when they're not. You know that every month, every meeting, these particular women went to this room, sat and discussed this thing. By the repeated sight of their names on a list of 'those present', they flesh out and become real. This particular maroon exercise book opens with Mrs C. Pitt in the chair, and we see her signature as she signs off each set of minutes as an accurate record. Across thirteen years her handwriting becomes increasingly wobbly and frail. It takes on a very specific kind of 'old lady' patina – becomes an approximation of its original self. By October 1973 the SLSC are discussing moving to the new pool for their summer season and Mrs Dumbleton is in the chair. What happened to Mrs C. Pitt? Where is she? Ah, here she is, under Any Other Business, being sent a 'get well soon' card. She makes a brief return to the chair the following year, but by 1977 has clearly retired from active duty and is made a life member. Through these flimsy pages, I have become connected to Mrs C. Pitt, maybe because I recognise her. I suspect if you're in any kind of club you'll recognise your own Mrs C. Pitt figure too, someone who keeps large chunks of it together; they tend to be called 'unsung heroines' in the local papers. They don't do anything 'brave', they're not saving lives, but they are quietly and conscientiously getting on with the work required to keep things running. In my club (South London Swimming Club) we have Doreen Fitch, who has been our Membership Secretary for decades. Doreen is an 'unsung heroine', she's my Mrs C. Pitt.

And then innocuous sentences send you spinning off into your own memories. A minute, recording how 'Mrs B. Smith sent invitations to the annual Swimming Club Dinner and Dance at Brocton Cricket Club' took me back to nights in the seventies when my parents would go to dinner dances at somewhere Unattainably Posh in Sutton Coldfield, somewhere with a long gravel drive and rose gardens and drinks on silver trays being wooshed under your nose. My parents' social life was almost fully occupied by being active members of an amateur theatre group, so going out usually involved rehearsing or performing or building sets and they took turns to be in plays because babysitting was a rare and precious commodity you couldn't squander. (They rarely paid for it except in emergencies. Instead, my mum belonged to a babysitting circle, which in theory sounds like a fantastic idea – parents organising themselves to offer a mutually useful free service – but in practice is not. Looking after your own kids can be boring enough but looking after other people's is a dreadful night out. I could tolerate it if there were better snacks on offer in someone else's home, but in the 1970s snacks were either three crisps on a plate or a couple of Rich Tea biscuits, neither of which are worth leaving the house for.) But once or twice a year, they'd prop an invite on the mantelpiece, with their names written on the dotted line. Mr and Mrs Philip Landreth. The pleasure of your company. Dinner, then dancing. It sounds tremendous and I can't for the life of me think why that fell out of fashion.

A small selection of long dresses for these occasions hung in my mum's wardrobe; we'd occasionally sneak up to peep and marvel at them, these glamorous frocks that represented another mother entirely. Up to a frilled neck, down to a frilled floor pelmet, in fabrics that don't exist any more and colour combinations that shouldn't. Great glossy exotic swathes poofing into sleeves and ruffles and bows and all sorts. A fabulous, bright, tiny-waisted collection that was rarely worn, and equally rarely added to. She'd get her hair set, pull out her best jewellery – brooches the colour of peacocks, clip-on earrings that pinched and almost-hippyish filigree pendants on long chains. She'd 'put on her face'. My father would dress in his tux, his maroon cummerbund straining harder year on year, smooth back his hair and become like a film-star man, really rather handsome, and oh, they were a picture. They'd drive off, my mum briefly wishing they had a better car or at least a clean one and my dad not caring, and we'd imagine them with other equally gorgeous couples sipping from delicate glasses, swishing about with a confident elan, laughing with a tinkling gaiety that showed their teeth. We didn't want to know about them dancing, that was peculiar and intimate, and no, we didn't want to think about that. Instead, the next morning we'd interrogate them on the menu, which was worlds apart from our everyday fare. If you've ever looked at a cookbook from the seventies, you'll see the kind of things we imagined. Things in aspic, things formed to not look like food, or in fake colours. Things rare and exciting, like prawns. It was like they were briefly on a different planet. Like once or twice a year, the characters my amateur actor parents played were aliens.

What none of the minutes show (and why would they? – they're the briefest of flirtations with what actually got said) is a tendency that Lady Dorothy, the *Swimming Magazine* ladies' correspondent, wanted to put a stop to. It's something you only ever see in women's clubs accorded to Lady D, rarely, if ever, in men's. That tendency is basic bitching. 'I refer,' she says, 'to a certain jealous vein which once rooted becomes a source of considerable bickering and is detrimental to the advancement of so many clubs.' Lady D goes on to state with certainty that the trouble starts with the club's 'foundress'. 'She has made the club what it now is and she has her own ideals and ambitions for the club's future welfare … and she resents opposition.' Then along comes new blood, who doesn't accord our foundress due deference. And 'if she is a woman with sufficient force of character to found or organise a club she will resent interference … and seek to overrule it'. Or, Lady Dorothy continues, she'll offer her resignation in the hope that no one will accept it … except they do. The whole thing is beginning to feel like a bad soap opera. But 'younger members are headstrong and thoughtless', she says, and 'do not realise that with their advanced ideas they utterly upset the conservative reasonings of others'. So is it disrespect that's the problem, or politics and new ideas? Is she repeating the line that everyone moves more to the right as they get older (a myth that gets no house room here)? Or is this the modernity versus tradition argument, like one Stafford Ladies had, about replacing the Long Plunge with something more fashionable?

Old women need to be less rigid, young women need to do less bickering, everybody just needs to get on and stop being spiteful: in attempting to police women's behaviour, Lady D plays into some hefty negative stereotyping. It's the classic 'women are their own worst enemies' canard, which is always handy for the times when women don't behave brilliantly to one another, and one that makes me yell 'and why do you think that is?' in response. I suspect the same rituals go on in men's societies and clubs, only in language with an entirely different set of stereotypes, all 'young bucks' and 'locking horns' and much more primal. So actually she could be describing any kind of societal structure, where the young rebel against the ways of the old to take charge of the tribe. But beneath the stereotyping about women that I don't recognise, there's behaviour that I definitely do. It's about kicking against everything and anything represented by older women. I wouldn't use Lady Dorothy's word 'jealousy' – that doesn't chime at all. I'd call it ageism. Where people might feel comfortable challenging sexism, they might not recognise ageism as something so urgent. Silly old bag. Get out, old woman. But it plays itself out in every public sphere. Old men are revered, they're pillars of the community, majestic old stags, silver foxes. The worst they might get called is 'grandad' when they roar 'you paid *how* much?' Old women are not accorded that respect, not by anyone. Old women are Just. The. Worst. Why should dynamic and headstrong young women want to listen to them?

And equally, why should I pay heed to what Lady Dorothy says? It's because she was one of the few women writing about women in a public sphere, so her words carried weight. It would take an extraordinary curmudgeon to disagree with her underlying message that we should all be nice to each other however old, but I wonder if seeing a woman castigate other women in print was as dispiriting then as it is now. And I wonder if women readers struggled, like I did, to see an accurate reflection of my own empathic and supportive experiences in women-only clubs. It's not until the end of the article that Lady Dorothy says something where I see myself. 'There are always troublesome and quibbling members in any club who argue for the sake of argument,' she says scoldingly. Yes, Lady Dorothy there are. I'm sorry. I'll try to be less argumentative in future.

Chapter 6

My Waterbiography
(Part II)

At the start of the 1980s, 'getting fit' hadn't really been invented yet, except for jogging, which people only did in America, a land far far away. Jogging was imported here by intrepid travellers, the few plucky individuals who ventured across to the States on journeys that took three weeks on massive ships that the whole nation would turn out to wave off from Liverpool or Southampton. Flags flapped, mothers waved hankies at their brave departing sons, brass bands played 'Anarchy in the UK'. Months later, most of the travellers would return – we'd always lose a few to the irresistible lure of massive salads served with a slice of orange – appearing at the top of the gangplanks in what we now know to be 'tracksuits', in which they would demonstrate the new fad of running slowly to get fit.

Of course, this is a fiction. Firstly, television existed, through which we could ogle at the strange fitness habits of people from faraway lands, and secondly, jogging had existed since Shakespeare (probably, it's always Shakespeare). But fitness wasn't anything like the business it is today. All we had was the Green Goddess. Trying to explain the Green Goddess is a little like telling teenagers about life before computers – it sounds unbearable, inconceivable, but it's all true. For those who don't remember, the Green Goddess was a set-haired cheery lady in a shiny lizard-green leotard who did exercises on breakfast television – and there was a point, sometime at the beginning of 1983 – when each part of that sentence was so new and exciting you wouldn't believe. Leotards! Exercise! Breakfast television! Even the 'green' part – just because television had been broadcast in colour for some years by then didn't mean everyone had a colour television. We were very late adopters in this respect; my older sister and I would go next door every Thursday evening to watch *Top of the Pops* on their spanking great colour set. Our TV wasn't just black and white either, it was in a box which had little doors so you could pretend it was something less objectionable, like a drinks cabinet. It was also coin-operated, something I find so peculiar in retrospect that I wonder if I have false memory syndrome. But no, it's true, I've checked with Landreth Google (my mum). Our TV was coin-operated. We rented it, but that wasn't uncommon then, buying a TV was a big investment, as unreachable as buying a new car. If you rented it, you could change it for a better one in time (the word 'upgrade' also didn't really exist), and you could rent video recorders too. As prescient as ever, my dad chose to rent a Betamax machine; this excellent display of business acumen illustrates why the whole rental business suited us well. If the TV broke down, a man in a grey coat would come and fix it. A different man would come and empty the little coin box at the side, a slot where you'd put your 50p, turn the key with a cratttccchhh and listen to the money drop. When it was nearly full, we'd itch to get into that coin box, knowing the great wealth that lay therein. Sometimes the TV would run out in the middle of a great programme, and we'd be scrabbling for Mum's purse in the hope she'd have coins.

I bounced out of home and into uni to 'do drama', where the combination of being Catholic (don't show off) with being on this kind of course (SHOW OFF!) ended up cancelling each other out perfectly. It was perfectly normal not to have stuff. It was people who owned things who were the exception – only one person on my corridor had a portable TV, which was about the size of a small fridge and which nobody watched except when football was on. My friend Paul was the only one with a car, and in those days you were legally allowed to squash in as many people as could fit, so he did. Not that anyone really went anywhere, just to college and back when we moved off campus. If we missed the lift from Paul, we would hitch. The notion that you'd stand on the side of the road at the university's semi-official hitching point, stick out your thumb and get a ride from a stranger going in the right direction is another unfathomable idea now. We did it regularly, everyone bundling around hopping in and out of random cars like nothing. Nobody thought it was risky behaviour, though the idea of a young woman doing that now gives me palpitations.

Nobody in my university tribe played sport; like my family, this tribe too was very defiantly arts and crafts. My friend Adrian had brought his badminton racket with him in the first term but one badminton racket is a lonely thing, and it got shoved further and further under his bed as the terms ticked by. I shared a corridor in halls for a year with some women who played rugby, and even though I identified with Jo from *Little Women*, quite the most robust and independent of the four, I still found their ways quite startlingly brusque. That may have been influenced by the fact they were training to be PE teachers and my view of PE teachers had not yet recovered from Mrs Hassle days. My only real contact with sport was during the holidays when I'd scurry home to my job in the lido cafe, serving Bovril to Two Spoons Gary.

Well, apart from that one time when my creative writing tutor suggested we all go nude swimming in the university pool (I hadn't realised there was one) and then we would draw on the experience for our writing. The tutor was an interesting-looking man – all vertical eyebrows and neck scarves, and rumour had it he lived on a barge. But hey, we were a bunch of pretentious idiots in pyjama tops and dungarees who thought we were going to be actors and writers, so we were well matched. We'd have to break into the pool, he said, and definitely not tell anyone, especially not those boring boss types. (At the time I thought this sounded daring and temptingly anti-establishment but with hindsight it's almost embarrassingly unsubtle.) Yeah let's do it, I said, with studied nonchalance. Please God, let's not, I thought – a cocktail of horrible anxiety and a desire to appear cool. Those feelings were partly about a lack of physical confidence. The thought that I might be joshingly dunked in rough play made me feel panicky. I couldn't stand my ground in water the way I could on land and the idea of being casually naked was simply not in my DNA. I'm from the Midlands! This is not how we do things! My repression bursts out in the form of anger, not confident strutting nudity! We didn't go swimming, in the end. We did play some games with this creative writing tutor though, and the fact that I've remembered them all these years later, when I've forgotten the names of my own children plenty of times, is significant. The games were to help us break down barriers, to engender trust, but the only thing they engendered in me was a lifelong hatred of trust games. One of the games entailed students placing everyone else in the room according to how they felt about them. When a fellow student put me under a table which had chairs piled on it, I sensed animosity. In another game, we all sat in a circle with one person in the middle. Someone in the circle would shout a category to end the sentence 'person most likely to', and the one in the middle would turn and face whoever they thought in the circle would fit that category. People did it tantalisingly, teasingly, or with great certainty. Person most likely to … be famous. Shoplift a ham. Take an overdose. Fun suggestions like that. Then it was the tutor's turn to be in the middle. Someone shouted 'Person most likely to … star in a porn film' to him. He deliberated. He spun, and spun again. And then he turned and stayed still, facing me. Given that I was mostly dressed in plumber's overalls with various bits of my head shaved and a furious scowl on my face, I didn't feel I screamed 'potential porn star'. It was the very opposite of the image I intended to project, and maybe he was playing with that. Or was I supposed to feel flattered? I wasn't flattered. I was crushed and I stared around the room measuring myself against the other women, thinking 'What about her? She's MUCH more …' which is some horribly divisive rubbish. Still, I hope the tutor appreciates that even though it's taken years, I've used the experience in my writing.

I wasn't the kind of student who backpacked round Europe every holiday. For starters, I didn't have a passport even though you could get cheap year-long ones. I didn't have the nerve. I didn't seem to be the right class, have the right confidence. It made me homesick just thinking of it. Going abroad was a rare exotic thing that other people did, the kind of people who got Minis for passing their O levels (I got a pen). My own children had passports before they were a year old, but then they, much to the utter bafflement of my mother, ate avocados as a weaning food. I present this as further proof of my glorious ascent to the middle classes. The first time I went abroad I was twenty-two, and it was a revelation. It was the first time I'd seen some sea that I might actually want to go in. I went with my mum and sisters the year after my father died. It would be good for us, we thought, a distracting adventure, though I suspect we were all terrified not just at going so far but at negotiating the terrain without my more-worldly dad. We went to the South of France for a week. It was hot yet they sold doughnuts on the beach, which seemed crazy and wrong. But here, the sea wasn't grey and bitter and frightening and the beach wasn't pebbly and hard, it didn't make you fall over like a Kinnock if you walked on it in bare feet. Here, it was sandy and the water was calm and flat and greeny-blue, like I'd seen in magazines. I wanted to be in that water. As I say, a revelation.

To say I went swimming would be an exaggeration. I'd wade in, enjoying the simple pleasure of being able to actually walk on the sand rather than stumble like a broken puppet over rocks, then I'd launch myself into the sea and swim to just inside my depth – no further, because I knew that tides could whip you right out as soon as look at you. Then I'd swim back and forth across a short section of the bay, my arms pulling in a proximity to breaststroke, my head up and sunglasses on, as worldly as a person ever was. Feeling for the first time the play of an intense sun on wet skin, seeing my laughingly pale body under the water, getting a heavy crush on that warmth. It was more about cooling off than swimming, but from the lofty heights of my early twenties, being able to play in the water was delightful, and brought with it none of the concomitant blue lips and twiggy shivering limbs I was used to. Those childhood days were gone, this was a new era now. 'I wouldn't really have called it swimming,' I said to a friend recently, and she told me that this is how most people swim – on holiday, sunglasses on, doing a few laps of some picturesque cove or tiny hotel pool. My perspective was skewed, my friend said, because I was now so obsessed. She said 'so obsessed' with that tone of 'there is something actually wrong with you'.

From then on, every penny I earned, which was never much so the budget was always very mean, went towards holidays by the sea with friends or sisters. Greece was my favoured spot, you could share a Greek salad between two and it was guaranteed hot, but the swimming still essentially served the purpose of making it bearable to stay in the sun as long as possible. We'd be on the beach by 9 a.m., and didn't like to leave until the sun set. Because this was all about The Tan. Getting a good tan was serious business involving sunbathing schedules and sun lotion regimes; the smell of Hawaiian Tropic can transport me back in a flash. We'd start on the highest imaginable factor for the first few days, which was factor 8. Now that my face is permanently slathered in factor 30 and I go around looking like I recently got bad news, this sounds like we were on a death mission, but we didn't know any better. We'd move downwards through factors 6, then 4, towards the final basting when we'd use baby oil (or olive oil if we were feeling truly Continental) on the last day so we could fly home with actually blistered skin. One particular friend had a cone of shiny metal that she'd put under her chin to reflect the sun up to her face. She'd also sunbathe sideways with her arms up, so her armpits could be tanned. It was ridiculous. We were ridiculous. Of course, if you're going to sunbathe like that you also need good sunburn remedies, and we'd lie at night with sliced tomatoes all over us or slathered in Greek yogurt, both of which were 'local remedies' we were reliably informed, but really just made us feel like hot salad.

The whole 'look' really needed to include tanned breasts. I did not want to be a prudish Brit, I wanted to be a Modern European, and Modern Europeans had their tits out. Whatever the age or shape – out. All it had taken for me was that first week in the South of France and boom, I'd moved from wanting to hide, to defiantly stripping it all off on holiday. It was an extension of character acting, and I had a degree in that. This was some powerful magic, except I always kept my pants on. To strip off completely was unnecessary exhibitionism (I danced a fine line of self-imposed regulations, riddled with inconsistencies), and anyway, you needed to wear bottoms to get a sharp tan line. Without an area of contrast, how could you really show the work you'd put in? I was a living 'before and after' – bikini bottoms showed the pale placebo section of myself, two ghostly buttocks so glaringly white they could have brought planes in to land. This is not behaviour on any level that I'm proud of, and even though I now know the science of dead skin I'm still secretly a Tan Fan. I've just toned it down a bit.

Very few photos exist of a young topless me, and I'm glad. It's all a bit ... embarrassing. I don't play that brave, insouciant character comfortably any more, I've accepted the fact that I simply was not raised to parade my body. That is for other, different people. More relaxed and open people, not ones from Catholic homes in the Midlands. People like the Finns. I try and find pools wherever I go abroad, for me it's as much part of the cultural experience as visiting museums and art galleries is, and on a recent trip to Helsinki, I wanted to swim. I knew that my family would not willingly visit a frozen outdoor bathing spot so I found a local indoor pool, Yrjönkatu Swimming Hall, for decades Helsinki's sole indoor pool – after all, why would you pay to swim inside when you have a multitude of outdoor places? While the elegant structure of the pool building itself felt familiar, its rules were a reverse of everything I know and hold dear. Bathing costumes have only been allowed since 2001, and it has separate swim times for men and women. Nude and segregated swimming is entirely the norm; in a land not so far away from ours, people are being raised to be completely comfortable with hanging out with their parents in full buff. It's enough to make Nigel Farage explode.

I went along to the pool with my teenage daughter and her friend, and signs in the entrance warned us that 'swim costumes are optional'. Had I been alone I might have tried to override my DNA and pretend to be absolutely fine swimming naked. 'It's gloriously liberating,' I'd have spouted unconvincingly, though in my heart I've never found that to be true. I think it's exposing and makes me worried things might swim up. I don't think my daughter would have found enforced nudity in the company of her mother to be gloriously liberating, so I saved us all from years of therapy and we put on our costumes, though in a concession to cultural difference, I left my swim cap off. The pool was busy when we arrived, and we changed on the side – no hiding in tiny plastic cubicles here, oh no. We weren't the only three in costumes but almost. There was a whole lane of elderly naked women with floats strapped round their waists, doing a kind of aqua-walk up and down the lane, and if swimming ever looks unnatural, walking upright in the water looks downright tricksy. I snapped on my super-professional snazzy goggles, and wondered why everyone else was doing this funny kind of head-up breaststroke. Why does no one have goggles on? Why is no one doing Proper Swimming? And then I swam behind a naked woman doing breaststroke in my lane. Every time she kicked and I got a view I thought, ah OK. *Now* I get why people aren't doing Proper Swimming.

Once I left university I moved to London, as is the law for all new drama graduates. Here I was, in my twenties, working in a creative city surrounded, suddenly, by people getting fit. Even some of my arts and crafts clique took to the gym. But still, talk about our own bodies was restricted and private, to discuss them would be prurient. I knew of feminist classes where everyone squatted over a mirror and examined their own vulvas, but that wasn't for me. If we did mention bodies, we generally meant those all-in-one tops women wore, a cross between a gymnast's leotard and a Babygro, that did up with press studs underneath. Bodies were meant to give you a sleek look with nothing riding up, but the reality was that they completely flattened even the smallest of boob, and when you un-poppered them to wee, the back flap would dangle into the loo and then there'd be an unseemly amount of contortion and effort trying to grab it again and popper the front and back together between your legs. Also, a wodge of press studs between your legs is fine for babies, with their delicate bits protected by nappies, but less fine for adult women. Ouch. But gradually, exercise was pushing its way to the front of people's agendas, and they began to do aerobics for fun. It was the era that saw the birth of the step class. Step aerobics was basically stepping on and off a milk crate repetitively. Except obviously you couldn't use an actual milk crate, you needed to buy a special bit of kit almost exactly the same as a milk crate only not. And thus exercise became monetised. You could tell the people who were doing step classes because in a matter of weeks their thighs would change from small spindly things that just hung there, to pumped-up bulbous monster thighs, from supermarket own-brand chicken drumsticks with a paltry string of meat, to organic corn-fed crazy-plump wahoo can't-eat-a-whole-one drumsticks. Suddenly, thighs were everywhere.

I didn't want to be left out of this fitness thing, but couldn't stand being told what to do, so I started going to the gym a bit and swimming, though the time of getting my hair wet in the pool was still some years off. Going to a private gym or pool at this stage was simply not an option, they were unattainable and few, reserved for a different class of person, or yuppies as we called them. Yuppies made me furious and I would have downright scorned any place they went to, however nice. I had as much aspiration to join a private pool as I did to become a member of a gentlemen's club, and about as much chance. Now we're overrun with private gyms and it's standard to pay silly amounts to swim in an over-styled pool the size of a bathroom sink, but then I swam in what I thought were grotty dives: council pools, council facilities, for council people, at a time when that really did mean something about community.

I thought they were grotty dives, and in many ways they were. Underfunded, too hot and too cold, clammy and crammed changing rooms, basic facilities, rubbish showers that dripped sporadically on your head, leaking pipes kept together by crusts of yellowing lava that grew round every joint, cracking plaster, crackled tiles, bits falling off, great behemoths of chilly water pumped full of chemicals that ironically might hasten a building's demise. The kind of pool my Aunty Mary first took me to. Places we should cherish because they speak to us about who we are. They were starting to rebrand as 'leisure centres', which is infinitely snappier than 'great Victorian pools of historic significance that are a crucial part of our architectural and social heritage'. I swam at Seymour Leisure Centre in Marylebone, Marshall Street Baths off Carnaby Street and Ironmonger Row Baths near Old Street – all London pools because I was becoming myopic and thought it was truly the greatest city on earth. The last two of these have been beautifully refurbished and are now part of the capital's best swimming offer, but at the time I regularly used them, they were distinctly harder to love. But then, our expectations were lower, *my* expectations were lower and my swimming bag was definitely more minimal. There was no point owning goggles as I still didn't put my face in the water, and, anyway, I had the wrong shape face for goggles, it felt like they were slowing trying to suck my eyes out of their sockets, like when you clamp a glass over your mouth and then have that slight panic because you can't break the grip of the suction and fear that you'll die ingloriously with a glass stuck on your face. Even wearing a Speedo costume I felt I could be done under the Trades Description Act. If there had been a range of swimwear called Slowo, I'd have been first in the queue to buy one.

I'd change into my one functional costume and spend a good twenty minutes kicking ineffectually up and down the pool. Always in the slow lane, head up, always on my own. It wasn't sociable, or relaxing ... it wasn't pleasant in any regard, truthfully. I didn't feel free in the water, I couldn't lose myself, it felt like an extended session of barely controlled panic, an elemental struggle that I was engaging in for reasons that escape me. I can't have been getting fit. The only thing I was definitely getting was wet.

The only modern place I used regularly at that time was the Oasis in Covent Garden, which had been reconstructed in the sixties and included a very small, very heated outdoor pool. This felt different. Being in warm water outside gave the Oasis the giddy decadence of being on some kind of holiday. There was a sense, swimming here, that I could make a different life for myself, a more glamorous one, one with heat *and* water, such extravagance. Going there marked me out as rather something, I thought. Hindsight being a marvellous thing, I could say it also marked the start of my love for swimming outdoors, but I'd be stretching a point. But I certainly loved the steam rising on a rainy day, the cold air on a hot face, the tippy-toed scamper from changing room into the water. Who doesn't? I didn't mind how busy it was, I was never in a hurry or had a goal of how far to swim, I was serving out my time in the water in what felt like the most pleasant way. I worked round the corner from the Oasis and even started to go with colleagues, in the evenings. We'd laugh up and down the slow lane, while a whole other breed of person entirely flung themselves sportily along in the fast lane. Who were these fast-lane creatures? They were the people who got picked for teams, who did sport on Saturdays, who cared about competing and winning. They were the rugby girls I'd shared a university corridor with. Those poor people and their uncultured lives, I thought, as if a competitive attitude was incompatible with going to fringe theatre a lot. I stayed in my slow lane, with my uncompetitive fringy friends, and I was happy there. We'd come out after a swim into the now-dark London streets, light our cigarettes and wander along wafting that particularly noxious combination of chlorine and smoke as we went.

By the mid nineties, I was pregnant with my first child, and swimming started to mean something different to me. It's no coincidence, the two things were definitely connected. I was working round the corner from Ironmonger Row Baths, at a time when being the Gateway to Shoreditch was not something an estate agent would boast about. (It wasn't completely untrendy – there was one vegan cafe that in my mind I am convinced was owned by Boy George but maybe I'm getting mixed up with a celebrity storyline from *EastEnders*.) A couple of lunchtimes a week, my colleague Claire and I would troll up to the baths and go for a swim, then visit a cafe (not vegan) on the way back to get an impossibly large floured bap and a bag of crisps to eat at our desks. Everyone knew that swimming while you are pregnant was a good healthy choice, even if you're not supposed to undo it all by scoffing an unfeasibly big lunch afterwards.

Ironmonger Row was in a pretty manky state; I've revisited it since it's been done up and it feels like a different place while still paying respectful homage to its history. The memories of how it was in the nineties have been wiped out by one successful refurbishment. Swimming while pregnant is a blissful thing, even if your waters break while you're there, as happened to a friend. I didn't have a pregnancy swimming costume, and if they had existed I certainly wouldn't have wasted money on one. I wore that same trusty Speedo, the rather schoolish dull navy-blue affair that entirely encapsulated my attitude to swimming. When I had a small pregnancy belly, it fitted fine. As my belly grew, it did not. By the time I stopped work it was stretched so out of shape that the midsection resembled a damp plastic bag that's carried a bit too much – practically translucent, sagging and almost at breaking point. Barely useable when it was on, utterly terrible when I took it off. I must have looked a right sight. As I got bigger, getting changed for swimming was like trying to put a sleeping bag back in its bag – everything starts off OK, but rapidly descends into a mad attempt to cram the damn thing in any which way. In the water, though, I didn't care. On those days when I could almost hear my skin stretching and straining, when I could barely stand up without feeling like I was going to tip forward and my whole body ached from carrying this busy and enormous bulge, getting in the pool was a blessed relief.

Pregnancy hadn't turned me into some spiritual mamma weaving flowers into my hair, but swimming felt like the right thing to do on a very instinctive level. In the pool, I felt weightless, I felt calm and I connected with my changing body. It helped me accept it. And I felt more connected with the baby too; as he swam around in water, so did I. We were both held in a bigger sphere, safe in a shared experience. Neither of us had to fight the pull of gravity and I could play with my sense of balance. We reached a mutual equilibrium. And I'd revel in the silly things pregnancy temporarily deprives you off – not just the grandiose things like a sense of my self, but also the more mundane; as l floated on my back, sploshing calmly up and down, I might get a glimpse of my forgotten feet. Feeling weightless is temporary, I'd realise when I'd try to spring up the steps and remember it had become more of a haulage process. I'd stand poolside, become physically grounded again and be thankful for the brief respite.

For the first time, swimming offered me freedom. I was physically capable above and beyond my immediate situation. I wasn't a pregnant person, I was a person, I wasn't lost. Though it sometimes felt like this bowling ball of a belly wanted to anchor me to the bottom of the pool, I could float and move without being hostage to it. I could escape.

Chapter 7

Women of the World

'There is a good deal to be said in favour of the French mode of proceeding,' the *Guardian* wrote in 1864. 'People walk about among their friends before [and] after bathing with the greatest ease and freedom and the bathing, instead of an unpleasant furtive parenthesis in the day, where nobody likes to be seen ... is freely undertaken of in company and becomes the means of much enjoyment and social pleasure.'

Oh, why couldn't we be more like the French?

I'm happy to report that the fight for women's swimming rights wasn't just happening in Britain. Happy because these things were happening independently of each other, something was in the air (or water) across the world and there wasn't a social media manager in sight. I do like a good old-fashioned zeitgeist. And happy because give or take a few decades, the fact that similar stories can be found across Europe and America strengthens the idea that there is a direct link between suffrage and other rights for women, a correlation between our participation in voting and our fight for swimming equality. Women needed to combat the same conventions in order to get access to sports, the same issues around social class and imposed cultural roles. So our swimming foremothers were unknowingly part of a global movement.

The push for public bathing in Germany and Austria began to emerge in the 1850s and 60s. Sweden was already ahead of the game – Gustafva Lindskog was the first female PE teacher in her country as early as 1818, though she couldn't be called teacher, she was called a 'Movement Giver', so it's two steps forward, one step back. Nancy Edberg put women's swimming on the Scandi map when she was employed as a swimming teacher at Stockholm's first women-only bathhouse in 1847, and went on to popularise the skill across the country, particularly when she taught the women of the royal family. And the Swedes showed their crazy feminist credentials most clearly when they introduced diving and swimming for women into the Olympics in 1912.

We had Agnes Beckwith et al., and America had their own amazing individuals making unprecedented treks, like Eliza Bennett who in 1877 swam across New York's Hudson River, which still attracts the same kind of questions that swimming in the Thames does – is it clean, is it safe, will I die? Actually, the American story of women's swimming mirrors our own in many ways. Like here, American beaches were the first place where the idea of women swimming came about. By the 1880s, there were a few private clubs women could join that encouraged physical fitness. The US bathhouses were initially for washing, and women faced similar restrictions in terms of what they wore and what activities they were allowed to participate in. When the number of public pools grew, so did the number of women who wanted to use them; they wanted to learn to swim for the same reasons we did: social, recreational, health and safety. The safety aspect played a significant role in the early days, and it was horrifically illustrated in an accident in 1904; one thousand women and girls drowned in New York's East River when an excursion boat, the *General Slocum*, caught fire. (The only other time I've heard the name Slocum was on *Are You Being Served?* and I sincerely hope that this piece of TV trivia won't detract from the seriousness of the story.) Educational establishments in the States led the way for women's physical education, and by the end of the nineteenth century most colleges had a PE department for women, promoting the view that good health was essential for academic success. The 1903 American publication *Athletics and Outdoor Sports for Women*, their version of our *Gentlewoman's Book of Sport* in which Mrs Samuda had so boldly paraded her swimming prowess, naturally included a chapter on swimming for women, written by Edwyn Sandys (who I'm presuming was a man). 'Setting aside the possibility of saving life,' he wrote, 'the actual value of swimming to women is well worth their serious consideration.' There were three main reasons he felt women should give it a go. Firstly, it's a 'highly beneficial and fascinating form of exercise'. You'll find no disagreement from me on that point. Secondly, it encourages a 'supple ease of movement which lends additional grace to the carriage'. I never found that to be the case personally, I could still trip over a leaf. And thirdly, he politely suggested that for those women 'able to dispose of a few pounds of surplus adipose tissue, it is one of the best of reducers'. Basically, if you're a bit of a fatty, Mr Sandys suggests you get in the water. Do I agree with this point? Debatable – any exercise is better than none when it comes to weight, but swimming does lead to a lot of cake. Am I fed up with people thinking that the way to sell an idea to women is by making it about their weight? Definitely.

Opening the Olympics to women is definitely a key part of our British story, so thank you, the Swedes. But probably the women who most influenced us and so were most significant to us were American. And perhaps the most significant of those was Charlotte 'Eppie' Epstein. She's already appeared in Hilda James's story, when she invited her over to the States, but Eppie's influence goes way beyond our own parochial interests. She was, after all, known as the 'mother of women's swimming in America'. Aside from her outstanding contribution to the sport, there are three particular reasons why I love this woman. Firstly, she wasn't a great swimmer herself, and I feel some solidarity with that. Secondly, she nailed her political colours to the mast by allying herself to the suffragette movement, and I feel solidarity with that, too. Thirdly, she sounds like she knew how to party. That's not a skill I possess so I find it particularly enviable and attractive in other people.

Charlotte Epstein was born in New York in 1884 and worked in the city as a court stenographer, a job that was seen as eminently suitable for a woman because it involved a typewriter. In 1911 a new organisation was set up, the National Women's Life Saving League (NWLSL), which as the name suggests had as its prime purpose encouraging swimming and life-saving for women. They ran free swimming lessons for women and children in municipal pools; their president in 1912 was Katherine Mehrtens who said, 'Teach a girl to swim and you place her in position to gain for herself a perfect body, and a perfect body is the natural abiding place of a healthy mind. It makes a girl hold her head high, place her feet firmly on the ground – and it gives her a wonderful complexion.' (My frustration at the last bit of this message may be simply through its repetition. Over and over, women were encouraged to swim through personal vanity, as if that's all we care about. If I could time travel, once I'd killed baby Hitler I might be tempted to go and wave a selection of our more vacuous beauty magazines around, yelling, 'Is this how you want things to end up? Is it? IS IT?') Charlotte Epstein joined the NWLSL, became chair of its Athletic Committee, then chair of the whole organisation, and by 1914 was appealing to the Amateur Athletic Union (AAU) to allow women to register in swimming events. At that point, the AAU was exclusively for men, but the NWLSL made a conscious decision to model themselves on similar amateur principles to the AAU, and thus be in prime position to leap in and join them as soon as the gates of maleaucracy creaked open even just a tiny bit.

In 1915, through Eppie's persistent efforts, a small door within those huge gates did open just a fraction when the Metropolitan branch of the AAU decided to recognise women's swimming. She was then able to organise the first ever 'Women's Swimming and Diving Championships' at Madison Square Garden. (It wasn't the same building we know now, but it had the same kudos and hosted similarly large-scale events.) New Yorkers gathered in their thousands to watch a display of women's ornamental and practical skills. It must have been quite the scene. Eppie kept on plugging away, and two years later, the national AAU followed the Metropolitan example and formally recognised swimming as a sport for women. It was the only sport that was given this accolade – it's a shame there weren't duplicate Eppies working for every discipline – but it did so with a clear set of limitations. 'All women contestants must wear bathing suits of a black texture that covers their body from shoulder to toe,' the AAU decreed. And 'in every event the women swimmers must wear bath robes that cover them entirely until just before they dive off'. And in case you were beginning to feel a little bit too much like an equal, huddled underneath your bath robe poolside with just your forehead showing, 'no woman must compete against a man'. It's not clear whose benefit that rule was instigated for; maybe they were looking out for the fragile egos of these women athletes. Or maybe – and I'm taking a shot in the dark here – maybe the men were worried they might get beaten by a woman. Imagine the horror.

I've already called other women 'swimming suffragettes' because of the sporting freedoms they fought for in the pool. But so far, none of them were directly linked to the fight for voting rights. Epstein did make that direct connection – she was most definitely a suffragette in the water and out. In the water, she fought for reforms in bathing costumes, arguing that women competitors needed greater mobility and speed, and for women to be able to take part in distance events. Out of it, she made public her belief in voting rights too. In the summer of 1915, the NWLSL staged 'suffrage swim races', where they dressed a dummy with a red sash declaring it to be 'anti-suffrage', while the swimmers themselves wore sashes in that familiar suffrage purple embroidered with 'Votes For Women'. They rowed the dummy out and dropped it overboard, whereby the League women raced to save it. The event made the *New York Times* with a headline of 'BRAVE SUFFRAGISTS SAVE "ANTI" FROM THE SEA'. 'Fully clothed and hampered alike by her garments and her principles,' the paper wrote, 'being an old-fashioned woman who does not believe it is ladylike to swim, she would certainly have been lost in the waves but for the gallant women who hurried to her rescue.' With a five-star review like that, it's clear what the *New York Times* official stance was.

In 1917, Epstein founded the Women's Swimming Association (WSA – a mercifully simple acronym). Eppie herself was a competent swimmer but was never going to be the star; what she did do brilliantly was marshal on behalf of others, attracting young female swimmers and taking them to the top of their game. The WSA ran under her leadership and the coaching of Louis B. Handley, himself a keen advocate of women's access to sport, who had worked for years developing the American crawl; it was Epstein, Handley and Ethelda Bleibtrey who taught the stroke to Hilda James in Antwerp in 1920. So our journey finds another link to theirs. The WSA produced outstanding champions like Gertrude Ederle, Aileen Riggin and Eleanor Holm, it dominated world-class swimming for decades, and launched numerous American swimmers into national and international fame. It was Epstein who saw the Channel as a potential winning swim for an American woman. She also played a crucial role in persuading the US Olympic Committee to allow American women to participate in the Olympics, and persuaded them to include the young Aileen Riggin, then aged fourteen, who went on to win medals for diving and swimming in 1924. Eppie attended the Olympics in 1920, '24, and '28, became assistant manager to the 1932 women's swim team (and was the first woman to be so named) and was honoured as the first female Olympic judge. The fact that she boycotted Berlin's 1936 Olympics in protest at Nazi policies makes me love her even more.

During her twenty-two years with the WSA, Epstein's swimmers held fifty-one world records. I call them 'her' swimmers, because it seems that's what she brought out in people, a deep sense of loyalty and commitment; she drove them on to do their best, because they knew she'd be there fighting for them if they gave their all. A kind of benevolent matriarchy. (Is there any other sort?) Aileen Riggin described her as 'a great influence' but I think she was more than that. Forceful, dynamic, focused and incredibly impressive, the kind of woman who never asked anyone to do more than she was doing herself. Leading by example, mixed with an infectious generosity of spirit. All of that alongside a clearly sociable and gregarious character, a side of her which comes out in Hilda James's story. Hilda and Charlotte had forged a friendship in Antwerp and the former was invited by Eppie to swim in exhibitions and races in New York. As we know, Hilda travelled there under the careful chaperonage of her coach Bill Howcroft and his wife, but Eppie played a blinder – she was respected by Bill and respectful of him and the restrictions Hilda was under, but knew when and how to bend the rules to give her friend some fun out of the pool. Eppie smuggled Hilda out to enjoy some shopping and a bit of what we might call gallivanting, all of it innocent but relaxed and unfettered by the watchful eyes of Bill and Mrs Bill. 'Good Sportsmanship is greater than Victory' was the WSA team slogan. And Eppie told her team to 'get points for the club, get in there and dive and never quit, never show off'. Every account of her presents a character who absolutely bounces off the page. I'm quite sure I'd have done exactly that had she told me to – I'd have got in, never quit, and never showed off.

Ethelda Bleibtrey was one of the champions of Epstein's WSA team. (Let that name roll around your tongue a minute. Ethelda Bleibtrey. So satisfyingly chunky, it would make a great name for a Pixar character. In the same way I enjoy pronouncing in utterly British tones the names Betty Crisp and Olive Marriage, I love drawling American names like Ethelda Bleibtrey. And researching Eppie I chanced upon perhaps my absolute favourite: Miss Fannie Binswanger. Now that's a name to relish, one that works best with the 'Miss' in front of it, to give it full momentum. Enjoy it.) Ethelda was an American swimming star, the first woman to win an Olympic medal for the US in 1920, and the first female contestant to win three gold medals at the same Games: the 100m freestyle, the 300m freestyle and 4x100m relay. This extraordinary achievement is all the more considerable when you realise that these medals weren't won in her strongest stroke. 'At that time,' she said, 'I was the world record holder in backstroke but they didn't have women's backstroke, only freestyle in those Olympics.' Of course, the times she recorded have since been smashed, but as she modestly said in an interview in the *Knickerbocker News*, a daily paper in Albany, New York, 'Records are like bubbles, they quickly disappear. But one of my swimming marks remains unbroken, by a fluke.' She's referring to her Olympian 300m record, which has never been beaten by the simple fact that there is no 300m race any more. The *Knickerbocker News* interviewed Ethelda in 1952, describing her as 'A Waterford undertaker's platinum blonde, blue-eyed daughter', and a 'gracious lady who led the aquacade of feminine water speedsters'. If the linguistic contortion of 'aquacade of feminine water speedsters' is not enough to make you spit your coffee out, then read on. 'The platinum of Ethelda's hair hasn't turned to the matronly gray' – Ethelda would have been fifty at the time of this interview, the poor old matron. 'It is somewhat on the straw or yellowish side now. But the famous Bleibtrey figure is retained.' Coffee spat out yet? Yes, mine too. So rude, and so irrelevant, the colour of her hair. Can you imagine them referring to any male star in that way? 'The brunette locks of Johnny Weissmuller are somewhat on the dull old codger side now. Maybe there's a shiny patch at the back, where his impressive skull peeps forth. But hurrah, his sexy six-pack is still just about visible.' The *Knickerbocker News* folded in 1988 and while I'm always sorry to see a news outlet go down, in this case I can barely muster a shrug and an insincere 'oh dear'.

Of course, Ethelda has a direct link to the British story as it was she, with the permission of Charlotte Epstein and Louis Handley, who volunteered to teach Hilda James the new American crawl, she who got herself back into the cold and mucky waters of Antwerp's Stade Nautique at the 1920

Olympics to help coach the British woman. She played an active part, too, in the story of what we wear in the water. Like Charlotte, Ethelda was a staunch campaigner for women's rights, and clearly a fan of direct action. In 1919, she was arrested under local decency laws for the crime of 'nude swimming'. You might imagine that meant she was swimming nude. No, all she had done was taken off her swimming stockings, at a time when it was forbidden to 'bare the lower female extremities for bathing'. I am not a biologist, but I don't think legs are something specifically female. I know what is specifically female in the lower extremities, and it ain't legs. Nonetheless, Ethelda had got fed up of swimming in what were essentially soggy leggings, so she'd stripped them off before going in, and was arrested for it. Her derring-do worked, though. The public outcry at her arrest meant that all charges were dropped, and the requirement to wear stockings in the water was phased out. So now, all American women who reveal their lower female extremities in the pool can thank Ethelda for stepping out and enabling that freedom.

It might be an exaggeration to say that she got a taste for protest, because it was nine years until Ethelda's next foray. (She was busy winning Olympic medals. I guess that can distract a gal.) In 1928, she was paid what was then a pretty whacking sum ($1,000) to swim in New York's Central Park reservoir (and if anyone is asking, I'll get in the water pretty much anywhere for about the same in modern money). It was a publicity stunt for the campaign to get better public swimming facilities in New York. She dived into the reservoir, where it was illegal to swim, for the assembled audience which included loads of press, and was arrested as she came out of the water and put in jail for the night. Again, there was public outcry – she was good at generating that – so the city's mayor got involved and bailed her out. Within a year, the city council had voted to open a public swimming pool, and while it might not fit with your image of New York, free summer lidos are now something the city does really well. We love it when our revolutionaries are successful.

Ethelda was disobedient, one of my favourite kinds of women. I love daring women too, and Charlotte Schoemmell was certainly that. At the peak of her career, she held twenty-one world championship records, as well as doing 'novelty stunts', like swimming in the Park Central hotel pool for seventy-two hours in 1928. Two of Eppie's rallying cries were to make women's costumes better suited to swimming, and to encourage women's distance swimming, and Mrs Schoemmell took both of those things a step further. She was one of the first women to advocate discarding swimming togs altogether in long-distance swims, saying that just wearing grease gave you more freedom. And why not? It's how the men swam, after all. In 1926, she swam 156 miles down the Hudson River 'clad in a bathing cap, a coat of black axle grease and nothing else', as *Time* magazine put it. The notion that this woman would slather herself in black axle grease and consider that to be better than wearing a costume says much about the kind of costumes on offer. And if imagining the sight and smell is not detail enough, she completed this marathon swim while being sustained by lumps of sugar soaked in whiskey. I picture her getting out of the water after 63 hours and 35 minutes stinking of old cars, utterly knackered, and pissed. Still, she did a good job of hiding it. *Time* magazine went on to report how she was wrapped in a sheet held up by her sister, then 'comforted her crying children, announced that next year she would swim the channel and back, took a bath, ate enough food for two men and went to a dance with her brother in law'. Hats off to you, Mrs Schoemmell. Hats, costumes, everything.

In the same year, Charlotte undertook the Manhattan Island Swim, and though she is recorded as the first woman to do it (in 14 hours and 21 minutes), it's not clear whether the actual distinction belongs to her, Amelia Gade or Ida Elionsky. Little is known about the last. There's just one intriguing piece of information about her. And that is (I'm drawing the moment out here) she swam round Manhattan Island (because you won't guess what's coming) in 11 hours and 35 seconds and (small drum roll) ... 'she had her brother tied to her back'. What the hell, Ida? Wasn't it enough to undertake this mammoth swim without strapping one of your rellies to your back? It's such a brilliantly bizarre bit of casual detail. 'Yeah, I did this thing. Yeah, quite tough. Yeah, Harry came with me. Tied to my back. Hmm. Yeah, maybe it was a bit strange, now you put it like that.' The Elionsky family clearly had a penchant for this type of thing, because two months after Ida's swim, Harry attempted a treacherous mile-and-a-half river crossing with two men tied to him. And in case that wasn't drastic enough, his hands were bound. So he swam with his ... chin? The men all made it across safely, but reports state how they nearly drowned. No shit.

Mrs Schoemmell's next big adventure was the Wrigley Catalina Island Swim, which became more popularly known as the Chewing Gum Swim as it was created by William Wrigley Jnr, multimillionaire chewing-gum king. (King of Chewing Gum – what a title. King of All Those Annoying Lumps of Chewed Goo on Pavements: less catchy, still true.) Wrigley had seen the kind of publicity that channel swimming got and wanted a piece of the action, so he created a swim to rival it that could also, entirely coincidentally I'm sure, boost tourist visits to Santa Catalina, an island he owned off southern California. The Catalina Swim was twenty-two miles (longer with tidal streams), and on 15 January 1927, 102 swimmers including Charlotte Schoemmell set off from Wrigley's island towards the mainland. The big story from this swim was not about women; it was a David and Goliath tale, where the biggest male competitor, world champion Norman Ross, was beaten by an underdog, a seventeen-year-old Canadian amateur called George Young. Charlotte didn't finish the race, leaving the water having 'only' swum for six and a half hours. But she'd certainly gained publicity for taking part. When she announced that she'd swim it nude, that 10lb of grease would be her protection, the race committee had had to hastily convene, before agreeing to allow nude contestants. Her actions were angrily denounced by the local chapter of the Women's Christian Temperance Union as an act of 'brazen vulgarity'. Somehow their very name suggests they'd be a bunch of sour-faced joy magnets. The fact that Norman Ross also planned to swim nude seemed to pass by unnoticed. The brazen vulgarity was all with Charlotte Schoemmell.

In the end, everything joins up. These stories about Eppie, Ethelda and Charlotte feel like history, but they still have resonances. The swims they did are still swum; the challenges then are challenges now. Times have got quicker, people are trained more in better costumes and with bigger teams of nutritionists and therapists and motivational gurus, techniques are video-analysed and worked on to within a millimetre of their lives. But swimming is swimming. The links remain between these women and more contemporary heroes. The Catalina Swim that Charlotte Schoemmell attempted was swum by the incredible Lynne Cox at the age of fourteen. Lynne now has many achievements in endurance swimming, including being the first person to swim the Bering Strait. The Manhattan Island Swim is still a formidable challenge – the first woman to swim round it in under eight hours was Diane Nyad in 1975; more recently, Diane became the only swimmer ever to go from Havana to Key West without a shark cage. Both Lynne and Diane have written books about their accomplishments.

And while these stars are miles above us, doing things us ordinary mortals might never even dream of, there are links between us everywhere we look. All the stories – the bravery, the swims, the fellowship, the achievements – are connected. They come together to form one long, continuous swimming story. A story we're all part of, on whatever level, and one that's still being told.

Chapter 8

In Praise of Lidos

A year or so back, my pal Becky and I wanted to take advantage of a lovely September morning and have the final swim of the summer at Serpentine Lido in Hyde Park, central London. If you're a member of Serpentine Swimming Club you can swim here early morning all year round, but it's only open to the public from May-ish to September-ish, and while I do swim outside all seasons, my loyalties reside with Tooting Lido. But at the risk of sounding like your nan, it's nice to have a change every now and then, and the Serpentine offers a different, more 'natural' experience. It's lakey. And it's right in the heart of town. You could be nearly naked one minute and in Oxford Street Primark the next. Hyde Park is a Royal Park, and it feels pretty royal, what with the Queen Mother Gates and the Princess Diana water sculpture thingy and Buckingham Palace just over there and royal horses being stabled nearby. So cavorting in your swimwear in the Serpentine can feel a little ... subversive. Rude, almost. Any minute now a royal cavalcade might trot past and there you'd be, barely covered by a wee scrap of a costume. It's as close to anarchism as some of us ever get.

Becky and I, competent organised women both, arrived at the lido to find we'd read the website wrong and it had shut to the public the day before. What a blow, we thought.

We were just about to slump off when we spotted that the big green metal gate to the water was unlocked, so feeling like giddy ne'er-do-wells, decided to have a swim regardless. (In the retelling, Becky casts me as the instigator, but it was definitely mutual.) We snuck in through the gate, nipped behind a tree on the bank beside the water and quickly got changed, both of us enjoying the thought of some hapless tourist being accidentally assailed by the flash of ancient arse. Looking over our shoulders to make sure we weren't about to be chased out by a royal gardener, an image which in itself could fuel us through the long winter months ahead, we skidaddled over to the roped-off area of the lake which forms the lido, and got in.

Things forbidden or snatched can feel delicious in themselves, but the warm water and sunshine combined with that thrill to engender a real sense of daring and freedom. We mostly kept our heads up, flicking our eyes furtively around, because for all our bravado it would have been ignominious and embarrassing to be ordered out. But nobody showed, so we swished up and down in the thick

Top: Sparkhill Baths, before demolition. A piece of architectural heritage, gone.

Above: I don't think the one bottom right was enjoying it much.

Right: Girls paddling by a bathing machine, during a hurricane. Must be summer.

Left: Important to co-ordinate your outfit with your bathing machine.

Below: This pose is meant to read 'sexy'. But to me it reads 'accidentally washed ashore'.

Bottom: That pose again. Now with added shower cap.

Right: This one's for all the men hoping this book would be full of half-naked women.

Below: Agnes Beckwith (middle) and her sisters. Do. Not. Mess.

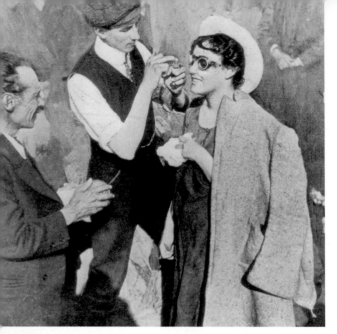

Left: One should always have a man handy to apply one's goggle grease.

Above: Kellerman in the water. Lovely big smile. Nageant-ing always makes people smile.

Left: A happy Hilda James, in her Olympic swimsuit.

Above: Agnes Nicks after a long cold swim. Spot the racist elephant in the room.

Right: Agnes getting well greased before her swim. He's really giving it some.

Below: Agnes and the Houses of Parliament.

Above: Chiswick Baths. Someone was contravening the dress code.

Below: Nice idea. But very annoying when the cards get soggy.

Above: A gang of cheery swimmers on their way to Hampstead Ponds, summer 1931. My kind of girl group.

Below: Modern Spartans breaking the ice at Hampstead Ladies Pond. I too keep my socks on til the last possible moment.

Above: June 1935, Serpentine. Timeless.

Below: Three Serpentine women, drawing admiring glances for their … gas masks?

Right: This, 1920s, looks positively modern.

Below left: 1926. Strong theme.

Below right: This won 'best individual costume' in a competition in 1922. Scandalously short.

Left: These costumes are in the 'Annette Kellerman style'. I would wear these. I LOVE a cape.

Below: Forming a queue for a little state-sanctioned slut-shaming.

Above: The amazing 1912 British Olympic women. Clearly loving this photo opp.

Below left: Australian champions Mina Wylie and Fanny Durack.

Below right: The 1956 British Olympic swimmers, including the wonderful Fearne Ewart (as she was then), back row left.

Left: Ethelda
Bleibtrey, being
appraised by
two 'gentlemen'
behind her.

Below: US Olympic
team ready to sail
in 1924. Charlotte
Epstein is in the dark
hat, in the back row.

Above: Before – Thomas Burgess slapping the lard on Gertrude Ederle.

Left: After – A greased-up Gertrude. Brilliantly fierce.

Below: Gertrude arrives home in New York, Queen of the Waves.

QUEEN Of the WAVES

Above: Mate. This is NOT the time.

Right: Mercedes Gleitze, the first British woman to swim the Channel.

Below: The indomitable spirit of Freda Streeter, on Dover beach.

Bottom: The heart of London on a beautiful day. Bliss.

Right: That's cold. (I prefer not to know til I get out. It can be too off-putting.) (I know.)

Below: The beautiful Tooting Lido, my spiritual home, as seen from the deep end.

Bottom: That's Jackie Cobell on the right, keeping warm before a cold swim.

Above: Beth French. This is what an adventurer looks like.

Left: My wonderful knitted swimsuit. (Clearly someone just told a filthy joke off camera.)

green sun-warmed water. Side by side, heads up, chatting like ladies, that very particular style that absolutely enrages lane swimmers in a pool. After twenty minutes or so, tired of filtering goose poo through our teeth, we got out, quickly washed the weed off under the poolside cold shower and got dressed again. When your skin is cold, it's quite difficult to wriggle out of a clammy costume and put on a bra without inadvertently outing a boob, but you don't get to be an adult woman without years of experience in these contortions. It could almost count as yoga. Then fully dressed and looking for all the world like responsible adults on an innocent morning stroll, we slipped out through the gate again; the only giveaways were a few damp hair fronds against our necks, and the soggy costumes in our bags. The little frisson of illicitness kept me tingling all the way home; it's a feeling I used to have often in my younger clubbing days.

Becky and I weren't the first women to have illegally jumped into the Serpentine. People have been swimming there for many years, the National Swimming Society held competitions there as far back as 1837, and the Serpentine Swimming Club has held races since 1864. But by people, I don't mean women. Those races were only open to men. Opening hours were early morning because the men were usually swimming nude, which was the norm. It was the lack of changing facilities that was the official stumbling block to women's participation; men could race, because they would happily change in the park willy-nilly. Women were undertaking all kinds of spectacular and incredible swimming challenges and performing in crowd-thrilling aquatic shows elsewhere but they weren't allowed in the Serpentine. Suffrage activist Margaret Nevinson wrote in the *Guardian* in 1930 about how, in the tropical days of the summer of 1881 with the thermometer soaring into the eighties, 'a poor woman of Coal Court, Drury Lane, was seen bathing in the lake [and was] arrested at once by a scandalised policeman, and dragged before a magistrate, while 200 male persons were left happily swimming'. A scandalised policeman my eye. Nearly fifty years later and nothing had changed, as Margaret wrote that 'another woman swam in the Serpentine and was fined for her audacity.' The 'audacity' of these women, inflicting such terrors upon poor innocent policemen who surely can't have seen a more shocking thing on the streets of London. How very dare they.

I don't imagine these women were selfish monsters unfit for common society; I imagine they felt pretty similarly to Becky and me, that they had the same sense of 'things forbidden or snatched feeling delicious in themselves' that we did. It's highly unlikely that nudity was the source of this audacity, as we know that women still wore more clothes to swim than we wear now on formal occasions. But while things might have been getting decidedly liberal at the beach, it was much more restricted in rivers, lakes and pools; the strict mixed bathing by-laws were definitely still in place in fresh water. The idea that salt water was somehow more intrinsically moral than fresh water was a puzzle, one which, Margaret wrote, was a conundrum for 'the logical mind of girlhood'. Why was it? The answer is hidden. Maybe it's found in James VI's *Daemonologie*, the one that proscribed women be drowned as witches? Or somewhere in an arcane passage of the Bible perhaps, where they talk about the water being purified because it had salt thrown in it? But the idea that laws about where women could swim might relate to impure water in the Bible is almost too mind-boggling to get your head round. Which leads me to suspect that actually it *was* as tenuous as that. Whatever, Margaret Nevinson went on to write how 'few realise the hard work that their mothers and grandmothers have had to get the taboo removed from fresh-water swimming for women. I remember how bitter it was in our childhood to be told, when we saw our brothers going joyously out to swim in any river or pond handy: "Little ladies may only bathe in the sea; God made the canals and rivers for boys. You are very rude girls to want to go."'

There were no ruder girls than the suffragettes. In April 1914, their movement, which was banned from demonstrating in Hyde Park, advertised a 'Water Carnival' at the Serpentine as a way of circumventing that ban. They'd announced their intention to take to the boats, but the authorities weren't having that and moored all the boats in the middle of the lake. The women, or 'Militants in Tights' as the *New York Times* referred to them (a reference to their swimming tights and a phrase I'm very drawn to), paraded around the lake with their sunshades. Sylvia Pankhurst recorded in *The Suffrage Movement* in 1931 how 'Others appear in dominoes, each carrying a letter of the word Suffrage on her chest. One girl in Japanese dress turned up in a rickshaw drawn by a girl companion in knee-breeches ...' (Let's take a moment with that image, let it sink in. It's April 1914, Hyde Park. A woman pitches up dressed in a kimono with another woman dressed in what was distinctly male garb, pulling her in a rickshaw. It sounds like some good old-fashioned lesbian role play to me, and all rather gloriously filmic.) Pankhurst continued with the tale. 'The Office of Works, shocked by the prospect of such merry advertising by persons who had banded themselves together for the commission of serious crime, had prohibited the Serpentine to all comers that day ... the boats being lashed together in midwater to prevent their use. Nothing daunted, the Suffragettes flung off their wraps, revealed themselves in bathing costumes, swam out to the craft and cut them free.'

It was reported in the *Daily Mirror* with rather more palpable excitement than Pankhurst could allow herself. The tabloid, which had positioned itself as a paper for women at the start of the century, described thousands of Londoners watching this 'remarkable swimming display'. Getting themselves in a right old frenzy, the paper reported how 'Suddenly the crowd had a shock. Two women ... whipped off wraps and in neat bathing costumes plunged into the Serpentine. While they struck out vigorously for the boats two oarsmen put off to intercept them. It was a frantic race that roused the crowd to cheers.' See? Much more exciting than Pankhurst's version. 'One woman swimmer succeeded in reaching the boats and, clambering into one, waved a suffragette flag' the *Mirror* report went on. 'The other woman was overtaken by the boatmen and both were conveyed to the boathouse. Hardly had they disappeared when a third woman in a bathing costume jumped out of a waiting motor-car and plunged into the water. Amid the crowd's wild cheers, she was captured by boatmen. A moment later two more women on the opposite bank plunged in and swam towards the boats. They too were captured ...'

Obviously, the women's intention was to highlight the suffrage movement rather than working towards equal swimming rights. That seems fair enough; I concede that getting the vote might take precedence. But it seems apposite that these militants in tights chose this 'shocking' act to highlight their cause. What could be more outrageous than a woman swimming where a woman shouldn't swim?

It wasn't until 1930 that the situation changed at the Serpentine when an 'official' lido was built to replace the more ad hoc situation, and this one had actual changing facilities, which meant that women would finally be allowed to get in. The idea and its execution came from George Lansbury, then the government's Commissioner of Works and later leader of the Labour Party (and also the grandfather of actress Angela Lansbury, for fans of unrelated facts). His plans mainly arose as a way of preventing innocent passers-by accidentally seeing naked men and the inclusion of women was the unexpected bonus. But Lansbury's plans weren't met with unequivocal support. As Chris Ayriss says in his book *Hung Out to Dry*, 'there was outrage over the prospect that near nudity was to be *encouraged* in the park'. Accidental near nudity is clearly one thing, but purposeful? THE HORROR! As is still so often the case, men took to writing letters to *The Times* to express their dismay at the wretched turn of events.

The upset of one particular man, a Mr Holland, petitioning *The Times* on behalf of some existing Serpentine swimmers, seemed nuanced at first glance. It was not the admittance of women he objected to, oh no no, he calls that 'a much needed reform'. What a terribly modern gent. Rather, he's upset that men would lose the right to dress and undress in the open air, and that 'some will not be able to afford any regular charge and many more will not be able to afford the time to wait in a queue for a vacancy'. My eyes may narrow at the specious arguments he employs to keep women out, but that final part is a sentiment I can relate to. I expect anyone who regularly swims in a lido will recognise how annoying it is on those three or four excellent summer days when there's a long queue and you're not afforded special privileges. You've put in the hours, swimming in rain, hail, snow and misery, and then suddenly, it's nice out, everyone wants to jump in the pool, and no, you don't get to push to the front of the queue. It's a terrible injustice.

144

Mr Holland goes on. 'No accommodation that can be provided will be sufficient to deal with the crowd that gathers on a summer morning between 7 and 8.30, especially when there is a swimming race.' Again, he's absolutely right, it's very frustrating, it still happens. But the Mr Hollands of this world are transparent; they might try to appear modern and accommodating, but still they put the rights of busy men, poor men and naked men above those of women. Bloody women, ruining everything.

Despite the objections, Lansbury prevailed, and the new roped-off area of the Serpentine was called Lansbury's Lido for a time in recognition of his achievements. On opening day, 16 June 1930, the queues started to form early. It was a big story across the country, with even the most distant regional papers reporting on it. 'There was great competition among London swimming girls for the distinction of being the first authorized "mixed bather"', one wrote. 'So great was it that though the starting time was 4.30 in the afternoon, two venturesome damsels plunged in at 6am and had to be ignominiously driven out by police.' 21-year-old Kathleen Murphy of Pinner was the first woman to officially swim; she queued from 5 a.m. and was awarded a medal for her efforts. Papers went on to report how 'Miss Murphy was loudly cheered by a crowd which had broken down the railings and rushed the police in its eagerness to see the innovation. A throng of other girls followed Miss Murphy's lead ...' These happy women were described as 'working girls in bright hued bathing costumes' – an especially vibrant image. From what it's possible to gather, Miss Murphy wasn't some terrible kind of radical feminist, she wasn't even a suffragette. She just wanted to swim. And in that blistering summer, who can blame her? Some rather glorious Pathé footage from the same year, snappily entitled 'Phew! Lansbury's Lido offers a refreshing spot during the great heat wave', shows a bunch of men and women leaping off the still-familiar jetty into the water. It's trickier than it would be today to differentiate between men and women in these bits of old footage – both sexes were dressed in similar singlet-style costumes, and the sense of great fun is evident in all the players, the lack of reticence entirely mutual. The women, with their short bobbed hair and scrubbed, open faces are as involved and happy as the men; they're all throwing themselves about in equal measures of forthright abandonment.

You'd think from the excitement and crowds and level of press reporting (reviews for the lido were printed across the world – the *Sydney Morning Herald* welcomed 'a new era in the history of Hyde Park') that Lansbury's Lido was unique. But it wasn't the first or only lido at the time; women already had (restricted) access to several lidos and ponds across the city. There's some fabulous footage from Hornsey open-air baths in 1929, called 'Water Witches' (cue sigh and eye roll), where more happy throngs of grinning women are clearly having a whale of a time in the water. So why the big hoo-ha here? Maybe it relates to the park being part of the Royal Park family, that same sense of near anarchy that

Becky and I felt all those years later? Or maybe it was the fact that Lansbury's Lido seemed to be formalising the idea of equality of opportunity? Giving it the stamp of officialdom. There is, after all, something about lidos that encapsulates a sense of equality. As Ken Worpole writes in *Here Comes the Sun*, 'lidos helped break down the barriers between men and women in public', barriers which were also coming down on beaches and very reluctantly in indoor pools. 'The proclamation "mixed bathing at all times" was a badge of pride and free-spiritedness worn by many of the new lidos,' he writes. 'The space around the pool in the lido resembled beach space in its promiscuous democracy of age, class, bodily shape and temperament.'

Much as it's a lovely thought, not all lidos started out wearing these liberated badges. At the beginning of the twentieth century there'd been a spate of building outdoor swimming lakes. Coinciding neatly with the passion for All Things Outdoors, digging a great big hole was seen as an efficient way to provide work for unemployed men. Initially these lidos offered limited opportunities for women. The standard offering was one short morning out of seven. The outdoor-swimming boom belonged to men and boys, not women. Tooting Lido was one of these work-creation schemes, and women were graciously allowed in on Tuesday mornings. In 1907, fifty-four local women signed a petition to get the hours increased, and fifty-four local women were flatly refused; I like to think I'd have been one of those women.

Things were a little more free-thinking over in west London, however. Chiswick Baths (which is what we'd now recognise as a lido, though the term wouldn't be used until twenty years later) had opened in 1910, and offered 'risqué mixed bathing', the only purpose-built outdoor pool in the country that did so. Again, there's some magnificent footage of women leaping in with abandon, and a particularly charming piece of film where four laughing gals arrive at the pool clinging together on a motorbike and sidecar. They look like real go-getter adventuresome women, very cool. In the 1921 film *No Coal Wanted Here*, there's a great still of four top birds enjoying a fag at the side of Chiswick Baths. One of the surprising things is how contemporary they look. They don't reflect the traditional stereotypes of Edwardian women. They look modern in the carefree, insouciant way they're holding themselves. They look free – maybe they belonged to the newer, more racy breed of woman, the flapper. The image is spontaneous, life-affirming, un-posed and entirely lacking in sophistry. The woman at the back is clearly telling a story, and I'd love to hear it. Apart from the cigarettes, I recognise these women in myself and my friends, if we were caught in a photo unknowingly. I want to know them. I kind of do.

These swimming women were not without admirers – and you need to remember that the idea of heated lidos were some kind of futuristic dream at this point. 'I rather question,' said one newspaper columnist in 1927, on his visit to 'the famous open air bath', 'if men … would be equal to doing what many of these aquatic Amazons do. I have never seen a male bather … eat an ice between dips. But this is what quite a number of the Chiswick Bathing belles were doing when I was there.' On top of everything else, it's the eating of ice cream that seems to have quite bedazzled him, and his appreciation for a feisty woman is noted.

Aquatic Amazons, bathing belles, venturesome damsels and 'nymphs of North London', a phrase used in *The Times* – women in water really brought out the romantic side of writers. Qualified professionals were keen to offer explanations of how women could manage the feats of both staying in the water and remaining afloat at all. In a newspaper article 'Girls beat Men as Bathers' in July 1929, one 'medical man' used his expertise to explain how women had greater powers of endurance. 'They have … an extra thick covering of skin, which enables them not only to resist the chill of the water for a longer period than men, but they are not so easily fatigued as men. Because of the physiological differences in the sexes they are much more buoyant.' We can only presume that this 'medical man' thought that women's breasts and maybe even our wombs were some kind of flotation device? Huge, if true. Also, extra thick skin? I'm not medically qualified, but even with my rudimentary knowledge, I'd find that one pretty easy to disprove. And how does thick skin stop you being tired? Surely it's worse, dragging the heft of all that extra covering around? And are we women thick-skinned and hardy, or feeble and faint? Are we stronger than men, or weaker? Is it only a certain class of woman who has thicker skin? Blimey, it's so confusing being a woman, with all this pernicious nonsense pretend-science we have to find a path through. Our medical man went on to solemnly warn the readers how 'One of my patients at Chiswick spent practically all her spare time in the baths and she became a victim of insomnia simply due to the enervating effects of prolonged immersion in the water'. The doctor's message: women, don't spend too long in the water, you'll be so tired you'll get insomnia. Thanks, medical man, that makes total sense.

It was becoming more acceptable for women to swim everywhere. We had women teachers, we had inspiring role models, we had the boom in ladies' swim clubs. But there was still a bit of a stumbling block. A vicious circle. Because women didn't have the same levels of freedom as their brothers, particularly as girls, they didn't have the same swimming abilities or confidence, so they didn't see swimming as something they could do or participate in, so they still didn't generally pitch up to these lidos in the same numbers. And after all, they'd had it instilled in them that swimming in a freshwater pool was immoral, so the reluctance to get in under those circumstances might be understandable. But maybe spurred along by the 'famous' Chiswick Baths and the desirability of their aquatic Amazons, other lidos started to broaden access for women. I say 'started to broaden access' as if it came from nowhere, as if to a man the generous lido owners (mostly municipal councils) woke in a good mood one morning, took pity on our feeble, excluded, thick-skinned sex and decided to generously give us more provision. No, that didn't happen. Again, there was manly foot-dragging every inch of the way. Concessions were hard fought and hard won and the campaigns were invariably instigated by women willing to stand up for a more modern approach, with the odd progressive guy like Lansbury being in a position to do something about it. We see that in the way women won the vote, and the same applies here. Gradually, apart from a few dinosaurs, men began to concede that women were people too. We were close to getting full suffrage, we were working outside the home in unprecedented numbers, becoming (gasp) full members of society, paid up with our own money. It was time we had our swimming suffrage. Again we can cynically follow that money. Maybe decisions were not just philanthropic or societal, maybe they were financial. After all, a woman's fiver has always had exactly the same value as a man's.

So it wasn't just a matter of a quick meeting, a quick wave of a patrician councillor's wand, and bosh, things changed in women's favour. This was where our swimming foremothers really worked for our benefit. Margaret Nevinson, the suffrage activist, wrote in her *Guardian* article about the campaign to get access for women into Hampstead Ponds: 'In North London a few enthusiasts worked hard for years to get some of the Heath ponds open for women at least one day a week,' which sounds very like the story of Elizabeth Eiloart fighting for that same right at

Marylebone Baths. 'At the first informal meeting,' Margaret went on, 'our plan was mocked out of court. All the men present sat back in their chairs and roared with laughter at the very thought. The crowds would be so great on the banks that people would be crushed to death, and the tramways and North London Railway would run special excursions to see such a sight. However, we worked on, heedless of ridicule, owing much to the influence of the few women on the L.C.C. and the Borough Councils.'

There's such a vivid picture painted in this short paragraph. You can imagine the dark wood-panelled room, the besuited men leaning back in their chairs, so greatly amused by the precocity of the notion of women swimming. The way the women would have had to steel their nerves before they walked in, *knowing* they were about to be roundly mocked. Having to sit resolutely polite and calm, we assume, listening to the idea that women swimmers was merely some sort of entertainment or sideshow that men would flock to gawp at. The rage and frustration those women must have felt, to have been so mocked and dismissed, marginalised, treated with patronising disdain – but carrying on anyway! The kind of dedication those women showed in the face of all that guff is inspiring. We owe them so much; it's down to them that we can do what we do.

Despite all the mocking that Nevinson describes, the campaign was victorious and in 1926 women gained access to No. 5 Pond, known now as Kenwood Ladies' Pond. Caitlin Davies's book *Taking the Waters* gives a full and vivid description of the pond's life from boom to slump and back again; from the early 'Modern Spartans' who swam year round, even breaking the ice to enjoy a swim, to its current incarnation as a treasured oasis of peace. It's still a women-only pond; going there can transport you back in time: back to the 1970s, when being women-only was a much more straightforward concept, and back to its early days too, because water doesn't really change much and neither does Hampstead Heath. As the mocking councillors predicted, images of the pond in its infancy do indeed show men standing round on the banks gawping at the women swimmers. But now it's surrounded by trees, and, anyway, access to women's scantily dressed bodies is better sought on the internet.

I've described women's access to the Serpentine, Chiswick, Hampstead and Tooting, London pools all, but it wasn't just in the progressive metropolitan that this was happening. Across the country, as the decade switched from the 1920s to the 1930s, fresh water was finally, by degrees, becoming as 'moral' as salt. Everything was slowly coming together to provide the perfect storm. Sunbathing was becoming popular. The idea of 'doing stuff as a family' was gaining credence, and you couldn't do that without acknowledging the contribution of women. The cult of physical fitness was gaining a foothold. By-laws on mixed bathing were being relaxed, and it was becoming widely acceptable. Outdoor bathing was the confluence of all those ideas, and lidos began to grow in popularity. As they did so, women gained more access; it happened at the same time. It happened *so much* at the same time that it's impossible not to draw a link. Women gained more and more access and the lido movement grew. Or, the lido movement grew and women gained more access; either way, it's hand-in-hand. From Prestatyn, Blackpool, Exmouth and Plymouth in the 1920s, to Skegness, Brighton, Penzance and Weston-super-Mare in the 1930s. These are just a few names, sadly most of them extinct now. Lidos organically became the centrepiece for equality of opportunity. Janet Smith, in *Liquid Assets*, talks about how lidos were 'deliberately classless. Unlike their indoor counterparts, there were no first or second class distinctions. As Sir Josiah Stamp, Governor of the Bank of England … declared at the opening of Morecambe's new open air baths in 1936, "Bathing reduces rich and poor, high and low, to a common standard of enjoyment and health. When we get down to swimming, we get down to democracy."' We're talking, don't forget, about a time when women had just recently won full suffrage. We had suddenly become full participants in that democracy, be it swimming or electoral.

For anyone who is a fan of lidos, either in principle or practice, it will come as no surprise that they play such a role in our swimming equality. Lidos were inclusive, progressive, modern – and they still are. In its heyday, London was served by nearly sixty of them; now just fourteen remain between over eight million people. They were, and still are, as close to the freedom of the beach as it was possible to get (while often being nowhere near it). This idea is doubly appropriate here, as it was on the beach, with the abolition of sex-segregation laws, that women first dipped freely.

But if, as Ken Worpole says, they merely resemble the beach, why not stick to the beach? We do, after all, have the sea all around us. But the sea has no changing rooms, or cafes, or (frequently) lifeguards and clean water. The sea is scary if you're swimming alone; things live in the sea, things that can swoop up from the bottom and grab your leg. The sea holds secrets. It has boundless horizon with all the fear that holds. The sea never ends. In a lido, we're stripped of all our baggage and its labels, stripped of all our layers – but, crucially, held by actual physical boundaries. There's also a sense of being held by a community, of belonging, absolutely literally within a set of walls. The community is defined by this one thing and nothing else: a desire to be here, doing what you're capable of, whatever that is. Once you're swimming, no one else is counting, no one muttering 'she didn't do much' or 'she's slow'.

From what they brought women then, to what they bring us all now: in an increasingly cluttered, cosseted, regulated world, lidos offer a safe and egalitarian space, a supervised wildness. It doesn't seem to matter what your costume is like; it doesn't seem to matter if you're old or young, big or small, if bits hang off oddly, or you don't have all of them. Am I a mother, a partner, a success or a failure? Who knows. It doesn't matter what the years have done to you. It doesn't matter what you've done or not done during those years. It doesn't matter, finally, if you're a woman or a man. They brought us equality of opportunity and experience beyond our sex. All you are at a lido is a swimmer, regardless of status. Julie Burchill put it well when she said, 'They seem to me to be the greatest expression of a very public hedonism, attractive and accessible to all, regardless of age, sex or social status. If you go to the theatre or to football, you can get a better seat by having more money or by knowing the right people. But at a lido, wherever you lay your towel, that's your home.'

By the 1930s, women swimmers were allowed to lay their towels, and be home. But let's not forget what it took to get there. As Margaret Nevinson said, 'it cost us a long and weary struggle to win, not the freedom of the sea, but the freedom of rivers and lakes and ponds'. It seemed that finally, in the eyes of the law, we were all equal in a swimming cap.

Chapter 9

We Are What We Wear

A recent survey, undertaken by a corporation who manufacture some of our most ubiquitous modern fabrics, revealed what women wanted from their swimwear. The results are interesting, and may not be quite what you'd expect. According to this survey, women firstly wanted more comfort, and yes, that's an easy one to get behind, comfort is important. Then, women wanted 'improved shaping performance', and while I know the meaning of each of those words, they're in a combination I find bafflingly jargonistic. The thrust is, I deduce, that women would like their costumes to make them a different shape. OK, that might be quite a big ask. We are what we are. But it's the third thing women want from their swimwear that's most bemusing. Because it is, apparently, 'more emotional satisfaction'. You what now? That's right, more emotional satisfaction. From our swimming costumes. I envisage the disappointed woman, gazing mournfully at a costume laid sadly, emptily, on a changing-room bench. 'Oh, my dear swimming costume,' she weeps softly to the unreceptive garment. 'I've tried so hard to love you. But you've given nothing back. It's not enough that you are comfortable. It's not enough that you have improved shape performance. If only you could have listened more, supported me emotionally, been there for me like I've been there for you.' Perhaps the most pertinent question to arise from these findings is: did they speak to any actual living women? Because the idea that there is a solid core of us out there yearning to have a more meaningful emotional relationship with a piece of well-crafted fabric is frankly ludicrous and perhaps a little scary. How on earth did we get to this point?

The history of what women wear in the pool is very well documented. None of the stories, individuals or achievements in the water attract as much attention as what we've been wearing; the commentary happens on every level, from high-culture coffee-table books using architectural language and sculptural images where you can barely discern which way is up, to cheeky cartoon postcards where what you mostly get is cleavage. This approach is not restricted to swimming (although it does have added appeal in that you get a lot of near nudity); as soon as there's anything written about women, in almost any context, fashion will feature. Wherever there are women, there is discussion about how they dress. You might be describing her life-or-death mission to remove landmines in a war zone, and her pumps will get a mention. 'This is Corinne. She's forty-two, and she's rescuing orphaned children from Syria (Blouse £18.99, Zara).' If you gathered together all the material written about women swimming, there'd be one huge pile marked 'outfits' and a tiny pile beside it, 'everything else'. Above and beyond every other detail, what people most want to know is 'but what did they wear?' And why not? It's a great and easy way into a story, a way of humanising history that people can get a grip on. I've already described some costumes of old, and all the lace and twill and fiddly bits of decoration and bloomers and jaunty whatnots quickly build a resonant picture. People respond to visuals, particularly ones with added bosom. It's also true that from our lofty twenty-first-century position, olden-day outfits are plain funny, and some of us put great store in the value of jokes.

I'm not immune to fashion. I've greedily pressed 'Next' on photos of outlandish outfits from the Met Gala. I've said 'What *is* she wearing?' more times than I'm comfortable admitting, and in a tone that wasn't always kind. But I've probably read more articles on 'Why fashion is in fact feminist' than I have articles on fashion, so if you're sensing any resistance on my part, it's because there is some. It's outside my area of interest. But it's also in my nature to kick against tropes, particularly the boring 'it's about women, we must include some scanties'. The idea that not only are women – apparently – only interested in fashion, the only interesting thing *about* women is their fashion. Except I have to fight my inclination to dismiss fashion as irrelevant, because in this case, it's not. Outside of all the frivolity, the way swimming costumes have changed is actually very relevant to our story. In fact, you might describe it as a visual depiction of the whole tale. It's physical, emblematic, symbolic. It's exactly as French fashion historian Olivier Saillard says – 'the emancipation of swimwear has always been linked to the emancipation of women'. Or maybe it's the other way round, that the emancipation of women is linked to the emancipation of swimwear. Maybe, dear Olivier, the politics came before the clothes.

We learn quite a lot about what society thinks of women by looking at the way it requires them to dress. Mostly, we're forced to conclude that for vast rafts of time Western society didn't really like women very much at all. For centuries, women's actual body shape was disguised so heavily as to be almost impossible to discern. They wore things designed to make them appear feeble, helpless and weak. More than that – clothes didn't just make women *appear* weak, they made it impossible to fully function. Clothes actively restricted women, limited the kind of things they could actually do. Like lift their arms up, for instance. Walk at speed, or any distance. Breathe in and out. The ability to do these things is not a radical request! But they sewed weights into the bottom of women's swimming skirts, for goodness' sake! The ostensible reason was that it stopped the garment floating up in the water and revealing one of the many layers worn underneath. But weights in a swimming costume? It doesn't take a Freud to work out the subliminal message. Thankfully we're past all that, and everything is just peachy now …

There is a famous mosaic, called *Ten Athletic Women*, attesting to the fact that Roman women in the fourth century were cavorting around in something akin to a modern bikini – a bandeau top and small knickers. (These women might be considered luckier than us – there is no corresponding 'Comments' mosaic beneath this one, where men have crafted crude demeaning critiques of the women's bodies in small ceramic tiles.) But it's not a fashion that sustained over the centuries – and imagine how different history might have been if it had. Imagine if we could have been fighting for things that actually mattered, rather than the right to wear what we want. Instead, it took us sixteen whole centuries to get back to where the Roman women started. In that time, we quickly went from the sublime and spent far too long in the ridiculous. When women started to get in the water in the mid nineteenth century, their costumes were absurd. Mr Hully in 1864 described the standard bathing dress as 'just long enough to make swimming impossible'. Bathing is different from full-on swimming – the accepted role of women was to bob around in the water clutching the rope of their bathing hut. But given what we had to wear, was it any wonder lots of women really couldn't get it together? Victorian modesty required garments in stiff fabrics (so they didn't cling when wet) and dark colours (which stood less of a chance of becoming translucent), mostly in the form of pantaloons with short over-dresses. With weighted hems, don't forget, if you were considering this to be a relatively carefree look. Australian women were informal by comparison, only being required to be covered from neck to knee, leaving the bottom half of the leg dangerously exposed. French women were stylish, of course. Mrs Cecil Samuda in *The Gentlewoman's Book of Sport* recalls a trip to France where she was determined not to be outdone. She relates how she 'selected a most ravishing "get-up" of pure white serge, handsomely braided, with a large white washing silk sash ... white silk stockings and sandals' before getting in for a proper swim. No clutching a rope for the ravishing Mrs Samuda. Unfortunately, she hadn't taken into account that this outfit was more suitable for promenading than actual swimming, and when she exited the water she found that the whole lot had become transparent. We've all suffered that particular ignominy. 'After a severe reprimand I felt considerably humbled,' she reports, though she doesn't sound like the kind of woman who'd allow such a thing to hold her back for long. Determined to get back in the water, she went shopping and bought a black serge bathing dress and was 'reduced to the level of the ordinary foreign sea bather'. Oh, Mrs Samuda. Not bothered about revealing your all, but entirely bothered by looking like a foreigner.

I suspect you'd be one of those 'speak as you find' types were you around now. In fairness to her, a black serge dress does sound drab and disappointing compared to her other terrifically fancy outfit.

Edwyn Sandys, writing at the start of the twentieth century in the American publication *Athletics and Outdoor Sports for Women*, felt the plight of women very strongly. He declared he had never seen anything more useless and absurd than a fashionable bathing suit, finding it to be the greatest obstacle that the female swimmer has to face. This sentiment, clearly stated in 1903, illustrates exactly what Olivier Saillard stated one hundred years later, and it's why what we wore is the physical embodiment of our story. Sandys felt so strongly that he decided to see how it felt in the water, dressed as a woman. I say 'dressed as a woman' – Mr Sandys doesn't show his hand quite so boldly. 'I once wore a close imitation of the usual suit for women' is how he chose to express it, obviously feeling the need to obfuscate, in case we surmised that he actually liked it. 'The suit was amply large,' he wrote, 'yet pounds of apparently dead weight seemed to be pulling at me in every direction.' He's referring to all the extraneous cloth that a swimming outfit would take. Most women made their own, and would be putting seven to ten metres of material into each one. Let's average that out at eight metres. Eight metres of fabric is nearly as long as a bus, more than enough for a fancy ball gown. 'In that gear,' Mr Sandys went on, 'a swim of one hundred yards was as serious a task as a mile in my own suit. After that I no longer wondered why so few women swim really well, but rather that they are able to swim at all.' Given that women were essentially swimming in ball gowns made in the densest fabric possible, I completely agree with him.

So did Australian Annette Kellerman. 'How could these women swim with shoes – stockings – bloomers – skirts – overdresses with puffed sleeves – sailor collars – in some cases even lightly fitted corsets?' she asked when she arrived on American shores in 1907. How indeed. Although Sandys was conducting his own campaign to change what women wear in the water, it was Kellerman who caught the public imagination, and she who is widely considered to have instigated changes in fashion. When Kellerman first came to Britain, female swimmers in Australia were permitted to wear short-legged, non-skirted costumes for competitive swimming. They knew that extra fabric caused drag, so why should women be hampered with it? Instead, Australian women wore men's singlets. On her arrival in the UK, Kellerman wore what she was used to, a gender-neutral singlet, but when she got a gig performing for a royal audience she was required to cover her legs in case the sight of her knees accidentally brought down the monarchy. So she sewed a pair of stockings to the bottom of her singlet, thus creating a black costume that covered her from neck to toe, but also revealed – in fact accentuated – her pretty fabulous figure. (I'm not making a value judgement when I say Kellerman had a fabulous figure. It was official. A

Harvard professor, Dr Dudley Sargent, bravely took on the thankless job of measuring three thousand women and declared Kellerman to be the Perfect Woman as her statistics most closely resembled the Venus de Milo. It is sincerely hoped that Dr Sargent was fully lauded and recognised for this most public-spirited and arduous task. Beyond my initial scepticism, it could actually be seen as a positive move for women, that the standards of female beauty were not allied to frailty.)

When Kellerman took this outfit to the States, it went down a storm – not in exclusively the right way. At that point in history, things were generally not going well for American women on the beach. They were being arrested for all sorts of spurious reasons: wearing a swimsuit under your clothes (like it's anyone's damn business), having revealing armholes (because if men knew women had armpits they might get all in a frenzy), wearing the wrong length of costume. There were even men who patrolled American beaches measuring the lengths of ladies swimsuits, making sure they were no more than three inches above the knee. What a job, eh, fellers, state-sanctioned slut shaming. Annette being Annette, a person who knew the value of getting press attention – it was her livelihood, after all – capitalised on the attention her outfit (and figure) got her by designing and marketing the first truly modern bathing suit, the Kellerman – a tight-fitting knitted suit, with a jersey skirt that came down to just above the knees as some kind of modesty panel. She tried to avoid censure by promoting it under the banner of health, but it still took some time to catch on – after all, Ethelda Bleibtrey was arrested for revealing her legs a whole twelve years later.

If it took a show woman to change things, it had been the sports arena that had influenced Kellerman, so credit must go to the liberal Australian attitude that had put her in a men's singlet to start with. The English competitive swimming organisations played a key role too, because over in their world of competition, the expectations on women were much less frilly.

In 2010, the Amateur Swimming Association issued costume guidelines for men and women. There had been problems with new performance-enhancing, non-textile swimsuits which apparently conferred unfair advantage to the wearer. These new revolutionary 100 per cent polyurethane costumes were said to compress muscle, add extra buoyancy and aid forward propulsion. It would take something more akin to a jetpack to propel most of us at anything like the speed of our nation's favourite swimmers, even on their off days, and I have considered wearing ten of them at once to get me above the pace of a plodding hippo. Regardless, the ASA's 2010 rules were clear. For men, costumes must not extend above the navel nor below the knee, and for women, 'shall not cover the neck, extend past the shoulder nor shall extend past the knee'. There's something quaintly biblical in their use of 'shall not' and 'nor shall' but, then, these are commandments that amateur athletes are required to pay very rigorous attention to, on pain of exclusion. The first costume rules produced in 1890 by the ASA were, as you might expect, a complete reversal of this. Where the modern version is all about things not being too long, the original rules were all about things not being too short. At the start, the rules only applied to men because it was only men who were allowed to take part in public competition, and they still mostly swam in the nude, which sore affronted public decency. The first ASA regulations for women came only nine years later in 1899 – which in terms of history is a relatively speedy turnaround. By 1912, ASA regulations insisted on the following: singlets for both men and women, in black or dark blue, buttoned at the shoulder. 'For LADIES [their capitals], a shaped arm at least 3″ long shall be inserted.' For men, the front of the costume was to be no lower than 2″ below the pit of the neck, whereas 'for LADIES [still shouting], the costume shall be cut straight across the neck'. The regulations insisted that 'drawers' were worn underneath the costume; because costumes were made of wool, which can be a little clingy when wet, these cotton drawers were to preserve modesty and there were strict rules about their design too, even though they'd remain (hopefully) unseen. And finally, 'on leaving the dressing room, lady competitors over 14 years of age must wear a long coat or bath gown before entering and also immediately after leaving the water'.

The men's costumes were designed from a starting point of nudity, and the women's from a starting point of overdressed nonsense. And they'd met somewhere in the middle (apart from the minor detailing of sleeves, necklines and an insistence that women wander around poolside shrouded in their dad's overcoats, looking like some ghostly pre-mechanised Daleks). Here was a place where men's and women's costumes were really very similar. We wore what men wore. Or maybe, men wore what we wore; yes, I think I prefer it that way round. So it seems that in the very narrow arena of competitive sport, a kind of equality had been reached. An almost level playing field ... in the water ...

Oh, if only it had been so simple. If only we could have just followed the example 'allowed' our sporting sisters. Because outside the competitive pool, swimming outfits here were as frilly and insensible as they were in the States. But hang on, were they? Or were things actually shifting? A woman writing in the *Daily Mirror* in the summer of 1915 talks of her 'pretty friend' who was 'charmed with a bathing dress she has just bought. The tunic is composed of black crepe broche with three full graduated flounces trimmed with kilted crude pink ribbons of a tartan effect. I exclaimed that this gorgeous garment was most unpractical.' And I exclaimed that this garment sounded pretty horrendous. Three flounces? Why, it's practically a puffball skirt. Personal taste aside, she continues to report their conversation, and the impression you might have had if you'd just read the first part of it – that the status quo remained and was terribly overdressed – is wrong. 'On the contrary,' her friend exclaimed. 'It is the most useful garment going ... When I want to swim off comes the tunic and voila! And she disclosed a black silk maillot underneath.' Aha! Women were catching on! The frills and flounces were for parading up and down the beach, and as soon as you wanted to actually swim, you could strip those off and be in something practical and simple. It sounds almost revolutionary.

Change was coming from overseas, too. Lady Dorothy wrote in the *Swimming Magazine* in 1914 describing a new costume worn by South African champion swimmer Miss Doreen Lyttle. Of course, Lady Dorothy said, Miss Lyttle wears a standard costume when she's racing, but once she's on the beach, 'like a great many ladies, she prefers to wear something other than regulation dress'. The outfit she describes has lots to commend it. It's a two-piece, knickers to the waist and a long jersey with short sleeves, generally made in dark colours with a contrasting border. It sounds positively attractive. You might cancel your order for a replica, however, when you discover it was made in worsted 'like the thick costumes many divers wear'. The two-piece hadn't been terribly well received in England initially because of worries that the jersey top may ride up in the waves and 'expose some inches of one's natural covering', by which she means skin. The South African ladies had sorted that problem, though, by sewing large buttons on the knicker bit, which fastened top to bottom and also 'ornament the dress'. Lady Dorothy exhorted the women of England to follow the example of these enlightened South Africans, and if you plan on bringing back this look, please remember to build in extra time to undo those buttons when you need a wee.

Things were definitely loosening up. We were edging, after all, towards a new type of modernity led by women who could be freer, bolder, could listen to jazz – the flappers. The women who sat at the edge of Chiswick Baths, telling each other tales and smoking fags. The contrast between that jazz-loving, rebellious, crimp-haired woman and her Victorian and Edwardian sisters could not be clearer. To be a flapper was to be young and (yes, class again) probably middle or upper class. Young, single, possibly wage-earning, a bit posh. Sounds marvellous, and apart from the jazz requirement, I quite fancy it. Alongside the new fashions came new attitudes, a new physical aesthetic that can simply be reduced to 'being fit'. For the first time, being fit had value for and in itself. Women's bodies were starting to be seen for what they were, rather than the feeble, compliant, inactive, constructed and idealised mannequin shapes fashion had previously embellished. We were getting our flesh out. That's easily said now, but it must have felt like a very exposing act then. Showing more flesh in public than you'd been conditioned to show would have played directly against your old role of condemning people who showed flesh. For the women breaking the rules, going against convention and conditioning, whether it was wearing trousers or putting on a smaller costume, it might have felt quite nerve-racking. You'd have to have had confidence, attitude – and a ring of women around you doing the same. The power that resides in the solidarity of women should never be underestimated.

By the middle of the 1920s, we had these two new strong images of modern women: the free-wheeling flapper, and the serious sportswoman. For a few brief glorious years women's bodies were mostly seen in the context of health, instead of sex. But it didn't take long for our bodies to become sexualised again, for our physical abilities to be downgraded in favour of feminine beauty. The swimsuit became ubiquitous; you didn't have to be a serious athlete to wear one. You didn't even have to get wet. Once the domain of sportswomen, they became associated with status, starlets, sex and glamour. Blame Hollywood, marketing, advertising, pin-ups, blame the invention of the bikini.

Those few brief glorious years coincided with lidos gaining mass popularity, along with sun-worshipping. Exposing your body stopped being so taboo once it was associated with paying homage to our new health overlords. Costumes became smaller, backless, shorter, and women started wearing two-piece swimsuits – although the gap between top and bottom still showed just the merest sliver of skin and certainly not the belly button (another part of a woman's body that had fearsome power to alarm and horrify). Women had won the battle for the vote and had shed many of the dreadful restrictions of womanhood. So you might almost imagine that everyone could just lay off. That in these halcyon days, we could relax, enjoy the freedoms, that there might be no more conversation about what was 'respectable' for women. No. And don't be surprised, a casual bit of woman-judging over a quick pint is still our national sport. The *Yorkshire Evening Post*, for instance, reported their own 'respectability conversation' in 1935 with some vox pop on what people thought of the two-piece costume. (When I'm in charge, vox pops will be banned from all forms of official media. If I want to know what some random stranger thinks about anything, I'll ask one. Until such a time I shall give them no credence, and continue to yell at the TV, 'What this person on the street thinks is not news.') After a barrage of comments about how the two-piece was 'ugly' and 'hardly suitable for a crowded bath', I could have hugged the Southport vox-popper who said, 'My experience is that women are the best judges of what constitutes respectability in a costume.' Yes, thank you, Southporter, we are able to make our own decisions. But s/he went on. 'If a woman oversteps the bounds of what is decent, other women are not slow to show their disapproval.' Damn. I'm not having any of that 'women judge women' nonsense, so I promptly withdraw the hug and reinstate my ban on vox pops.

People were always talking about what was respectable for women – why was nobody talking about the men? Well, a few men were trying really hard to. In 1929 (and I'd like you all to join me as we belt out 'And then a hero comes along') the Men's Dress Reform Party was created, ostensibly to free men from the restrictions their clothes imposed, and to improve the choices of what they could wear. The party lobbied for reduced clothing for swimming and sunbathing as if they had seen that women's clothing was becoming more emancipated and thought, 'Hmm. Not fair. We are becoming mere accessories to these newly liberated women.' As I'm a woman and can therefore multi-task, I am now playing a tiny violin at the same time as flicking through a catalogue of men to accessorise myself with. I'm also affording myself a small fond chuckle at this short-lived and ultimately unsuccessful forerunner to modern men's rights activist groups.

'The emancipation of swimwear is linked to the emancipation of women.' I've been emancipated time and again in a parade of costumes large and small. I've had colourful scraps of bikini with the tiniest straps and bottoms that tied at the side. I've worn hi-legs that ride up your bum, so-called boy shorts, and retro big pants that covered my sexually provocative belly button. I've had ones with beads and mirrored bits and clasps. I've worn costumes I could fit in a matchbox, I've worn a tankini. I've tried complex costumes that I couldn't quite work out and am still convinced that I put on upside down. I've looked at costumes and thought 'she can't actually swim in *that*'. I've worn costumes that have chafed and pinched and gaped and costumes that have fallen off when I jumped in. I've worn costumes till you could see through them. I've paid too much for some costumes, and I've not paid enough for ones that split on the third wear. I've bought ones that faded through overuse, and ones where the colour stayed bright because I didn't really wear them. I've bought costumes from all over the place so I can now make sweeping generalisations like 'American women are short in the body' and 'Australia makes the best costumes'. I've bought ones with support panels, ones with superfluous zips, ones with useful zips. Ones with high necks, ones guaranteed not to rot in chlorine, ones I've popped out the top of. I've bought ones with adjustable straps, removable straps, straps that cross over and no straps at all. (Those ones I found too much of a worry.) I've had ones I loved so hard I thought I'd never want another until I found a better one. I've had ones as gifts, and I thought stripy or black ones were my favourite until I got a neon-pink one. I've even had one with a strange net lining that I bought on the King's Road but I didn't like the lining so I cut it out and then the costume became so transparent I experienced the same shame Mrs Samuda did in France, so that was a waste of money.

I've felt a lot of things about some of these costumes. In line with the survey, some of them have been comfortable, some have had 'improved shape performance'. But what I've never, ever got, from any of them, is emotional satisfaction. Until now.

Hilda James's mother knitted her a swimming costume, and my friend Jemma, who is infinitely nicer, volunteered to knit one for me. I have an ambivalent relationship with knitting. I've had times of rebelling against the whole 'women doing crafts' thing, when I wanted to reject anything that represented a traditional women's role, or was a 'feminine art'. And I've had times of celebrating it, because it's an amazingly creative skill. But mostly my ambivalence is because I can't do it. I am not a knitter. My hands just don't go the right way. For me, knitting is like trying to thread a needle in a dream when your fingers are actual sausages. I can do the thing with the needles, but I don't have the patience or the dexterity to do anything more complicated than row after row and even if I achieved the world's longest scarf it would have more holes than a chunk of supermarket Gouda, an edge that's windier than Snake Pass and somehow more stitches than I started with. I did knit a whole garment once, when I was twenty and on a summer holiday with my family in an isolated cottage in the New Forest. I knitted a jumper; it was grey-and-yellow stripes and a funny box shape because going in or out on purpose was beyond me. The family would go out on excursions for the day, and I'd stay in, crossly knitting. The sun beat down, I was hunched inside over my needles, cursing. The only time I huffed myself outside was to go and find a phone box to ring my boyfriend and moan about being on holiday with my parents. Or when they watched the Royal Wedding (it was Charles and Di, this was 1981) on the tiny rental TV and I was not willing to participate in such a 'charade' so I sat in the garden, under a tree, knitting. I didn't just knit, I also taught myself to play Christmas carols on the jangly cottage piano; my mum recalls coming up the path after a beautiful day on the beach to hear me clonking through 'The First Noel'. I don't have the jumper any more but I can still play 'The First Noel' with two hands, so it was definitely not time wasted.

I've never been fitted for a piece of clothing, so when Jemma came round to fit my knitted swimsuit it was a new experience for me. I tried it on and she tweaked and measured and decided where she'd pull bits in and sew bits up. The dog wanted to join in, snapping at strands of hanging wool. It was more fuss than I'd made about my wedding outfit. (To be fair, I made precisely no fuss about that because we sneaked off to get married at Marylebone Register Office on a work day and told only three people. I wore an Ally Capellino purple tunic that I already had, and my trusty leather jacket. The thought of a bunch of people, even ones I knew, all staring at me in a white wedding dress was a ghastly proposition.) Jemma and I had chosen a pattern together, and, being a swimmer herself, she put thought and effort into avoiding the sag potential. The pattern reassuringly said 'Don't be afraid to go into the water in this swimsuit', and I wasn't. If it sags, I figured, what's the worst that can happen? If I inadvertently revealed my breasts, nobody would die, including me.

The costume she made and I am thrilled to call mine is a thing of beauty and a joy forever. Blue shorts (of the kind that are usually called 'boy', though why shorts need to be gendered is a mystery) and a red-and-cream chevroned top, a hoop of red to tie in a halter, a little red belt and a swooping back leaving my shoulders and back free from straps. It even has a little diamond-shaped gusset. But it's one thing marvelling at the incredible skill that went into making it, quite another to see if it stood the test of water. So came The Day I Tried It Out, which had to be at my beloved Tooting Lido. I put it on, and like some siren call, various women gathered to marvel at Jemma's skill. I am not a fan of attention (see note about my wedding, above) but this was different. It looked amazing, it fitted me, it suited me, and for the first time ever I felt like parading. Not in a parody of glamour, with fifties shades and a pair of kitten heels. Just as me. I wanted to show off, actively invite the gaze. I could take the compliments gleefully without having to counter with any 'oh but's. This was such a new and exciting feeling, I got a glimpse of what other women feel when they post a selfie, an unfettered 'Look at ME!' What a genius garment this is.

It was a little toasty wearing wool on a lovely summer's day, so I was keen to get in the water. I had imagined that swimming in wool would be, at best, hilariously dreadful, so I got in cautiously. Nothing happened. I swam a width, and it felt utterly fine. More than fine. What was on my skin felt soft and enclosing, nothing rubbed or clutched, not like the cling film effect of Lycra. It wasn't dragging or ballooning or round my knees, I was still carefully wrapped and tied in a small woolly parcel, but there was a sense of freedom, better than nudity even, because there was a gentle touch on my skin and no sense of risk. I swam to the steps to get out, and I had imagined this might be the danger spot, that my naked form would emerge, trailing behind it a sodden wool bundle still tied round my neck with a straining halter, like an old shire horse tugging a reluctant plough through a wet field. If this were fiction, I'd definitely say that happened. But it didn't. It did get a little clingy and from my view looking down, I became a bit 'titty', which made me roar with laughter. Apart from a slight gape at the side, which might have revealed the side boob of a more-endowed woman, the costume was fine. And now I want to wear it to everything. I want to wear it to Glastonbury and Glyndebourne, and if I could have worn this to be married in, everyone in the world would have been invited. I've never felt better in a thing. A friend took some photos, and in every one I'm smiling my head off. Someone said I should frame the costume, but I don't want it behind glass – if you love something you let it be free. And I love that swimsuit. I love what it gave me: physical confidence, comfort, freedom and happiness. It's as close to emotional satisfaction as I could possibly imagine, and yes, I wish that for us all. And it only took four days to dry out.

We can't go back to wearing knitted swimsuits. We never go back, we just try history out for fun. Instead, we stand here freer than we have ever been. On the day I tried out my swimsuit, there was a model shoot on the other side of the pool, beautiful young women showing off tiny bikinis in tiny bodies. And in my knitted swimsuit, I understood, at last, their sense of confidence and pride in themselves. This is our freedom, the right to show ourselves ... as long as we're 'bikini body ready'. Personally I am always bikini body ready, in that I have both a body, and a bikini. But sometimes, when I read the sheer volume of guff written about how women should look in public, I wonder what emancipation really means. Because the expectations and judgements we get today, about our bodies and how we dress them, might be as stifling and restrictive as we think knitted swimming costumes were, in those more covered-up times. But we move forward. And this is progress. This is privilege. Yes?

Chapter 10

Olympic Flames

I wish I believed in homeopathy. I wish I believed that if you dilute a thing until it's no longer traceable, it will leave a 'memory' in the water. I wish I believed that water had a memory. Because if I did believe that, I could also believe that when I went swimming in the London Aquatic Centre after the 2012 Olympics, I might have taken homeopathic doses of Rebecca Adlington.

I was reminiscing about that Olympic summer with my daughter, recalling the feelings that the whole city was caught up in, the comradeship, the possibility and excitement. About how it was as if we'd subconsciously decided, as one, to defy the stereotypes of what being a Londoner is. How for one summer we weren't rude, unhelpful, surly and uncommunicative, but instead qualitatively added to people's experience of the city, and practically led sing-songs on the bus. How we stopped tutting at people standing on the wrong side of the escalators, and hugged them instead. (I've gone too far. There's no way London became a city of huggers, thank goodness.) People cited the spirit of the Blitz, as if that was appropriate. But, snatching this phrase back from the mouths of opportunists, we really were all in it together. I recalled how frustrated I was that my own cynicism had stopped me signing up to be a volunteer helper on the basis of … well, I can't actually remember. I can remember being opposed to giving my time, but not why. How utterly ridiculous, and how self-defeating cynicism can be. The idea of being negative was bafflingly pointless long before the brilliant Opening Ceremony started. 'I loved that summer,' my daughter said. 'We spent the whole time watching TV.'

By the time I decided I did want to go to an Olympic event after all, the only tickets available were so expensive it would have been cheaper to go on holiday. So we did indeed spend a summer watching TV, armed with a complex schedule of events, including those we had no natural leaning towards; there was a brief window of opportunity that summer where I could wax lyrical on the virtues of shooting as an Olympic sport, although that information, like fully understanding how futures can actually be traded, has absolutely no brain-stick and now all I can muster is 'because it's hard to point a thing at another thing and hit it?' We ignored the siren call of the beautiful weather and stayed on the sofa, except for a two-hour slot when we went to support the runners along the Embankment and it rained so hard we might as well have gone swimming fully clothed. We loved it. And then, even though we were worried we would never feel with that intensity again, loved it a second time when the Paralympics were on a couple of weeks later.

Once the Games were over, builders moved back in to the Aquatic Centre to strip it of its Olympic specifics. The huge area where athletes were drugs-tested became the public changing rooms, the two spectator areas right at the top on either side, the ones that had formed the very tips of the building's stingray wings, were taken off; the second pool, which we never saw on-screen because it was where the athletes did their warm-up and warm-down swims, was revealed behind a new glass corridor. Having admired it so many times on TV, as soon as it opened to the public I was in that queue. I've swum in other Olympic pools, but swimming here is special. I think the experience may be similar to the one religious people talk about when they swap their usual humble parish church and go off to a cathedral. The actions are the same, but there's bigger feelings. Everything gets elevated, inspired by sublime architecture that's on a scale you thought was reserved for a different class of person. Somewhere in your psyche you instinctively understand the architectural language even though it's way above your head in every sense. The fluid undulations of the ceiling like the underside of a great whale. The way the diving boards rise organically from the ground like something incredible unearthed in an archaeological dig. The massive curving banks of glass, even the way lights are set up the stairs, and the stairs themselves. The discreetly natural forms centring an intensely unnatural box of water. The purposeful imperfections of the concrete feeding my long-term love affair – I love you, concrete. I stood beside the diving blocks, ready to do a clumsy jump in rather than the athletes' smooth starting dives, but still, somehow, was part of the same thing they were. I could be part of the continuum, because it was mine. We all can be, because it is ours. In a culture that strips back everything that belongs to people, our railways and our health service and our libraries, public legacy is quite a concept to get your head around. And while one doesn't want to get too teary-eyed and start singing the Internationale, legacies are getting hard to come by. The Aquatic Centre was, and is, a fantastic place to swim, partly because there are only a few fifty-metre pools in our capital city (though we're lucky, most UK cities don't have any), partly because it belongs to us, and partly because I'd felt so passionately about what happened there that summer. So maybe water does hold memories, after all.

In the 2012 Olympics, men and women took part in an equal number of swimming events, as we might expect. In fact, the Games were heralded as 'the Women's Olympics', not least by the International Olympic Committee (IOC) who called it a 'historic step towards gender equality'. Because this was actually the first Olympics where women competed in all events. The first Olympics that saw women from Saudi Arabia, Qatar and Brunei competing, Qatari women being represented in the water by the splendid Nada Arkaji who talked of how 'it meant a lot … because since I'm the first Olympic swimmer maybe that would encourage other girls'. It was an Olympics that saw Nicola Adams crowned as our first female Olympic boxing champion. But this gender equality has taken a long time coming, almost a hundred years to the day. It wasn't until 1912 that women were allowed to swim in the Olympics at all. And they achieved that despite objections, as we might expect.

I must be feeling in a generous mood. If it's taken us a hundred years to get equality, then the 'mere' sixteen years it took to go from 'zero women' to 'some women' swimming in 1912 suddenly feels like a very quick step. And swimming was comparatively 'lucky' – in field hockey, for instance, women weren't competing at Olympic level until 1980, and at the 2000 Olympics, women were still excluded from boxing, wrestling and baseball. These were 'men's sports'; genteel tennis and golf were much more suitable for ladies. The first modern Olympic Games was in 1896 and woman-free, but at the second, in 1900 in Paris, there were twenty-two female competitors (out of a total of 997) who took part in those two sports. The 1900 Games used live pigeons for the shooting competitions, so there were more birds than women present but at least the women didn't end up dead. The idea of including women swimmers in the London Games in 1908 was briefly considered but they settled for a diving display from Sweden's Miss Ebba

Gisico and Finland's Miss Valborg Florström instead. (The rules for new additions to the Olympic roster are complex, but one basic stipulation is that athletes have to put on a demonstration of their sport at an actual Games if they want to be considered for inclusion in the future.) So 1908 became the first year that women's water skills were celebrated at the Olympics, if purely decoratively.

For early women Olympians then, winning was only part of the challenge; a big part of the achievement was in taking part at all. Particularly given the animosity towards women athletes held by president of the IOC, Baron Pierre de Coubertin. Coubertin is heralded everywhere as the 'father of the modern Olympics', a title which will surely annoy all those fathers who value their daughters as highly as their sons. He made it very clear, repeatedly, that he did not welcome sportswomen, that he wanted to keep the Games as 'the solemn and period exaltation of male athleticism ... with the applause of women as the reward'. I'm not in a position to judge whether male athletes were happy to take part just to hear women clap and for no other prize, but it seems unlikely. For Coubertin, as with many men of his generation, athletics for women was 'against the laws of nature', and it was a position he held firm to. He used all sorts of tactics, claiming that women destroyed their feminine charms if they engaged in sport, and that no one wanted to see women's horrific expressions as they exerted themselves (an idea which made me pull ugly faces even though nobody was looking). When that wasn't working, he appealed to men, saying that allowing women in their sports feminised both the men and the sport. This was a dire warning – being feminised was an awful suggestion. But it wasn't long before Olympic events were organised by the host countries and those lovely feminist Swedes took the initiative to allow women in. A powerless Coubertin kept banging on, looking increasingly like a tragic man at the office party having to tell his sexist jokes to the photocopier because everybody else has got tired of them. In 1935, when women were firmly established in the competition, he was still spouting off about how the primary role of women 'should be like the ancient tournaments – the crowning of victors with the laurels'. Were the Baron still around, I'm sure there'd be a long line of volunteers happy to 'crown' him with some 'laurels'.

Baron de Coubertin was not the only one who was resolutely against women participants. Over in the States, his brother-in-sexism James E. Sullivan refused to allow a female swimming team to travel to the 1912 Games. Sullivan, described as a 'self-made man' (which seems to be code for 'massive controlling reactionary bully'), had enormous personal influence which he used to exert absolute control over individual athletes. He was president of the American Athletic Union, and they pretty much ran the American Olympic Committee, so women like swimmer Ida Schnall stood no chance. She railed against Sullivan in a letter to the *New York Times*. 'This is not from a suffrage standpoint,' she wrote, though of course we'd have no beef if it were.

'I read in the newspapers wherein James E. Sullivan is again objecting to girls competing with boys in a swimming contest. He has objected to my competing in diving at the Olympic Games in Sweden, because I am a girl. He objects to girls wearing a comfortable bathing suit. He objects to so many things ... he must be very narrow minded.' Ida love, I applaud your ability to remain polite. I suspect my own letter would have been full of f*** and w****r.

It wasn't just men who didn't approve. Looking at the feminist credentials laid out in the biography of Australian Rose Scott, president of the New South Wales Ladies' Swimming Association, you'd imagine she'd have been so keen she'd have rowed the women there herself. You'd be wrong. Although she'd campaigned vigorously for women's voting rights, Miss Scott was implacably opposed to women and men appearing in the same space in their bathers. She raged against mixed bathing on beaches: 'there is too much boldness and rudeness now', she said, 'and I'm afraid this decision [to desegregate beaches] will have a vulgar effect on girls'. It seems she didn't hold men in very high regard. 'It is not a compliment to be stared at by a man,' she said, and there are many women who would agree with that without then suggesting the solution lay in women not appearing in mixed gatherings at all. 'It would be alright, perhaps,' she conceded gracelessly, 'if the men would behave themselves properly, but a lot of bad men would be attracted who would make all sorts of nasty remarks and who would rather go for the spectacle than for the skill.' Again, there's plenty to agree on in that sentiment. But her response – to modify the behaviour of women, rather than to tackle what she saw as predatory men – is essentially anti-feminist. The answer surely did not lie in her next step – attempting to ban Australia's top women swimmers, Fanny Durack and Wilhelmina 'Mina' Wylie, from going to the Olympics, because they would be (gasp) watched by men. Rose ended up resigning her presidency when it was finally agreed that Fanny and Mina could attend, even though the deal was that they had to pay for the trip themselves. In fact, Miss Scott's opposition worked against her – ha HA! It gained publicity for Fanny and Mina and so they were able to raise their travelling costs via public donations. It's a really good job for Australian swimming that Rose didn't succeed, because Fanny Durack became the first woman to receive an Olympic gold medal for swimming at the 1912 Olympics, and Mina Wylie took silver.

Women like Fanny and Mina, having to raise their own travel expenses, play against the popular image of the early Olympics as being a little bit *Chariots of Fire*, stuffed with the gallant gentleman amateurs driving around in top-down jalopies with picnic hampers in the boot, dashed good fellows at heart, ready to rescue a puppy from a stream without a moment's thought for their own safety. 'Oh, Jeffrey, you saved Binky. How can I ever repay you?' Reports of the first American women taking part in the 1900 Games don't help dispel that image. Essentially, they were a bunch of wealthy socialites, their lives ones of absolute privilege. Because the

1900 Games coincided with the Paris Exposition, most of them were already in town, 'doing the season'. What luck! Tennis finalist Marion Jones, for instance, was the daughter of a millionaire. Of the golfers, all five were either already living in Europe, or on extended vacations organising educational experiences for their children, like one does. Bronze medallist Daria Pratt happened to be in France organising her daughter's wedding to a count. None of this detracts from their sporting achievements, but there's no doubt their journey there would have been first class, in stark contrast to the experiences of Fanny, Mina and the women in Britain's swim team. They were there not through any kind of birth right or privilege, but through what has been called 'athletocracy' – it was their sporting merit and commitment to training that got them through to competitions at the highest level. It was their performance, not their background, that mattered. They were there through hard bloody work, against the odds and against the expectations. There's a purity to their achievement because of that struggle which I find deeply admirable. It's the same principle that has me always rooting for the underdog.

Annie Speirs (from Liverpool), Irene Steer (Cardiff), Isabella 'Belle' Moore (Glasgow) and Jennie Fletcher (Leicester): in 1912, they became the first British women to bring home Olympic gold medals in swimming, for the 4x100m relay. What an achievement for four ordinary women. Four pioneering women who in their official photo are the very models of a self-conscious modernity, their arms crossed over swimsuits designed to give them the best competitive chance rather than protect their modesty. Nothing fancy, just the same slick one-piece suits as the male competitors wore, costumes that they were responsible for supplying themselves, along with all their own training costs. Years later Jennie Fletcher said she hated that photo – and maybe that's because it shows the outline of her breasts and knickers, revealing, not hiding, her sporting body. It's certainly more 'daring' than Kellerman's had been, except here, in this sporting arena, there's a different, desexualised message in these bodies. 'This is what competitive women swimmers look like,' they say. And 'get used to it'. We can use our bodies for sport and competition, and we will. Standing behind the four women in the photo is their chaperone in a demure full-length gown, buttoned up and, let's be honest, a tad grumpy. Maybe she was hot. Or maybe she knew that she was part of something gone. Because if this is a representational photograph, the chaperone represents the old days, and the competitors are the new. She's how women used to be seen, trussed up and cross, and they are the new reality, open and capable. She's the role women have fulfilled, and they are what's possible in the future. Because after these four took part, the principle of women in the Games could not be questioned again. Once a thing is done it cannot be undone, the hardest thing is being the first people to do it. And it was hard. Jennie Fletcher, one of eleven children, had to fit training in between her six days a week twelve hours a day shifts as a cutter and machinist in a hosiery factory. Belle Moore, the eighth of nine children, had to walk two miles to the pool and back every time she needed to train – she remains Scotland's only female gold medallist swimmer. You might think, why do we non-Olympians owe them thanks? They opened the doors for other women to take part in the Olympics, but that's for a higher elite, not the ordinary woman in the pool. But every step along this trail is relevant, what each woman achieves changes the perception of what we are capable of, and what we would be allowed to do next. That was applicable then, and it's applicable now. If these four women could get in and compete at the highest level, we can certainly be free to dandle around in the shallows.

Let's not forget diver Isabelle White, who brought home the bronze medal for plain diving in 1912, even though the official report of the Games, which runs to an astonishingly dull 1,426 pages, described how she 'has great speed but is too back-swanked during her passage through the air'. Back-swanked, yes. A phrase that's pretty difficult to look up on the internet without attracting a whole host of sites that aren't answering the question you asked. Looking at the photo of White's dive, I'm forced to conclude it means her back was too arched. She may have been back-swanky, but she was a bronze winner nonetheless. Apart from diving, women only had two swimming events – the 4x100m relay and the 100m freestyle – as opposed to the men's seven. While men swam distances up to 1500m, no woman swam more than 100m, so 'nowhere', says Chris Love in *A Social History of Swimming*, was 'the cultural belief in the greater strength and stamina of the male versus the general weakness and frailty of the female more clearly illustrated'. A 300m event was added to the Antwerp Games, but its addition just underlines Love's point, that women simply couldn't (or shouldn't) do the same distances as men.

Sixty-five women (including Hilda James) took part in the 1920 Olympics, and so did 2,500 men. Stuff that, thought Frenchwoman Alice Milliat. Stuff women being considered inferior and not being allowed to compete. So between 1921 and 1936, Milliat put on a women's Games, to build on the networks of women's sports and protest their exclusion. Nobody thought it would be much of a success – why would anyone come to watch women, apart from those leering men that Rose Scott was so concerned about? Why would anyone want to see women's ugly 'trying hard' faces? Well, it turns out that plenty did, and the Games were a roaring success, both in terms of audience and because they accelerated the acceptance of women's sport into the full Olympics. After putting it on four times, Milliat had forced the hand of the IOC to include more women's athletics. And here we are now, with the IOC proclaiming their gender equality. Except ... I wonder how long it will be before men force the hand of the IOC to be included in synchronised swimming? Introduced into the Olympics in the 1980s, this is one of two sports they can't compete in (the other is rhythmic gymnastics); while swimming displays started as exclusively male, synchro was hived off as a natural fit for women because it could be decorative, and seen as less strenuous. As we know, as soon as something becomes a 'women's thing' it's entirely marginalised. But it seems confusing – either it's easy, therefore just for women, or difficult and therefore an Olympic event suitable for all. Which is it? Are men being denied the right to be decorative? Anyone who thinks it's easy has never tried it, and anyone who thinks it's pretty has never seen me attempt it. In my mind, I'm swooshing around with the natural grace of the dancing fish in the underwater sequence in *Bedknobs and Broomsticks*; in reality it's more reminiscent of the football scene where large mammals lumber ungraciously around the pitch bumping into each other, boof. I shove my foot up above the surface while paddling underneath it like a desperate drowning goose then burst to the top and gasp for air like it's my last breath. It's hard enough looking pretty just standing still; doing it at the same time as swimming elegantly and in time with a group is nigh on impossible.

We can know so much about our contemporary Olympians – it's discoverable in a few clicks, alongside a heap of stuff we would rather not know. (Sometimes when I glance accidentally at the Internet of Bad Things, I find myself thinking fondly back to times when *Heat* magazine was all we had and if we wanted to fully discuss the Circle of Shame, we had to ring each other up. On our landlines. Which are phones you can't take to the shops.) And even though we hold our Olympians in massively high regard, the press still persist in dropping pointless nuggets of their personal information into our gaping maws. In some sense our interest is not surprising, we're almost as invested in their success as they are (only without the effort or financial outlay). And they do appear to be almost a different species from the rest of us, their achievements and commitments almost unfathomable. I was once in the same pool as some German Olympic swimmers at a training session, so I can confirm that they are human, just more so.

We know so much about modern athletes, but what of the ones who came before *Heat* magazine? What about the hidden women? I wanted to know. And then a thing happened. I had an entirely fortuitous conversation in the pool with a fellow swimmer, and I think it underlines the joys of how communities sometimes fit together completely by chance. She asked why I was timing myself in the water, so I explained about Miss Emma Dobbie, leaving out any reference to my unpleasant competitive streak. 'Oh!' she said. 'I have an Olympian staying at my house this week. Would you like to meet her?' Why, yes, I said. Yes, I'd very much like to meet her.

Which is how I came to sit and talk with Fearne Spark (née Ewart), about her experience representing Great Britain in the 1956 Melbourne Olympics. It may have been confirmation bias, but there was something about Fearne's bearing when she opened the door that made her look exactly how I'd imagine an Olympic star of the 1950s would look: casually chic and relaxed. A tall slender woman with effortlessly excellent posture, Fearne generously told me her story, and in terms of possibility, she certainly had a better start than Jennie Fletcher et al. Brought up in Sri Lanka (then Ceylon), a perfect climate to be outside year round, she was swimming every day. 'I think that this must have had a benefit,' she said, 'because if you compare this with other people, brought up in England, you had to actually go to the swimming pool and learn to swim and it was very different.' By the time she was nine, 'my dad used to drop me at the pool in the morning and collect me at lunchtime'. That sense of freedom was familiar to me – like Fearne, we used to disappear out of the house in the morning and come home when we were hungry. The difference, I suppose, is that while Fearne went swimming in a tropical outdoor paradise, learning what was then called the 'Australian crawl' and getting involved in her first races, we went down what we called the Little Lane, which was, well, a little lane which led on to a scruffy field and then a golf course, where we threw sticky grass at each other, climbed trees and found abandoned porn mags in the bushes.

It would have been just after the end of the Second World War when Fearne came to England, to boarding school in Sussex. During games time Fearne would go swimming, and there's a slight sense that this might have been a lonely option. While everyone else was in a team playing hockey or netball, Miss Ewart was off at the pool in Hastings on her own. 'I'd go about three, four o'clock in the afternoon, after lessons, train and come back at six o'clock or whatever,' she said. And then on Sundays, aged twelve or thirteen, she'd take the train to London, again on her own, to East Ham Baths. 'But a lot of it was disapproved of by girls' boarding schools in those days, because you got polio still from swimming pools.' None of that stopped Fearne, and the school's disapproval (which was based on expert advice of the time, that polio was considered to be spread via public pools) never blossomed into a ban, and before long Fearne was swimming in county championships, then at national level and in her first international competitions by the age of fifteen, in Denmark. 'The competition site was a fenced-off area of the harbour,' she recalled. 'The water was just brown and horrid. It was hailing. The water temperature was about fifty-six degrees, I think.' It sounds pretty grim, and redolent of Hilda James's experience at the Antwerp Olympics. But still, she was lucky to have been there at all. 'It was the week of the O levels. And the school rule was that you couldn't leave the school during that week, even though [the competition] was a weekend and I wasn't going to miss an exam. So my dad said, "Well, she might never get chosen again. It might be the only chance she'll ever have so she's going." So I left school. And I had to take my O levels in the November, privately.' Had her father not stepped in, her career could have screeched to a halt right there, but instead, Fearne won and she allowed herself a brief moment of pride when she said, 'I was British champion at 100 metres, I beat Johnny Weissmuller's time,' before retreating back to modesty, talking about how you can't measure the times people achieve today with those in the past, because every aspect of the sport has changed so much. I made a mental note not to brag about how I was faster than Miss Dobbie. I was talking, after all, to a woman who beat one of the biggest swimming heroes of his time.

Fearne was nineteen by the time her Olympics invitation came along, and the way she described finding out that she was selected would not have been satisfactory for me. I'd expect a team of trumpeters marching up my street bearing a gold letter on a red velvet pillow. Fearne got a 'scrappy little bit of paper' saying 'You've been selected to swim in the Olympics', and that lack of a fanfare bears out through the rest of her story. There was no team of nutritionists and physios and managers, not even a little pamphlet on 'how to train for the Olympics', or any advice on what to eat, meaning that for Fearne, who'd left school and was now working, it was often a Mars bar and an apple. It was just Fearne, training once a week in East Ham and being left to herself the rest of the time, relying on her own dedication and self-discipline. 'You just pitched up and went,' she said. She just pitched up at the airport in her Olympic blazer, and went to Melbourne. It all sounds pretty ... well, amateur. 'The last of the really amateur Games,' Fearne concurred. And although the women were highly chaperoned and didn't leave the Olympic compound, it was also 'tremendously exciting, to be there and in the Olympic village. Everybody was friendly and you met all these people in other teams. It was hugely exciting.'

I can picture the world Fearne described. I've seen photos and films of how the world looked and how women looked. I can picture the girls' school in 1940s England, the horrid woolly costumes, her sitting alone on the chugging train from Hastings to East Ham every Sunday. Grabbing a Mars bar and an apple and hurrying back to her job at an insurance company. But what does the current chapter of her own waterbiography look like, now she is in her eighties? I asked if she still thought of herself as a swimmer, and her husband Philip joined in the conversation. 'You certainly swim very well,' he said, and Fearne agreed that 'yes, rather than anything else, I suppose I'd say yes'. I could understand the reluctance; Fearne is not one of nature's braggarts, she'd talked about how she was discouraged by her parents from becoming a 'big-head' and at the use of the word, I can feel a small bubble of something approaching injustice. Why can't we say 'I am good at this'? What's so wrong with a bit of self-belief? Why do we rail against holding ourselves in any kind of esteem? Woe betide anyone deemed too successful – we've given our natural inclination to cut them off at the knees a charmingly horticultural phrase, 'tall poppy syndrome', because we might not like a big-head but we're damn good at gardening. Fearne told me how other competitors in her Olympics didn't hold back. 'My heat was against Dawn Fraser, and she told us all before we started that she was the greatest and she was going to win.' And on some level, I asked, you believed her? 'I think you do,' Fearne replied. 'You say you don't but I think you do. She was full of confidence.'

We've taken that confidence, called it big-headedness, and sold it as an unattractive quality, particularly for women. Be a big-head, I want to say, or I'll be a big-head for you. Perhaps we need to create an informal network whereby we can be big-heads on behalf of others who find it difficult. I'd suggest that we call it BOBO: Big-head On Behalf Of, except that teeters on the edge of being terribly twee. Philip is a BOBO, for his wife, and it was a pleasure to hear. 'Fearne never tells anybody she swam in the Olympics,' he said, 'but I tell people. I'm proud of her.' They swim every day at their home in Portugal and Philip told me (because Fearne never would) how in the pool 'you get young girls of nineteen, twenty, and Fearne will beat them'. '*Some* of them,' she batted back. 'You get in the pool and you're swimming and then a young man is swimming next to you and you think, "I've got to keep up." And then I think, "Why am I keeping up? He's only twenty-five or something. Why am I trying to keep up? It's a funny thing, this competitive spirit,' she said.

Despite all the evidence to the contrary, I still loudly and regularly declare that I'm not at all competitive. Really, I say unconvincingly, I don't have a competitive bone in my body. I claimed to only ever do the mothers' race at my children's school sports days to show them how to lose with a smile on your face. That it was the taking part that mattered. I certainly didn't, like some mothers, train for it or wear proper running shoes. If there was a competition for least competitive person, I would probably win it. But still, I sometimes do exactly what Fearne does, have races with whoever is beside me in the next lane of the pool. I realise I'm swimming stroke for stroke with them, and, before I know it, the urge is upon me. I glimpse a chance for some meaningless victory, the possibility that if I really went for it, I might be able to touch the end before they do. Sometimes they sense it and speed up, but usually they're unknowing, which adds to the fun. It doesn't matter if the person I beat is only ten years old, it all counts. Fearne's right. It is a funny thing, this competitive spirit.

Chapter 11

My Waterbiography (Part III)

Picture the scene. We are slap bang in the middle of the 1990s, and for a few years women have been telling themselves that they can have it all. They can have it all, they can do it all, nothing is going to hold them back from striding like great besuited colossi over all man-made obstacles. They are going to have demanding jobs and brilliant relationships and gorgeous families and run homes and be sexually available and basically I'm tired just thinking about it. Whirring like overwound clocks, we are all very busy doing everything, gaily proclaiming to anyone who will listen that life certainly isn't going to change 'just' because we've had a baby. So busy in fact that nobody has time to stop and consider that maybe doing everything isn't actually progress. In a world of slogans we are stuck with Having It All, while ahead of us lie the ghastly popification of Girl Power and the invention of the Yummy Mummy.

If yummy mummies had been invented in 1995 when I had my first baby, I wouldn't have been one. I'm not being immodest about my ability to clip through Peter Jones in a pair of kitten heels, I'm being allergic to the words, when they're used on their own and most particularly when in that combination. There's something odd about the way people start using infantile language around women who have children, and about the way perfectly sensible women use it to describe themselves: 'I'm X's mummy.' And 'yummy' is just about bearable as a child's description of a cake, but a distressingly puerile way for adults to label each other in public. Put the two words together and they make such a demeaning sugary phrase it practically gives me diabetes.

Women giving their children skills that they don't themselves possess is part of the motherhood deal. Women teaching their children to swim is part of our swimming history. So, feeling as definitely un-yummy as sleep-deprived new mothers do, and with a brain only working on half-speed, I decided, when my son was about six months old, that he needed to be taken swimming. In theory, this is an excellent plan. In practice, it's also an excellent plan. It gets you out of the house and makes them tired, and most of parenting is about the most efficient way of getting them tired. In that sense, it's quite similar to having a dog. It wasn't about the passing down of skills because I didn't have any to pass down, and anyway, at six months old that would have been a frankly thankless task. And it wasn't about him having better opportunities than I'd had, because I didn't feel that I had been deprived in any way. But it was getting a bit trendy to take a baby swimming, for which I could blame Nirvana and their album *Nevermind* with its iconic cover image of a smiling baby underwater. That cover sent a clear and direct message: make your baby swim, it's cool. I was clinging on to the notion that I could still be cool. Clinging rather desperately, one might say. I was so keen on staying cool that I thought I should have a water birth. They were quite the speciality back then, as freakish and bohemian as delivering your baby at home. Water birth was radical, it was new, it was RIVEN WITH DANGER. I'd done dangerous things before, like ordering a vegetarian meal in France, so it had appealed to me; I quite fancied opening like a flower and it being all being calm and floaty. Sadly there was only one birthing pool in south London and when the time came it was already in use by some other devil-may-care cool woman, so I got in the bath instead.

Despite this tiring drive to appear effortlessly cool, going swimming with a baby was, for me, on a par with going to those great big hangars on the outskirts of towns called TIGER ADVENTURE! or HAPPY TOWN! that they paint garishly and fill with ball pools and climbing frames and play horrible fake pop and you sit there eating a sad little tuna sandwich and staring for about an hour until your child cries or hits another child and you can go home. It's just not my idea of fun. I offer that in defence of what is to come.

Only a miserable curmudgeon could fail to see the joy that swimming with a baby offers. There is something so deliciously, pleasingly tactile in it, new skin glossed with water becomes silky soft – yummy, you might almost say. Being skin to skin with a baby makes me sigh with pleasure just at the memory of it. You could do it at home in the bath, but in the pool you can jump, move, dance, swoosh them around in a circle, laugh at their expression as they meet the new resistances of water, they can splash and make someone's face crinkle, make their own face crinkle. You can throw them up in the air without that dread fear that you might not catch them on the way down, here, in fact, you can positively dandle on the edge of not catching them. And if it's a delight for parents, it's a positive thrill for them. Look, their eyes say, if their mouths can't form words yet. Look, I can jump into it! It holds me, and for those seconds when it doesn't, when I fall through it, there is always someone to bring me gaspingly, excitingly, to the top again. I can clamber up my mum in it, and somehow she becomes a much better climbing tree in water than she ever is on land. Unalloyed freedoms, expressed in smiles and laughs, the sheer enjoyment of having unrestricted limbs out, ready to be randomly flung. Water presents such a pure raft of opportunities, before they've learned how frightening it is, before they've learned about drowning, or competition and not being fast enough or the trials of bilateral breathing or about what lies beneath. Until then, all there is, is fun. And when they start to be free from your arms, start to float independently and try a few strokes on their own invariably some way under the surface, when you can dip under the surface together and one, two, three SMILE! underwater at each other, legs and arms splayed out or reaching towards each other, it is, without a doubt, utterly blissful. (It's particularly important to try and hold on to that bliss when one is engaged in possibly the most difficult task a human adult ever has to engage in: the putting on to a reluctant four-year-old of a verruca sock.)

But while swimming with a baby is sometimes a delight, it is also often most definitely not. And that's the bit no one tells you. That, actually, great chunks of it are deeply boring, and at worst it can feel like a terrible exercise in futility. People tend to keep that side of things to themselves because they don't want to be the first to mention it. But balancing the good with the bad is why the whole procedure is so damn complex.

For starters, my body was post-baby and my costume was late-pregnancy. I reckon it takes a good fifteen years for your body to get back to how it was pre-pregnancy by which time you're so old you don't give a fig and nobody's looking anyway. At the point I started, six months in to being a mother, I was not in my physical prime, and mentally I was less than present. Everything from my brain down sagged except for my breasts which were either as hard and misshapen as lumps of garden rockery or as limp as the overused pockets on an old corduroy jacket. At least in a costume if they leak nobody sees it. The last thing I wanted to do was get this body out in public, but chin up! Soldier on! So I dug out that old costume which I'd worn while I was pregnant, the one all stretched and see-through from where I'd crammed my belly in. This is the bit they don't show on the Nirvana cover, I thought – the woman standing just out of shot, ready to catch the joyous baby, the woman almost hallucinating from sleep-deprivation, a shapeless bag of what was once elastic.

Off I went to our nearest 'fun pool', two words which in combination are as dispiriting as 'yummy mummy' and which are an extra circle of hell. And I am not some amateur throwing a bit of snark at a much-loved public space, I am a professional swimming-opinion-haver, I have swum in many, and I know. They are hell.

I'd lug the small happy child and various bags from the car to the changing area, which presented a dilemma. Who to change first – me or him? (This is repeated on the way out, only with each party colder and more tired.) Either option was tricky; in the days before he could walk, I had to find some way to balance him, and in the days when he could walk he'd try to escape and bump his head before we'd even start. I'd find a large cubicle with a plastic tray fixed to the wall where I'd strap the wriggling boy down like a punishment in order to remove his nappy and clothing and dress him in his trunks. There was very limited product available in those days for the Swimming Baby. Nowadays it's a whole new spending opportunity, the market is flooded with special suits and floats and buoyancy stuff and hats and skincare and it's all terribly pink and blue and cute. Then we didn't even have nappies specifically designed for wear in the water (a very welcome invention as they prevent you from swimming into a slurp of a stranger's baby poo). You couldn't really 'make do' with ordinary nappies because they would bulge alarmingly within seconds of hitting the water. Have you ever dropped an ordinary nappy in a bowl of water? No, of course not, why would you? They swell up until they are as heavy as a bag of damp builder's sand, and then release these strange clear gel balls that have a lifespan of about 10,000 years and are malevolently cursed to clog our landfill sites. Stripped off, I'd drop him in a playpen while I quickly changed and shoved our masses of attendant paraphernalia into various lockers. By this time, he'd be furious at having been dumped, and would be pulling himself up on the bars of the play prison, yelling for attention.

We'd go through to the pool, which had a galleried cafe area above it with open railings so in the background you could hear the perpetual relieved chatter of parents who'd already been through the ordeal. This gallery arrangement seemed to be specifically designed to encourage inquisitive children to poke crisps through and watch them waft down to the pool below. The lifeguards would be on constant duty picking up soggy Monster Munch before children in the water dived and scrabbled in the race to reach them, like starved seals in an unfriendly zoo.

The interior theme of the pool was tropical paradise, and the designers were presumably working on the basis that everyone would be so exhausted they might be fooled. The designers were wrong. A couple of pathetic plastic plants wilting in front of a garden-shed sauna, feebly-coloured parrots on the tiles, a tragic palm that looked like it had survived a hurricane – 'South London Despair' might have been a better theme. There was a teaching pool to one side, which was very hot and extremely chlorinated, a combination that, when mixed with copious quantities of baby wee, can strip the top layer of your skin. The main pool was a free-form shape tagged onto a standard rectangle bit which was deeper and had lanes and was where you could go if you wanted to experience a near-drowning experience when they put the wave machine on, which they did sporadically and entirely on the whim of a teenage lifeguard. The children's entrance was a sloping 'beach' which was so slippery you couldn't risk letting go of your child's hands even though they would tug and tug to be free. To one side of the beach was a large grey plastic elephant, its trunk split to form a slide, and a plastic turtle resting on the 'shore'. The turtle is now extinct and I'm not surprised: it was a completely pointless hazard, an unattractive hard lump of slippery ridged plastic that children weren't allowed to climb on because when they did they inevitably fell off and would land on their heads on the hard tiles of the beach. There was a constant pip of whistles from lifeguards trying to stop kids climbing on the turtle hazard which was essentially there to teach toddlers several lessons. Lesson 1: if something looks fun, you won't be allowed on it. Lesson 2: sometimes adults don't think things through. And Lesson 3 (for all participants): that not everything that looks fun is actually fun.

There was a ritual to our swim which went like this: I'd encourage my child to get into the hot and grubby water. Child would fall over on slippery tiles. I'd get cross at the inevitability, at the tile design, at myself for failing in my supervisory duties. Child went in the water. This was when you had to make a decision – should you get your shoulders under to keep warm, which is quite tricky as the water is about one foot deep, or remain standing up ankle-deep in kid wee, which makes you feel quite existential? Once I was submerged I tried to bounce around a bit aerobically to get some benefit. I'd get very cold. Child would go to the steps of the slide, and I'd anxiously hope he didn't slip through the rungs, and stop other bigger children from pushing past him. He'd stand at the top, being scared. I'd stand there trilling enthusiastically, 'Come on! There's other children waiting! Come on! It's not scary.' My enthusiasm would wane, I just wanted him to come down the wretched thing. I'd give up being nice and turn into the mother that other mothers warn their children about. OH, FOR F***'s SAKE COME DOWN THE SLIDE, I would think. I never said that out loud, I said it with my eyes, which is apparently more scary. I'd try not to look at the clock, but eventually I'd give in – we'd have been in the water for three minutes. We'd bob some more. I'd try and invent games. The games made us both feel lonely. I'd try and make eye contact with other bobbing mothers. They were too busy making eye contact with their own children. Child discovered he loved the slide and goes up and down up and down up and down a hundred times. I lay on the pool floor waiting. Eventually, it was time to get out. Child wouldn't get out. I dragged him out by one arm. At least one of us was crying. Then came the final dilemma, a repeat of the first: who do you dry first? Do you stand shivering in your wet things while you dry a child who then sits in a puddle and tries to grab your pubic hair while you get dry? Or do you do as you would if this was the oxygen procedure on a plane and dry yourself first before sorting out the child? Either way, neither of us would be actually and satisfactorily dry by the time we stumbled exhausted to the cafe where we'd recover, me by taking in more caffeine and staring blankly at things, and him by throwing crisps down on the people remaining in the pool.

And then I had a second child, so the whole delightful palaver began again.

What use was I to these children? I couldn't swim well myself, and there was no Aunty Mary on hand so, once he was old enough, my son went to after-school lessons at our local pool. A non-fun pool. As well as giving him the rudiments, these lessons provided a whole new range of emotional opportunities for me. I became a prototype helicopter parent, hovering anxiously on a nearby bench. Fear and panic, when I watched helplessly as my beloved baby headed out of his depth. A barely contained fury: can the teacher not see he's out of his depth? Delight, as he learned to do stuff, mixed with a bit of jealousy, because I couldn't do that stuff myself. Relief, that I was off the hook as far as teaching him to swim went. Crossness again, when the teacher failed to recognise that my rather brilliant and amusing child needed special attention. And for the twenty minutes or so he was actually in the water, I would experience concentration of an intensity I had never felt before, as I willed myself to absorb the lessons through the very pores of my skin. Running through it in my head, over and over, as if by watching hard enough I could do the technique myself.

Swimming lessons are part of the state primary-school curriculum, and, like most state schools, at my children's there was no pool on site. Imagine going to a school that did have one, what an extraordinary privilege that would be. Having great facilities available on a daily basis could certainly skew your view of the world and your place in it, and please read my subtext. So, alongside the private lessons, my kids were bussed to the nearby pool with their classes on a strict rota for one term of the year. The class would be split into two groups of about fifteen kids: swimmers and non-swimmers, categories that basically defined two very different worlds. Parents who could supplement, and parents who couldn't. Parents for whom swimming was accessible and relevant – financially, culturally, socially, whatever, and parents for whom it wasn't. There were children who could butterfly up and down with ease, and in the same class, one or two who had never been to a pool before, or whose style was really more akin to vigorous hopping. Whatever the levels of ability, being with your school friends in the water remains an extremely exciting event; my son always came back home giddy with exhaustion, someone else's shorts on, and his jumper back-to-front. But if we hadn't supplemented those few lessons, I doubt he would have left primary school able to swim.

Yet the ability to swim 25m by the time you leave primary school is actually a national curriculum requirement. More specifically, the ability to swim 25m in a recognisable stroke, which quite a few of us might struggle to achieve and does not include 'being towed on a float by your best friend'. Recent statistics show that many children can't actually do this, that up to a third leave primary school with a fundamental life skill unlearned, even though it's on the curriculum. But it's not surprising, if you consider the pressure schools are under. A decrease in facilities, financial impoverishment, stresses on the subjects that are linked to league tables ... valid reasons why swimming might slip down the list. Schools struggle to find time, space and money for the bare minimum, and if they provide on average six lessons a year, that's six lots of about twenty minutes pool time. That's two hours of swimming PER

YEAR. And once those two hours are done, a whole other year goes by before you do the next lot of two hours. And a year is a pretty big proportion of your life when you've only had seven or eight years anyway. To say it's inadequate is an understatement; for children who don't have additional provision whether by dint of financial, social or domestic circumstance, the amazing thing is that any of them learn to swim at all.

Despite the inadequacy of school provision, we've gone, in a relatively short space of time, from my generation being thrown in at the deep end to some kids now doing triathlons, which I'm not sure I approve of (it seems a little ... excessive. What's wrong with slumping in front of the TV?). And coincidentally, public swimming pools have also really changed. We've moved away from the standard and traditional baths to a plethora of fun and leisure pools.

The first ever 'leisure pool' was built in Bletchley, Milton Keynes, in the 1970s, to replace a standard outdoor pool of the kind we now cherish (I now cherish). It feels like a cruel joke deliberately aimed at people like me, that design and fashion replaced the thing I love with the thing I hate. Bletchley got an iconic pyramidal building, since demolished, and it marked the start of a whole new wave of 'free-form' pool design. Free-form basically means no straight edges, something designed to have a 'natural' feel, though the word 'natural' feels like a terrible impostor in this case. If you look at what was happening socially at the time, the 1970s–80s, a kind of sense to it emerges reluctantly. Youth culture was well established as a social factor. People had started to holiday abroad en masse. The concept of 'leisure' was in its second or third generation. If people had spare cash to splash, they didn't want to splash it in a scraggy old pool built by men returning from the First World War, reminding them horribly of history and death and the past and how awful things were for their grandparents. Somewhere the family could go and have fun together had to work hard to attract their money, had to tempt in an audience whose expectations were on the rise now they were all familiar with what was on offer abroad. You could have your two weeks in Spain, and then bring your new, modern, well-travelled attitude to the fun pool on your doorstep. It would feel a bit like a holiday and could take your leisure cash all year round. This generation, they wanted something new. People liked 'modern'. People didn't like 'heritage' or 'refurbished', they liked forward-thinking, space age, futuristic. It was tomorrow's world. Eyes were firmly on the horizon, and the horizon had a jacuzzi.

That the first leisure pool in Bletchley replaced an ordinary outdoor pool was a situation mirrored round the country, from Stafford where the old brine baths were replaced with a leisure centre, to south London, where the traditional Latchmere Baths built in the latter bit of the nineteenth century were demolished in favour of the free-form Latchmere Leisure Centre. That drive to constantly change everything, that desire to look 'up-to-date', reflected well for leisure pools; our heritage stock was never going to measure up against contemporary requirements. Preserving the old pools, the idea that we need to nurture what we had rather than replace it with something glitzy and temporary, became an absurd, old-fashioned notion. Up and down the country, the same story. The old had to go. The old ... reminded us of something? Didn't fit in with our new shiny image of ourselves as go-getters, forward thinkers? Didn't reflect us as modern citizens who flew abroad every year? Whatever, the new was where it was at. Places like the Latchmere were new. And fun, if you like that kind of thing. I think it's clearly established that I don't.

And then, new social patterns emerged which suited the leisure pool equally well. From 'the family' being central, it was a couple of short steps over a decade or two and a little twist in perception that brought us to a child-centric view. Anyone who's ever tried to have a quiet cup of coffee in a cafe with a buggy park can see the cult of the child first-hand. Look how sweet little Oscar is, dressed like a junior banker on dress-down Friday and clutching his babyccino. It's still the family pound, but now companies get their mitts on it via the child. It's not just children demanding and getting, the old pester power; it's parents centring the kids under the banner of 'wanting the best for them'. And who can argue with that? We all want the best for our kids, right?

Adults who go to Disneyland without children confuse me. In the same vein, why would adults choose a leisure pool if they don't have children with them? Because what leisure pools effectively do and do effectively is put the child centre stage. Centre pool. It's an inherent irony: as the number of leisure pools grew so did the amount of swimming products and lessons and the push for children to be water athletes before they could even walk – yet these pools are not conducive to actual swimming. More, they actually set 'proper' swimmers against the leisure user, because the things that attract a serious swimmer are not the things that attract the family, and if you can't please both, which sector are you going to go for?

So how does one survive the fun-pool years? The key is remembering that all things pass, and particularly quickly where children are concerned. The era of the verruca sock is but a tiny blip on the continuum of parenting, and there are much, much worse things ahead (school music concerts). If only we could remember to focus solely on the joy of a situation. But human nature isn't like that; human nature gives the bad memories as much brain-stick as the good ones, and, anyway, the bad are often more fun in the telling.

With alarming speed you get to the point of longing to go swimming with your recalcitrant teenagers, and wondering how the hell that happened. There was a brief period in my son's teenage life where he would regularly go to the lido with me, but it led too rapidly to a time when he would go to the lido only as long as I wasn't there. 'Are you going to the lido, Mum? What time are you going? How long will you be there for?' are just ways of not saying 'I'll go in as soon as you come out'. I mean, what teenager is robust enough to welcome their mother, waving gaily in her swimming costume or even just trying to coolly pretend she hasn't seen you? Not mine. When we did end up in the same place at the same time, we were both thankful it's a long pool. He could be down the deep end (it's the law that teenagers hang out at the deep end) and I'd sit by the cafe, peering from a distance at unrestricted teen limbs splayed against the sky like startled starfish in mid-air as they flung themselves in. The visceral heart-clenching pleasure I'd feel, watching his childish enjoyment of the water, played into some nostalgic flashback to times when things were simpler, and he was closer.

Am I glad my children can swim? That's a very easy yes. Because above all the other things that swimming gives a person, all you need is the most basic statistic: between forty and fifty children drown each year in the UK (and I don't write that 'between' lightly; I know that within it lies an unimaginable pit of pain). In that number, there is no conclusive data that can show how many would not have drowned if they could swim, or indeed whether or not they could swim. There is no statistic that shows how many children didn't drown because they could swim. All any person really needs to know is that although drowning can happen to children who are good swimmers, the risks are lessened if they have even the most basic skills. I may have lessened their chance of drowning. And parenting is all about the 'lessened risks' and the 'may haves'.

So in the cold light of keeping children as alive as possible, my personal truth – that I loathe a fun pool and found it tedious bobbing about in milky wee soup – is irrelevant. Life is about doing stuff for your kids that might not be so great for you, and I wish someone had told Hilda James's mother that it wasn't about her. I wish someone had told me. What else it gave my children is not my job to quantify, best left for their own waterbiographies. Are my children now super swimmers with an innate feel for the water? No, now they make their own decisions it's tolerated at best. Maybe they'll come round, there's always time. Perhaps were I starting it all now – now I have a Positive Mental Attitude that borders on the obsessive – they'd have been infected by that rather than being hostages to my soul-sapping ennui. Sometimes it's a shame it's not actually Groundhog Day so I could do it all again only better. Maybe one day they'll look back and thank me for bothering. But I don't need them to. I didn't do any of it for thanks, and I'm not holding my breath.

Chapter 12

The Channel

Here's an idea for the British nationality test: if you are driving towards the coast, and everyone in the car is craning to see water so they can be the first to yell 'SEA!', then you are British. The same test can apply to the sighting of farmed animals. COW! SHEEP! and more rarely HORSE! This works even if you are an adult and alone in your car. Maybe you're trying to be cool so you don't yell it out loud (which takes more willpower than I have) but you still think it – this also counts. I imagine that actually living on the coast or among farmed animals renders this game unplayable and I am sorry for your loss.

I was being driven down to Dover by my friend Lucy and as her mind was on the road, I won the game. SEA! I yelled as we crested a hill and saw Dover's sturdy harbour walls, concrete arms in a hard embrace, and the Channel beyond.

It was a stunning May morning, one of those days when the reflection of a bright blue sky flecks the cool iron grey and makes the sea glint with a thousand tempting winks, a day when from a distance the water looks almost welcoming and you could be fooled into thinking it would be warm in there. Lucy was bringing me to Dover to experience what she'd been through several times – a training session for Channel aspirants, some of whom would be making their attempt that summer and so were now starting, at the beginning of the season, to become acclimatised to temperatures and get a feel for the challenges of that particular body of water. To be clear: I am not a Channel aspirant, a phrase I repeated several times that morning. I am an interloper. Those who try it are mighty. I wanted to gaze upon their works, these mighty, and admire, and you can't properly do that from the car park.

If you've seen it from a ferry, the idea that such an ugly stretch of water is a globally iconic swim is hard to get your head around. I'd want *my* globally iconic swim to be extraordinary, amazing, a visual feast. I'd want beauty, charmingly clean water (possibly twinkly, and full of lovely creatures who wave at me as I surge past, as we're in fantasyland), the chance of a great back tan. The English Channel is not those things. It's full of ferries, for a start. It's also full of what we might politely call detritus. Or shit. And jellyfish. And rubbish. And it's gloomy and horribly choppy. It's a purely functional body of water, with no redeeming features. It's also just a bit … boring. But the things I find 'boring' conspire to make the Channel one of the biggest challenges in the swimming calendar. It's a combination of tides, currents, our delightfully unpredictable weather, distance and water temperature. Maybe this is part of the appeal – if you can make it here, you'll make it (tap-tap) ANYWHERE. Also, in the way the 2012 Olympics were 'ours', this too belongs to us, and they haven't privatised it … yet.

Now, Lucy is one of those swimmers who roots you to the spot if you see her in the water, as you try to figure out what she's doing that's so different from what you're doing and why can't you just do that? Because what she does is beautiful. She glides past (and she will surely glide past) with barely discernible effort, like she was made for it. If swimming was a kind of art form, mine would be contemporary dance, all baffling arrhythmic movement and incomprehensible actions that leave audiences wondering when it's going to end. Lucy's would be ballet. So it should be no surprise that she has swum the Channel in a relay of six people, then a double relay in partnership with her husband Al, as well as making two solo attempts. It's those attempts we're talking about in the car to Dover. Both times she tried, Lucy 'failed'. The first time she caught the wrong tide and was essentially swimming on the spot for several hours, which must be like being trapped in a cross between a terrible cold grey nightmare and the worst quiz show invented: 'Can you guess what's hitting your face? Is it a jellyfish or a floating used condom?' On the second attempt she became

221

so hypothermic she lost consciousness in the water, was hoiked out by her costume straps and woke to find herself on board her crew boat with Al wrapped round her, trying desperately to warm her body with his. (Hypothermia is a danger for cold-water long-distance swimmers; fat is useful insulation against it but training ups the metabolic rate for most people, so you need to eat much more to put on weight. While Lucy was training, she managed to go from very slender to slender. She used to set her alarm for 2 a.m., get up, stumble to the fridge and eat a large tub of full-cream ice cream with extra squirty cream and maybe a dash more cream and then go back to bed, working on the theory that it would give the calories the best chance to settle in. That might be your actual dream life but in reality sitting at a silent kitchen table in the dark, eyes drooping as you shovel in fatty gloops of cream, loses its appeal by about night three.) For both of her attempts, Lucy trained for hours in the sea in Dover every Sunday, did extra hours of swimming in cold lidos and indoor pools and juggled work requirements and small children. (Literally she juggled children. She's incredibly strong.) She would not have been allowed to undertake her attempts unless one of the two official Channel swimmers organisations, who authenticate and observe all swims, deemed that she was capable. People can't just set out willy-nilly. And yet: what strikes me most clearly about both of these swims is the word 'failure'. In what sense is Lucy – and all the other Channel aspirants who don't reach the other side – a 'failure'? I ask if that's how she feels, and yes, she says that at the time it felt like failure. Now that several years have passed that feeling is receding, maybe because she's reconciled to not making another attempt. Still, Lucy concedes, 'it's a disappointment'. We need to find a new way to describe this, because it isn't failure. Stand on the beach at Dover on any morning and stare across that water and tell me that swimming for hours and hours in challenging conditions and not reaching the other side is failure. Like Lucy, I'll concede that it's a disappointment. I won't accept that it's failure.

Lucy and I arrive at the beach, and there's a group of swimmers readying themselves to get in, Vaselining up. It might feel intimidating, this collective buzz of incredible possibility, if I didn't suspect that most of them were trying to resist a tug of anxiety as well. I spot women I know – of course I do, the web of swimming friendship encompasses many waters – and we hug and I bat back their quizzical 'what are *you* doing here?' questions with quick jokes and excuses. There's a pull, a desire to feel part of something, except … I may gaze upon these mighty swimmers and admire, but I do not gaze upon the Channel and feel like swimming it, not even on this glorious May morning when the sap of optimism is rising. What I don't say to these people on the beach here and now, because it would be undermining, is that capabilities notwithstanding, there's not much I'd like to do less than swim the Channel. But I know we each draw our boundaries differently: that for some of us, putting the heating on in June is risky behaviour; I know that most people can't even contemplate the ridiculous idea of breaking the ice to get into water while some relish it. We all have our eyes set on different prizes and for a select few it's the Channel, the cold, grey, filthy, dangerous Channel, that is the most coveted. Today is not such a challenge, anyway. It's a glorious day. And as it's the start of the season, the requirement is comparatively slight – over to the harbour wall and back, then a break and the same again. How innocent those words 'then a break and the same again' sound. But therein lies the true pain. The pain of getting out from your first swim, going up the beach shaking your hands to try and get the feeling back, not even noticing the stinging stab of pebbles on your soles because your feet are numb, hunching over a Thermos of warm tea trying not to shiver too much and slop the tea over the rim of the plastic beaker, stripping off one damp cold costume and hoiking a dry one up on sticky uncooperative skin and then, just as the feeling returns and the shaking stops, getting back in the water. That's the pain.

Who decides that we should swim to the harbour wall and back, or keep going for three hours or six? Today, it's a woman called Emma France who, as the representative of the Channel Swimming and Piloting Federation, is sitting on a deckchair with a clipboard, counting people into the water and out again, watching closely to ensure they're not doing too much, or too little. Emma has taken over the role from Freda Streeter, who set up the CSPF as a splinter group from the Channel Swimming Association and subsequently sat on that beach every Sunday in the training season for a good thirty-plus years. Freda had started by coaching her daughter Alison, who went on to complete more Channel swims than any other individual, an astonishing forty-three solo crossings as well as a variety of doubles, a triple crossing and a raft of other incredible marathon swimming feats. And things just snowballed. 'I was down there on the beach with Alison,' Freda recounts when I meet her later that day, 'and someone approached me and said, "Look, I've attempted this Channel four times, will you help me?" I thought in for a penny, in for a pound.' Lucy tells me how Freda was 'a swim guru for not just Ali but hundreds of Channel swimmers training for a crossing. She understood people. She would sit on the shingle beach in a deckchair chain-smoking, working out why each person was choosing to undertake this event and how to help them across it, persuasively, gently (certainly with me) or plain bullying.' Freda chuckles as she recalls one of her more defiant swimmers. I'll preserve his anonymity and call him Charles. 'Charles was a nightmare,' she says. 'He was a joker, he was always doing wild things, I could not keep him in the water.' I get an image of Charles being the naughty boy at school. 'And one day he got out and stood [further] up the beach so that we didn't see him,' Freda goes on. 'I said to Barry, "Are we going to ignore this?" So he said, "Come on." We walked over to him, he got hold of one leg, I got hold of the other, we dragged him all the way over the stones, we turned him over, we kicked him in the water and said, "Now you stay there, you bastard!"' And he swam? I ask. 'He swam,' says Freda. I wondered if Charles had been successful. 'He didn't complete his first Channel swim,' Freda says, 'so the second one, he took a horrible picture of me, and he had it blown up poster-size and laminated and put all round the boat, so he didn't dare get out.' So Freda has been an inspiration in whatever way it took. But she's protective of 'her' swimmers, in the same way that Charlotte Epstein was of hers. 'They are my swimmers,' she says. 'In fact, I think I can go as far as to say it was eight years before I had my first failure, our first non-completed swim, I don't like calling them failures.' I don't either.

Freda's methods may have been unorthodox, but 'she'd be there', Lucy says, 'in rain, sun or sleet in a pair of thin shorts, surrounded by volunteers who serviced the swimmers with Vaseline, Maxim drinks and encouragement'. Now that Emma has stepped in to Freda's considerable flip-flops, it's she who decides how far we'll swim today. We go to the water's edge, a space enclosed by these two great old harbour walls and the swimming area marked out with buoys, outside of which there are bloody great ships coming in and out. We get in with varying degrees of enthusiasm. I'm bounding with it – I have precisely zero invested in this swim – but by the time I'm up to my knees, I've modified my intentions, it's colder than it looks. Everyone else zooms off as per instructions, and I take the path less travelled, which is slower and shorter. I don't care that I'm the first out of the water, I hip-hop up to my towel and get a chance to watch the others as they come back in and huddle under their post-swim coats, like a colony of fleeced seals on a pebbly English beach. Lucy and I decide to forego the pain of getting in again, and we leave as the rest are preparing for it – there's a few groans but mostly the mood is positive. They've a long season of this ahead. Some of them will succeed, others … well, others will experience disappointment.

There are many days when I feel I could use a Freda, sometimes gently persuading me and sometimes grabbing hold of my legs and chucking me back in. How different it might have been for swimmer Lillian Smith if she'd had the same, or Annette Kellerman, or any of the women who 'failed' to complete a Channel swim after Captain Webb's first achievement in 1875. The first woman to attempt it was the Austrian Baroness Walburga von Isacescu, in September 1900, who *The Times* described as 'plucky but vain', a phrase which might cause you to throw things unless she was actually swimming while simultaneously admiring herself in a mirror, which is doubtful. Was Captain Webb described as 'vain'? (Rhetorical.) In 1913, Lillian Smith showed ovaries of steel when she boldly stated that she was going to 'swim the Channel in order to demonstrate that woman is the physical equivalent of man. I am going to put a stop forever to all this twaddle about the weaker sex.' Oh, Lillian. If only! And where other women had not allied themselves to a broader political context, Lillian had no such qualms. 'I'll swim to France to win Votes for Women,' she said. Though she was a non-completer, Lillian remains a proud swimming suffragette in both senses, and I salute her.

The twaddle wasn't actually put to rest until thirteen years later. Hang on, let's be clear: the twaddle still exists. But the question remained: who would be the first woman to swim the Channel? 'When a woman swims the English Channel, it will have to be acknowledged that there is no physical feat in which she may not compete with man,' the *New York Times* wrote in 1922, echoing Lillian's words. 'It is the supreme test.' Between 1875 and 1926, many men had tried and only five succeeded. In the four years from 1922 to 1926, eight women, from Argentina, Austria, England, France and the US, tried. By the summer of 1925, the waters were comparatively busy, the race to be the first woman was well and truly on. On 16 July, the Argentinian swimmer Lillian Harrison made an attempt but was reported to faint mid-stroke. According to Jabez Wolffe, who'd made twenty-two unsuccessful attempts himself so could be considered somewhat of an expert in how not to do it, it was her vegetarian diet that was to blame. On 5 August, France's Jeanne Sion made her attempt, but was defeated barely a mile from the finish, just outside Dover (they swam the other way at that time). She blamed neither the cold nor fatigue but 'a stroke of *cafard*', a sense of melancholic apathy, an answer that could not be more brilliantly French and which we must all use henceforth when we phone in sick. 'Sorry, I can't come in to work today, I have a stroke of *cafard.*' 'I'm sorry to hear that. May your *cafard* be fleeting.' Gertrude (Trudy) Ederle was the third one to attempt it that summer, at the instigation of Charlotte Epstein. As soon as the conversation moves to an American woman swimmer from the 1920s, you can guess that Eppie would be somewhere in the mix, and the eighteen-year-old Trudy, a member of the WSA since she was twelve, was one of their strongest swimmers and already a gold medal winner from the Paris Olympics in 1924. Three days before setting sail for her first attempt, she had swum twenty-one miles from the southern tip of Manhattan to New Jersey's Sandy Hook and broken the men's record. So the signs for success were all there. Her first attempt may have been a failure – a word which seems so much kinder in the use when you know that success follows – but it sounds a blast. Alongside her crew boat was another, packed with reporters and a jazz band, which would certainly make me swim faster if only to get the damn thing done all the quicker. Expectation, press cameras, a band: it's quite the party atmosphere. But it didn't sustain. Conditions were tricky, the jazz band got sick and Trudy struggled. Her trainer was Jabez Wolffe and the two had not got on, even though Trudy's diet, as the daughter of a butcher, was heftily meat-based. Wolffe claimed she became unconscious in the water and Trudy claimed she was resting, but too late, he'd sent someone in to rescue her. The rules being the same then as they are now, as soon as someone touched her, the swim was essentially finished. As was their relationship.

The more women who tried and didn't succeed, the greater the promise of honour for the first one to achieve it – honour for both her country and her sex. So then came 1926. And with it came an even more determined Trudy Ederle, her goggles waterproofed with candlewax and a swimming costume that sounds suspiciously like a bikini, designed by her and her sister Meg and consisting of trunks and a bra top, the best way to avoid chafing and drag and still offer protection from photographers. This time there was no jazz band but a new trainer, Thomas Burgess, who at least had the distinction of having completed his own Channel swim, in September 1911. His numbers of attempts are recorded at somewhere between sixteen and thirty-two, but whatever the actual number, enough to convince me that Burgess was either determined or obsessed. One account of his successful swim seems at times to read like a cross between a variety review and a menu, featuring as it does a lot of food and a list of all the songs his chums sang to him from the boat. And Burgess himself clearly had a taste for the dramatic. 'I was never unconscious on the way,' he said, 'though I sometimes go to sleep in the water, but had hallucinations and saw all sorts of horrible things, too horrible to describe.' Interest levels: piqued. Scepticism levels: also piqued. 'I was stung thousands of times by jellyfish,' he continued, 'particularly big yellow ones.' And in a final flourish of campery, he asked for twenty drops of champagne every hour and 'not another drop, if I go down on my knees for it'. I can imagine some poor chum dispatched with the task of dripping the champagne through some hastily fashioned pipette. It might have been just the thing to help Jeanne Sion through her *cafard*.

And so, on 6 August 1926, after 14 hours and 39 minutes, Gertrude Ederle became the first woman to successfully swim the Channel. I wonder what Lillian Smith made of that news? I hope she punched the air vigorously many times and went prancing round whooping and hollering with glee. Trudy did it for all of us, passed the 'supreme test'. She sailed home to a hero's welcome and her own ticker-tape parade. For a time, she was a sporting legend and, as President Coolidge called her, 'America's best girl'.

Iconic woman, iconic swim. Once Trudy had done it, other women could come after. And come they did: the first British woman was Mercedes Gleitze in October 1927, on her eighth attempt. A few days later, another British woman claimed that she too had swum it, and in a quicker time. She admitted a few days later that it had been a hoax, but Gleitze got caught in the crossfire and doubt was cast on her achievement. To prove herself, Mercedes set out again in a vindication swim, and it proved to be a marriage of canny woman and fast-acting advertisers when Rolex leapt on the opportunity and gave her a watch to wear. After eleven hours the watch was still going but Gleitze wasn't, and she was pulled out of the freezing water – this was October, temperatures would have plummeted by then and the weather worsened. Her determination meant that people were ready to accept she'd achieved it first time, as she'd stated. It feels so demeaning that she'd had to prove herself but a short piece of Pathé film shows an undiminished woman, her beautiful smiling face with a curled plait around each ear. The film is called 'A Splendid Failure'. That word again.

The glory subsequent women gained may have been less, but my admiration is not. There's a roll call of fantastic achievements. The Queen of the Channel is undoubtedly Alison Streeter. The youngest girl to have done it is Samantha Druce, who was twelve years and 118 days at her crossing in 1983. (What were you doing aged twelve? I was lying around in a Madame Cholet T-shirt reading Agatha Christie novels by the wheelbarrow-load. I was not training for a Channel swim.) Samantha's record will stand for as long as the current rules do, which now state you must be over sixteen to do a solo swim. At the age of fifty-nine, Sally Minty-Gravett became the oldest woman to swim the Channel and back again; the oldest solo swimmer is Susan Oldham at sixty-four. This engenders the opposite feeling to the one you get when you see a policeman and he looks twelve. Sixty-four definitely doesn't sound old enough to be 'oldest'. Two other successful Channel swimming women in particular caught my attention. The first is Dr Julie Bradshaw MBE. The reason she drew my eye? Because she swam it butterfly.

I certainly could not swim the Channel, so already I'm in admiration of her. But I really cannot do butterfly. I cannot.

I have tried, and I cannot. There's the flinging of your arms, which is a no, trying to get your mouth out of the water to breathe, also a no, but then mostly there's the undulating. This is a problem. I was not raised to undulate. My body refuses, it's like trying to force a stiff little stick into a gentle curve: eventually something's going to snap. I am more see-saw than flexible willow. But if I have one motto it is 'work with what you have', so I've reached a level of happy acceptance of this fact. Also, I feel 100 per cent differently about people butterflying in the Channel than I do about that man butterflying up the narrow lane of a crowded pool and washing us all up into the gutter. Watching it being done properly is like seeing people who are further evolved than you are. In the future, our great-grandchildren will all be butterflyers.

Julie had started swimming young, and aged twelve was caravanning in the Lake District with her parents. It's an image I associate with pervasive dampness, overly close proximity to people you don't want to touch, nothing quite working, a flimsy undersized kettle that makes plastic tea, a sense of freedom for the first three hours followed by deep claustrophobia, holding everything in, and a rising desire to go home. 'I saw a sign saying "Cross Windermere",' she says. 'So obviously, when I was fourteen, I swam the length of Lake Windermere.' I can't help but interject. 'You say "obviously". That's not immediately obvious to most teenagers.' 'No,' Julie concedes. 'While a lot of people I knew at school were going out, I was swimming.' After

Windermere, Julie decided she wanted to swim the Channel and achieved that a year later in an incredible 10 hours and 9 minutes. 'So what made you look again and think, "I'm going to do that butterfly"?' I ask her. There's almost a pleading note to my voice – 'Why, Julie? Why would you do that?' When she put the idea to her supportive dad, he said, 'Don't be so stupid; you'll get burnt shoulders.' But Julie is not the type to get deterred by such comments. Living in Canada she started to build up her fly, racking up the lengths in their open-air pools. She came back to England, butterflied across Windermere and then went for the ultimate: the Channel.

It was August 2002, Julie was 38. 'My pilot was Reg Brickell,' she tells me. For Channel swimmers, the name Reg Brickell will have meaning. Pilots are an essential part of this crossing, it's their boats that accompany swimmers, they who have the expert knowledge on tides and currents, they who'll decide if the conditions are safe to go on. It's making my heart beat faster just thinking of these facts. Julie had to wait for the right tide and weather, sitting day by day waiting, ready, scanning the sky, watching the horizon, the sea, willing it to get in alliance, this set of unpredictable points. Then, 4 August, Reg phoned Julie and said, 'Yes.' She was green-lit to go. Julie had tried this swim before and been unsuccessful because she had shoulder issues (Dad was right). And on a long swim, staying positive is a challenge; when the tides start to work against you and it takes hours to swim a couple of miles, well, 'That's when my mind's got to go very positive: even more positive, especially if it's dark and all you can see in the water are little dots of light,' she says. 'People on the boat say, "Oh, it's not far. It's just over there." Well, your eyes are squinted in goggles; it's dark; you've got a different perspective in the water than they have on the boat. But Reg is good. It's when he got out the dinghy to put me to shore, that was the time I knew that it was near, the end of it.' I'm so exhausted at the thought I need a lie-down. She'd started at 8 a.m., 'and I finished fourteen hours, eighteen minutes later which was brilliant. It was dark when I landed and I just remember sitting on the shore and just listening to the waves and thinking, "Thank goodness that's done." And I got some pebbles and then came back on the boat.'

I got some pebbles and then came back on the boat. I got some pebbles.

Me, I'd have wanted millennial-level fireworks, a luxury liner and Donny Osmond (maybe with Jimmy as backup) feeding me proper buttery croissants with blackcurrant jam. I'd have wanted a statue of me butterflying erected in Gracechurch Shopping Centre, Sutton Coldfield, maybe across the front of House of Fraser. I'd have wanted more than pebbles. I'm in awe of this incredible achievement and this woman.

The second woman I particularly admire is Jackie Cobell. The first time I met her was on a winter's day and I was sitting in the sauna at Tooting Lido in my favourite spot, top bench, left-hand corner. I'd probably swum all of 30 metres. She came in and we started chatting, like people do in this sauna, about everything and nothing. I had no idea who she was, it's never relevant. We all kind of look alike anyway, you're seeing a different version of a person in their swimming costume. Jackie had swum considerably more than 30 metres, though I didn't know then that her incredible ability to withstand cold has led her to Ice Swimming Championships across the frozen bits of the world, and I asked her how she felt. 'Like a pork chop out the freezer,' she said – a phrase that went straight into my Top Ten Phrases. I also didn't know then that she had swum the Channel in the slowest recorded time, a total of 28 hours and 44 minutes. Take a moment to think about that. That means she set out in the dark and swam into sunrise. Swam through the whole day. Swam through the sunset. Through the entire black dark night. Into sunrise again. And then a bit more. And all in the English Channel. Can you even imagine? No. The horror. It's an astonishing thing to have achieved, and I'm now waving a banner for slower swimmers, because Jackie was swimming for twice as long as it has taken others. It could almost be called twice the achievement, though she wouldn't be so bold.

I ask Jackie how she got started, because unlike Julie she hadn't been a teen natural but instead was what is called 'middle-aged', a term I'd happily throw in the sea because it's so often used as a pejorative for women. 'I've always loved being in the water,' she says, 'but my self-consciousness about my figure stopped me.' Damn all your bikini-body adverts. Damn them to hell. 'I decided to get fit by swimming. I assumed Channel swimming was merely for athletic elite swimmers but then I heard that *anyone* could put their mind to it. Soon after, I was invited to swim in an English Channel relay. I was over the moon and couldn't believe my luck. The relay was fabulous. We all swam into France on the final leg. It was one of the best feelings. I thought, if I felt like this on a relay, swimming a solo must be ecstatic!' The positivity that radiates from Jackie is extremely infectious, enough to make a woman start flinging exclamation marks around with gay abandon! Jackie began to make plans for a Channel swim, and, again in contrast to Julie, didn't have parental support. 'I told my father that I was going to swim the Channel, and he said, "Shame, you're too old and fat, you'll never do it!!" I'm glad he said that because I was jolly well going to prove him wrong. He was so insistent, he bet me £1,000, patted his back pocket and said his money was safe. The bet was on. I thought, good, the money will go towards my charity [Huntington's Disease Association].'

Jackie trained with the help of Freda Streeter, and the two women, I venture, share some characteristics, both determined, strong and formidable. I wouldn't mess. Jackie has massive respect for Freda. 'She gave her time and expertise for free, was passionate about her charges, she was truthful and honest. She didn't have time for fools, or for swimmers that were full of bullshit or didn't put the training in. She told them – shape up or bugger off! Freda is also a caring and kind person, and takes you into her heart.' I wondered how Jackie coped mentally with the process during such a long swim. What went on in your head? I ask. How did you keep going? 'I knew I would take a long time, I'm a plodder. I'm a big ol' barge that goes on and on, as opposed to a sculpted, fast speedboat that runs out of gas.' I'm a keen study of self-deprecation, but Jackie really gives it a great wodge of welly. She also had a tactic, borne of experience. 'I decided that I would never look forwards or back and would not ask the time. I would just put my head down and get on with it. When I swam the Channel this was my mindset: it was just a day out of my life, a day of work, just as hard as being in labour. The pain and the ecstasy. The end result being so worth it. I didn't know it had taken me that amount of time, for I asked no questions.'

In a 28-hour swim, there are going to be some worst moments, of this I was confident. 'The worst moment was when a rogue wave caught my arm and twisted it behind my back,' Jackie remembers. 'My coach, Tanya Harding, threw some painkillers at me and told me to get on with it. Tanya is pretty formidable as well.' Another one for our army of no-nonsense women, getting on with doing their thing. 'I just kept swimming until my tits dragged on the sand – this was one of Freda's favourite mantras.' And until you felt your nips in the grit, you never gave up? 'I never gave up, because I had too much to lose. I didn't want to let anybody down who had believed in me or my charity.

I certainly didn't want to let myself down. I decided that if I was not frozen solid, not hit by an oil tanker or fifty-foot waves, there was no reason to get out. I had done my training, years of back-to-backs in Dover harbour and believed in myself ... eventually.'

I ask her next how she looks back on what she achieved. 'Swimming the Channel has been so positive for me, and I have to pinch myself for the wonderful opportunities it has given me. I feel very lucky and humbled,' she replies. 'I think that women of a certain age seem invisible,' she adds. 'But it is up to us to stand out. We are often not taken seriously enough. I wasn't, at first, because I was very slow. I was first in but always last out and got a bit of a ribbing. I felt down a few times, but I had people who lifted me up, encouraged me and believed in me. My coaches had so much faith in me. They told me that what I lacked in speed was made up by my stamina and determination.'

I think you're a role model, I tell her, and she accepts it briefly then passes it on as if it was a boiling hot baton. 'Women do get inspired,' she says. 'I'm inspired all the time by women of all ages, creeds and cultures. And I'm chuffed to say I have inspired several women to swim the Channel. I've coached and crewed for them, and it's the best ever feeling seeing them jumping for joy or cartwheeling on a French beach and being with a new Channel swimmer.'

Everything Jackie's said, that spirit, that determination, that down-to-earth sense of being fully alive in the moment, along with her humour, I find utterly inspiring. But it's her willingness to work for and celebrate another woman's achievement – to me, that's the supreme test. Lillian Smith might have stated her feminist intentions boldly, but I find in Jackie's words an unheralded embodiment of sisterhood. She's not bad for a 'big ol' barge'. I ask my final question, to which the answer is yes. Yes, her dad did pay up.

Chapter 13

My Waterbiography (Part IV)

Some parents have the art of standing in the school playground down to a T. They can stride purposefully across the middle of it with a casual toss of the hair, make friends, chat to other parents, do that tinkly laugh that's so attractive people hear it wafting along on a breeze and are irresistibly drawn to it. They can suggest things forcefully yet politely to teachers, without crying or apologising for their dreadful child. They say 'I'm terribly disorganised!' but they're really not. They double-park without feeling guilty. They like to take charge of the school's summer fair and can turn their hands to make bunting *and* Christmas wreaths. They do petitions that succeed. They always have handbag tissues. When they ask the school caretaker if he could just manage to squeeze in this teeny little job, like re-tarmacking the whole upper playground during his lunch hour, he does it. They don't try and sneak sugar into their children's lunch boxes and have never had to resort to the emergency corned beef. They smell nice.

Other parents slink round the side of the playground in case anyone notices them and asks them to Get Involved in something. They don't ever say 'I'm terribly disorganised' because that's implicit, they absolutely ooze disorganisation. Their hair is rarely brushed. They did do a petition once, but it wasn't an issue people could quite get behind so it was quietly buried (well, not exactly buried – the paperwork got lost; it's still in a pile in a corner somewhere and will be thrown out in ten years when they move house). They dread the teacher approaching them because they live in constant fear of 'Oh God what's he done now?' They wouldn't ask the school caretaker to do any extra work because they already think he's taken for granted and would rather re-tarmac the upper playground themselves over the weekend than have to add to his already overburdened schedule. Their laugh is a bit … noisy. It certainly doesn't tinkle. They never have a hanky. Their children's lunch boxes would be kindly described as 'creative'. These parents smell … natural.

It's easy to tell which group a parent may belong to: just ask them how they feel about being in the playground. The first lot will look at you with a puzzled expression, what is the meaning of this question? and the second will curl into a ball and moan. The first lot, the confident striders, are the ones who always got picked for school teams and have carried on being picked for things ever since. That's what gives them their self-assurance, the sense that they have something to contribute, that they are inside the loop. The second lot is me, and I'd like to know if the feeling that you're never going to be picked for the team ever leaves you. It seems that you can cling on to your 'outsider' status as hard as you like, use it as justification for all sorts, but there comes a point when you have to acknowledge that being the outsider can be a bit lonely. And that part of the thing about being an adult is knowing you can't always wait to be picked. Sometimes, you have to pick yourself.

Old habits die hard, and if you've never been picked for the team, you don't always recognise when people are trying to pick you. A few of the friends I had in the school playground were the type of women who were definitely always picked, and to my great good fortune, as well as being confident striders they were good 'team players'. From about May, after we'd dropped our kids at school, I'd go home for a coffee pretending to relish the silence, and they went to Tooting Lido together. I was constantly being included in the general call-out. 'Come, Jenny,' they'd say. 'You'll like it.' But I'd be full of excuses. I've forgotten my stuff. I'm busy. I can't. These women were good swimmers, I knew. They were sporty, capable women, they were not like me. So I resisted, like a self-defeating fool. I don't know quite what I imagined would happen, but there was a niggling sense that I didn't want my sporting inadequacy to be laid quite so bare. 'Oh, I am rubbish' was my shield, in a context where I didn't need a shield. These were women I knew well – we were in a book group together for goodness' sake, and as anyone in a book group can testify, there are no bonds so strong as those among women who have mutually loathed a popular novel. So one day I thought, to hell with it, I'm going. Enough of feeling not-good-enough, the only person excluding me was myself. I packed my swimming costume and joined them.

At first sight, Tooting Lido is both glorious and intimidating. At its most basic, it's an enormous blue box of water, the largest lido in the country, 100 yards (91 metres) long and 33 yards (30 metres) wide. (Jesus Green Lido in Cambridge is as long but not as wide.) Along each side are rows of cubicles with doors painted in bold red, green, blue and yellow. Beyond the trees on one side is Tooting Common, and on the other side, the train rattles past now and again, off to Gatwick and the suburbs. There's inelegant council paving round the sides, a cafe, two circular communal changing pods, and the kind of tiered fountain that will be familiar to lido aficionados. All that paraphernalia round the pool acts as a lure to local artists but the water is the thing. There's just so much of it. And it's not heated.

If you're not a super-athlete, and maybe even if you are, when you first swim at Tooting the deep end feels like another country. Actually, that feeling never completely goes away. In summer, arriving through the turnstile at the shallow end of the pool, it's all laid out before you. You see right up there? That's how far you have to go. It's so far that the water takes on a different quality up there; it's darker, foreboding even, if you've a bent towards the dramatic. There are clearly no monsters in the shallow end, but in the deep end, that's where fears could grab you. If you're used to swimming in a 25-metre pool, the standard length for most modern public facilities, you have four good push-offs to help you swim as far as one length here, and you really don't appreciate the power of a push-off until it's gone. Getting to the end can feel interminable, particularly if you're doing a slow breaststroke and struggling with the cold. It just never gets closer. The sun could be dappling the surface under your hands but the water is sharp and you can't put your face in because no goggles and you've been going for ages and you haven't even crossed the heavy black halfway line yet and just keep going it's OK and how the hell do your friends manage to make it look like poetry? how do they do that? and oh! I'm there! I'm in the cold deep holding on to the bar and grinning at the meagre accomplishment and now all I have to do is swim back to the shallow end which beckons me so glitteringly like swimming home.

A person cannot keep swimming breaststroke with no goggles forever. A person cannot. A person eventually realises, guided invisibly by the excellent company of other swimmers, that it would be entirely fine to keep swimming breaststroke with no goggles and there would be no judgement, ever, but that other things are possible. A person eventually succumbs. Perhaps a person succumbs here more readily than in a drab standard pool because the lure of a lido is qualitatively superior, but whatever, succumbing happens. A person realises that swimming properly might actually feel good. A person realises they need to learn.

The Scourge of the Goggles was the first place to start. Of all the pieces of kit, they are the things that swimmers can become truly evangelical over. Costumes come and go, caps are two a penny, but once you find 'your' goggles, they can inspire true loyalty. But I couldn't find any that fitted my face. Every time I would try other people's for size, I'd be left with the sensation that they might irretrievably slide into my eye sockets and become embedded. That's not relaxing. They would briefly work if I pulled an expression of great surprise but it's not a look any un-Botoxed woman can maintain honestly for more than about thirty seconds, even when her beloved children are recounting their dreams. My conclusion was that I have the wrong kind of face for goggles. As there was no way to get a different face, I thought I was doomed.

Then I found the right goggles. And my life changed.

I became evangelical about my goggles. So evangelical I could go into schools to preach about the Importance of Getting the Right Goggles to rapt audiences of teenagers who would raise me on their shoulders and parade me round the school showering me with confetti or more likely

Wotsits chanting Jenny! Jenny! Jenny! Jenny! because I had shown them the Way of the Goggle.

Or maybe not.

Once I had these goggles, which look more scuba than swimming and are so big they actually cover most of my small face, I began to try putting my head under, and once you start doing that and not drowning, a whole set of new possibilities line up in front of you. For a start, the view from under the water is magic. Perception changes; I began to swim *in* the lido's blue, not on it, and it felt like being put right inside a photo. Ahead of you are tiny legs hanging like tights on a washing line, kicking in a wind. The batik patterns of light on the floor break and blur as you pull through them. Other people's shadows are the hull of a boat, the body of a sea mammal. Stopping for a moment and dipping half down so your eyeline is flat along the surface of the water, you get the perspective shot they use in films like *Piranha*, which is perhaps not the best example to invoke. But it's an evocative shot, flicking your eyes down to the blue silence that lies beneath you and then up and along the surface. The water does things that feel counterintuitive. The surface bows, the colour is more concentrated at the top, a planetary horizon. And apart from taking satisfaction from that view, I started to understand why swimming pulled people in. It was the germ of an addiction, not the first cigarette, the one that makes you gag, but the fifth, sixth, tenth. I started to feel part of something. The first stirrings of a physical connection like new synapses forming, pushing you to get back in the next time, and the next. I began to appreciate what the water did for me, how it held me, what it gave me; I started to feel a kind of freedom. And my Goggles of Glory made me think that instead of doing breaststroke I could actually try and get better at this. Why not? I had nothing to lose. I thought I would just be able to do it by sheer dint of watching other people, but after some spluttering, flailing half-drowning attempts, realised I was mistaken. You can't learn things by osmosis. Homeopathy can't help you swim. I needed to get lessons. So I went on a swimming week designed for 'Improvers', working on the basis that it's always easy to improve on nothing.

I am not daft. I did not pick an Improvers week in Swindon. I picked one in Greece, because it's sunnier in Greece and the salads are nicer. I went with my capable friend Jackie, though her swimming was in a different league to mine and I wasn't sure how she could possibly improve. It was the first time either of us had been away without our children and the sense of freedom was electric, giddying and entirely tempered by an hourly stomach punch of longing. The sort where you find yourself interacting with the children of strangers and have to stop because they're looking at you weirdly. Imagine you loved tightrope walking, and your family were urging you to walk across a steep canyon on a taut piece of wire. The desire to do it would be strong, your body would be pumped full of adrenaline and fear and elation as you inched across, the whole mental and physical process would be entirely about you. Not you as a parent or a partner or any status label, just your absolute self. And behind you, on the bank you are leaving, stand your children and you just know without looking at them that they are trying very hard not to call you back or cry and not to spoil it for you. It feels like that. Only without the jeopardy. You're not going to fall to your death in a deep jungly cavern on a swimming holiday in Greece. OR ARE YOU? (No, you're not.)

You are, though, going to face some of your fears. The week's activities included lots of instruction, and pool and sea practice, and within a few days I was swimming from one beach round a headland to the next, mostly using a tentative uncertain crawl but with my trusty breaststroke as backup. 60/40: I was getting there. Then the instructors upped the ante. 'While we're here,' they said, 'let's try and tackle some of the fears you might have in the water.' I had a list, and top of it was night swimming. Night swimming: just the thought of it sends a gush of panic to my belly. A skinny-dip in the dark is one of those dreadful activities that is supposed to be sexy but that I find so scary I wonder if I'm suited to the world of romance at all. I have tried it, but found that trying to suppress panic and ignore the 'flight' messages screaming through every fibre of my very being just didn't quite do it for me, sexy-wise. (What on earth is so hot about wading into black water with your naked loved one when everyone knows that all the bad things come crawling out in the dark? That things unknowable from the deeps are drawn to your pale legs like moths to a lamp; that through the inky water they silently glide, things with scary staring glutinous eyes and rack on rack of pointed teeth and scratchy claws that scrape your skin and nip nip draw blood that attracts bigger, scarier things that grab your limbs and try to tug you down to live beneath the waves with them and be their wife. Why would that put anyone in the mood for love?) Night swimming, I blurted to the instructors. 'OK,' they responded cheerfully. 'Let's go night swimming.' Should have kept my mouth shut.

Breathe through it. Breathe. It'll be fine. Breathe.

Darkness falls late in summer, giving ample time to allow the nerves to really get jangly without the calming effects of alcohol. But I've played cool in worse situations, and my studied insouciance as I shrugged and said 'yeah yeah, I'm totally fine, let's get this done' was only slightly undermined by the pitch of my fake laugh as it veered off and up to an entirely unnatural register. We set up camp in a small sheltered bay, dark boats bobbing in the gentle waters, soft sloping sands. I was bolstered by the power of groupthink; we stripped to our costumes and waded in. From the beach the water looked dead black, but once I was in it, I saw that it was a less-terrifying lively inky green. We swam out to the edge of the bay and stopped for a minute. I'd done it! I was night swimming! The fear washed out, I could feel elation starting to bubble. We chatted out there like it was nothing at all, and as we did, I watched one of the group across the circle dive under the water. Seconds later, something from

250

under the water pulled my leg. In my head, I knew it was him. But my response wasn't in my head, it was in my body. Panic came ripping through me like it had been shot from a gun; it felt like a terrifying attack and I needed to get out of that water as fast as I could. Gasping for breath and cry-swimming, I fled for shore – and what do you know, I was doing crawl.

I didn't look at that member of my swim group again that holiday, let alone exchange words. I think he probably mumbled 'sorry' but I couldn't hear it. I understand that when one's natural conversational path is littered with quick jokes, a person might mistakenly believe the joker would appreciate a prank around a deeply held fear. That said joker would eventually chuckle and punch your arm and say 'oh, you'. That they'd see the funny side. They won't. There is no funny side. No one ever appreciates a prank. I'm not going to use his actual name because I instinctively know there's something more appropriate for him. Let's call him Dick. Thanks to Dick, I haven't been night swimming again. Why would I?

I had thought that after an Improvers holiday, I'd return to the lido and flash up and down the pool like a pro. That was the dream before I went. I came back with a more realistic goal – swimming one whole length doing crawl. That's 91 metres non-stop, and if you can already do that, if you can crawl and crawl to your heart's content and only stop when you've reached the horizon, it might be hard to think back to a time when you couldn't, but it's like heading for a beach that never gets nearer. The water chops and your breathing goes and you're thinking LEGS then ARMS then HEAD then ARMS then BREATHE and all the instructions muddle up and suddenly you're a blobby sloth clawing your way along, and every time I tried, I ended up spluttering and stopping and going back to the start and trying again, over and over. The only thing in my favour was that I didn't care. I knew no one would look at me meanly and think, ha ha, she can't do it. I knew there were people at all levels of ability in the pool, and nobody was ranking them in order. Then I spotted my pal Al, who is married to the wonderful Lucy (who took me to Dover) so a man who life has rewarded for his niceness. He asked me what I was doing. 'Trying to swim a length of crawl,' I said. Now, Al is a fantastic swimmer and a charming man, he is the opposite of Dick. 'Try this,' he said, chucking me over a pull buoy (one of those figure-of-eight-shaped floats that you shove between your legs). 'Won't that be cheating?' I asked. 'No,' he said. 'And go slowly.' So I shoved the buoy indelicately in place and set off, keeping close to the edge and counting my breathing. One. Two. Breathe. One. Two. Breathe. 'Keep going!' I heard Al say, as he paced me up the pool. I was going to do it. The trick now was not to get distracted by a mouthful of water. I kept on, counting and breathing and turning my arms over, raising my head only to see how far I had left to do. Then smack, my hand hit the rail at the end of the pool and I grabbed it. First length of crawl of Tooting Lido – done. Done! It had only taken me four and a half decades, but maybe I was nearly ready to call myself a swimmer.

I leapt out of the water, the bee of delight buzzing in my limbs, and Al was there applauding me. I gave him one of those awkward hugs that a wet body gives a dry one. And I took something from his pleasure in my success. That is: you should keep your Als close, but keep your Dicks at a distance. If you get the opportunity to be an Al to someone else, take it. Don't be a Dick. Fortunately in swimming and in life, there are many more Als than there are Dicks. More people who want to support and encourage you than people who seek to exploit your vulnerabilities. And you don't have to go night swimming to work out which is which.

Chapter 14

Exceptional Women (Part II)

Part of the pleasure of talking about history from a different perspective is including stories that have been overlooked. The cartoonist Jacky Fleming puts it this way: 'Women have been retrieving each other from the dustbin of history for several thousand years now.' It's a happy task, pulling from the bin individuals or achievements that somehow got lost. Margaret White Wrixon is just such an individual, an exceptional woman whose swimming story deserves its moment.

Margaret's is a story of being first and youngest, and it centres itself around the Thames Estuary. Picture England, pinpoint London. Now go east from there, following the river to the sea. If you wanted to slice the south-east off from the rest of the country – and let's face it, we've all wanted to give that a go at some point, for a host of reasons – this is where you'd start. Here, under the belly bulge of Suffolk and Essex, the first cut has already been made. The estuary, which has Essex on the north side and Kent on the south, is eleven miles wide, a busy shipping lane and not your average delightful swimming spot; it's similar in some respects to the English Channel, though if you swim that, at least you end up in France. If in mitigation we say that Margaret was conquering it in the 1960s when it would have been less hectic and the ships less like silent superstates, we also have to put the case that she had none of the benefits of modern equipment and high-calibre training expertise. Newspaper reports have her 'well-greased with mutton fat and lanolin', which could only be seen as a step up from Charlotte Schoemmell's coating of axle grease if you prefer the smell of rancid sheep over old cars. All told, it's not a popular swim. The first person to do it was Norman Derham back in 1925, on his second attempt. He had failed the first time despite having had unorthodox help. 'Several miles from the shore,' he is reported to have said, 'a large porpoise rose to the surface beneath me, lifting me completely out of the water.' (This charming image sounds like the kind of psychedelic animation favoured by sixties prog rock bands and makes you wonder what drugs he was on. 'There goes Norman,' his friends in the pub would chuckle, winking and nudging each other, maybe doing that annoying finger quotes thing, 'he's off "riding the porpoise" again.') When you think of how many bucket lists include swimming with dolphins, it's odd that the lure of potentially getting a lift from one failed to draw many participants; by the time Margaret swam thirty-five years later, she was only the fourth person to do it.

Margaret had been a member of the Leigh-on-Sea swimming club since she was five and had set her sights on the Channel early, seeing everything she achieved before that as 'training swims for the big one'. In August 1959, she became the youngest person ever to swim the Solent from Portsmouth to Rye. Aged sixteen in 1960, when she swam the Thames Estuary one way, from Southend in Essex to All Hallows in Kent, she was the first female to officially complete it and, again, the youngest person ever, though the record wasn't important to her at the time. I ask if it's more important to her now. 'As I get older I realise these achievements are more important to me,' she says. 'I suppose the word legacy comes to mind.' The legacy has been a personal one, in that 'the self-discipline I acquired through all the training and swims I've applied to my careers and life in general', Margaret says, and then succinctly adds, 'For me, there is a huge difference between earning it and buying it.' For me too. And she certainly did earn this one, through quiet graft, modestly spoken of. That it is a legacy with further reach than just her own life and career is in no doubt, because every swim that a woman achieved made it easier for the next woman to swim, and the next. But for it to be further-reaching, it needs to see the light, and it's a pleasure to be able flick the light switch on here, and shine some attention on her achievements.

And so, in June '61 Margaret became the first person ever to swim the Thames Estuary both ways, Southend to All Hallows, then All Hallows to Chalkwell Beach. It's a very tricky challenge, not just because of distance. 'Swimming across the Thames Estuary two ways is difficult as one has to contemplate the tides,' Margaret explains. 'The outgoing tide is difficult to swim against and one had to swim fast enough to time getting there and back on the one tide otherwise there was a danger of being stranded on the return.' Swimming on permanent alert, and in race mode, sounds extreme, but it paid off. Her success in this 'training' swim led to her ultimate challenge, and later that same season Margaret became the youngest person ever (at the time) to swim the Channel. 'Why should a pretty girl want to swim the Channel?' one magazine asked her, as if sporting achievements were something only ugly girls need resort to. 'I've always liked swimming,' she replied, showing great composure, 'and if I like to do something, I like to do it well.' I suspect the answer I might have given at seventeen – 'I mean, what the HELL? What do a person's LOOKS have to do with something? GOD, you're such a FASCIST' – may go some way to explain why a career in PR was never going to be my thing.

Since Margaret's achievements in the sixties, there's been a whole raft of amazing women completing tremendous swims. A few Olympic types have their deserved success, their names everywhere and their column inches (and the concomitant vicious scrutiny over unnecessary things like how they look and who they date). Others are less visible. Like Ness Knight, the first woman to swim the length of the non-tidal Thames, or Helen Beveridge who swam all 23 miles of Loch Ness in 18 hours, or Anna Wardley and her Five Island Swim Challenge which ended in a 60-mile swim round the Isle of Wight. To include every name and every achievement would be to render this book unliftable even by the toughest swimmer's arms. But sometimes a story grabs you. Because while history is about shining a light in a particular direction, waving stories in people's faces gleefully yelling 'Look! LOOK!', sometimes there's another layer. It comes alive for you because you feel a more personal connection. Those personal connections help us to the heart of a story, help us listen to them more fully, see them more clearly. I feel that about Beth French's 26-mile swim from Land's End to the Isles of Scilly.

Beth is a long-distance swimmer with an incredible 'repertoire' of achievements, but with this one particular swim I felt a click, an 'oh yeah, I get why she'd do that'. I connect with it for the smallest of reasons – a tiny family link with the Scillies – and sometimes that's all it takes. I didn't know about the family link when I first went there on holiday with Rosemary Lowe and her family aged thirteen, wearing that blue-and-white cotton bikini and with a blue-and-white bandana to stop my thin and straggly hair whipping into my face. I didn't know it all the times I holidayed with my children around Land's End and stood on a clifftop staring across the sea trying for a glimpse of these low-lying islands as far from us as we are from France. Standing there all wind-blown and inscrutable, I imagined myself as some kind of modern-day French Lieutenant's Woman, dressed not in a moody cape but probably some three-quarter trousers from Fat Face with multiple pockets, full of useless things like tissues that had been through the wash. Maybe my mum had tried to tell me when I was a teen but I'd stalked off, affronted at the very idea that I'd be interested in her stories. Or maybe she just never said. Because mine is not a family that has yelled its history. Things remain ... not secret, but unspoken. To talk of ourselves, to put ourselves in the centre of the picture, is self-aggrandisement, a vanity. I didn't find out, for instance, that my father was in Palestine in 1948 until two years after my husband had written a book about the place. 'Why didn't you tell me?' I asked my mum. 'I didn't really know much,' she said, 'he never talked about it.' In one sense that position is a luxury, never to be called to defend yourself, never asked 'why are you here?' or 'where are you actually *from*?' But at the same time it has a humility that makes me cross. So humble, its eyes cast down to the floor, it's a bit too 'know your place' to sit comfortably with me. For families like mine, it might be the stories we don't tell that form the most revealing part of our history.

As my mum has got older, so have her stories, her focus has shifted further back in time. That, or I started listening. My connection to the Isles of Scilly is one of those 'look what I might have been!' stories. Mum might have been, anyway. She might have been born there, because both her brothers were. It's quite the tale.

My grandfather had been in a hurry to sign up and serve in the First World War, and became Private Wilfred Nicholson of the Royal Warwickshire regiment just short of his sixteenth birthday. (He was tall.) In August 1918, two months before the end of the war though nobody would have known that, his mother was sent a telegram. He had been killed in action in France. Imagine getting that telegram, announcing in the briefest of ways the loss of this young life, one of your children; imagine the grief that was both intensely personal, and shared across the country. This moment is not worth playing out, however, as I've already told you he was my grandfather. Clearly, he lived. A week and a half later, my great-grandmother received another telegram: they were mistaken. He had been shot and had lain on the battlefield for days, dreadfully wounded but not dead. It was an actual miracle. And in one of those little twists that feel apocryphal but aren't, he had been saved because the bullet was deflected from his heart by the cigarette case in his pocket. Smoking saved my grandfather's life. I'll just leave that there, please resist bombarding me with your 'yes buts'. My mum has the cigarette case if you need to see it before you believe the story, and very good luck going to her with your doubts.

My grandfather returned home to work in Birmingham's council offices, where he met and married my grandmother, Jessie Sherwood. But his health was poor because of his war injuries, and the doctor advised him to seek outdoor work. So he and Jessie and another family went to work at a tulip farm on St Martin's, one of the Isles of Scilly. There would be no fresher air than here, no work more further removed from his office job for Birmingham Council. I admire their willingness to try it. Their family grew. The other family grew, too. But the farm didn't, it could only support one family, so a coin was tossed to see who would stay. A coin. Heads or tails. A simple action that might determine which end your team played, now in the employ of a family's future. How else could they do it? The coin was tossed, my grandfather made a call and lost. So the Nicholsons – my grandpop Wilfred, grandmother Jessie, my uncles Tony and John – moved 'home', from the Isles of Scilly to Erdington, Birmingham. From right out there, far off the south-west coast in blissful rural isolation with lives entirely circumscribed by the sea, to the industrial heart of the country, as far from sea as you can get.

I only know my grandparents' story because my mum decided she'd like to visit the Scillies around her eightieth birthday, and I asked why. Families can sometimes feel as tricksy as politics, you'll never get the right answers if you don't ask the right questions, but knowing the right questions is a mystery. From Penzance, Mum and I caught a small plane to the islands, which her parents would never have done. This wasn't about recreating their adventure, this was about getting our journey over as quickly as possible, and my mother's violent dislike of boats (which I possibly should have noted before going on an island-hopping trip where they are the only mode of transport) is marginally higher than her morbid fear of small planes. Our base was St Mary's, the main island, in one of those cute cottagey bed and breakfasts where for the first twenty minutes it's amusing that everything including the kettle in your room is so tiny, but after that you feel like a clumsy giant whose feet are too big; the kind of place where you hope for home-made jam with breakfast but it arrives in tiny pre-packaged pots. On our first day, we took a tourist boat over to St Martin's to find my grandparents' house, and that trip was fun. What with my mum clutching the side of the boat eyes tight shut and muttering 'Don't worry about me, don't worry' unconvincingly, much as she does in the car when I drive over 25 miles an hour, and me failing to rein in my mean impatience, other trippers were soon looking on askance – has the cross one kidnapped the elderly one? Should we stage an intervention?

On St Martin's, we found the house easily; it stood in a narrow lane among a small clutch of other cottages just up from the beach where the boat picks you up. This was the unassuming place that my unassuming grandparents had called home for six years. Someone had added a porch. We stared through the windows – not too hard, Mum didn't want us be nosy, didn't want to attract attention but at the same time absolutely did, absolutely wanted to be asked, wanted to tell her story and make a connection. Nobody came. I took photos of her standing in front of the house, dwarfed in an anorak, her face keenly smiling out of a pulled-tight hood, before the sense of anticlimax kicked in. So that's it, then. We sat on the beach and imagined Jessie and Wilf arriving on this island, a young couple struggling up a track with their cardboard suitcases, maybe a trunk. My mum talked about Jessie, about her laugh and her zest for life, how she'd read people's futures in their teacups, and we imagined her here with her glamorous cloche hats and fake-fur collars, perhaps missing Birmingham and office clatter and her friends, and then maybe chasing her small boys up and down the sand, my grandfather watching them, always with a cigarette in the corner of his mouth. Smoking had saved his life, after all. We talked of the particular hardships that their lives would have been full of, which my mum has a better understanding of than me, having been an evacuee, having lived on war rations, when all I've done is the seventies. We pictured them watching the sea from the windows of the cottage, waiting for boats that brought necessities, letters from 'home', the occasional visitors. Where was 'home'? Was it ever really here? Mostly, we hoped they'd been happy. We imagined they'd been happy.

If I'd done the swim from Cornwall to the Isles of Scilly, my grandparents would be the 'why'. But really, do you need a reason to do a swim? Does there need to be a connection?

I wondered what made Beth French want to swim it. The answer is much less tangible than a personal connection; it's 'because maybe it's possible'.

Beth's story is really rooted in Beth herself. She went from leading every sports team in school, to being in a wheelchair by the age of seventeen, felled by ME. 'My body had been taken away from me,' she says, feeling like she was 'trapped in a stranger'. For a person who had been wanting to swim the Channel since she was five or six, and would keep getting in the sea over and over to the point where her mum stopped taking her to the beach – you can feel the exasperation – this diagnosis seems infinitely cruel. Beth doesn't use the word 'recovery' and ME is still part of her, both in the sense that she 'manages' the illness and now mostly lives symptom-free, and in that everything she achieves she puts down to pulling herself through it. It's almost unbelievable, reconciling that broken girl with a 'failed body' with the woman she is now. You're extraordinary, I tell her. She laughs. 'I'm doing this for ordinary women,' she says, 'I'm an ordinary woman.' I believe you, I say, meaning 'I believe that you feel like that'. And yes, she might read as ordinary if you bumped into her down the shops. Much as it would be excellent, heroic women do not stride the earth accompanied by a soundtrack and all lit up with neon signs and flashing arrows above their heads. It all goes on inside. She might read ordinary, but, actually, there's nothing ordinary about her at all.

Beth's 'compulsion to get in the water from as early as I can remember' helped her. The water 'gave me back my body and I fell in love with what it can do'. Firstly, it took her across the Channel, at last. She loved every minute of that, loved swimming through the night with no sense of direction and just the 'sensory feedback of the water'. She talks of how the sun rose and 'the colour leached back into the world' and she felt like a new person. That new person then went on to become the first British woman to swim the 26 miles of the Molokai Channel in Hawaii. So what adventure would be next? Someone suggested Cornwall to the Scillies, a swim that had been done the other way – including by Queen of the Channel Alison Streeter, but nobody, including Alison, had successfully completed it the way Beth planned. Which was against the tide. Beth had wondered, briefly, if Alison couldn't do it whether it was possible at all. But her mind then told her 'if I don't know it's impossible, maybe it's possible'. And 'maybe it's possible' was enough.

So she tried it, and it was possible, and she became the first person ever to swim from Cornwall to the Isles of Scilly. When you look at it on a map, there's a great big gap at the bottom of the English foot, where massive American waves could sweep right in and totally wipe a person out. Actually, it was something much more prosaic that nearly did for Beth. The swim was great and conditions perfect, she recounts, but 'these swims never look like you think they're going to, they're never pretty'. She was swimming next to a crew boat that was chucking out noxious diesel fumes and they started to seriously affect her. 'Medical problems certainly sharpen the mind,' she says calmly. It would be stating the bleedin' obvious to tell you there is a small window of opportunity to grab a swimmer once they become unconscious before they drown, and one of Beth's crew kayaked beside her, ready to take that opportunity. But she has this spirit, this ability to absolutely welcome the relentless, to see uncertain outcomes as the space where adventures happen. So she reflected on whether she'd rather be in the water or on the boat and the water won, because 'water is where the world makes sense to me'. She threw up the toxic cocktail ('Trying to make yourself sick in the water is *hard*,' she says, like the rest is a breeze) and carried on further away from the boat, gradually putting her swim together again. Seventeen hours and 28 minutes after she'd started, covered in jellyfish stings, she landed on St Mary's. Done. The press went wild. 'WOMAN COMPLETES SWIMMING CHALLENGE' one national paper flatly reported. 'THE AMAZING BETH FRENCH COMPLETES ASTOUNDING SWIMMING CHALLENGE' is what it should have read. There, I fixed it for you.

How do we want our adventurers to look? Like great beardy conquerors in woolly socks, one foot on a rock and a hand clasping a flag while they look off into the distance at the next challenge we mere mortals can't even see? Like ruddy rugged buggers with chapped lips and hair that needs a good brush? People in 'technical clothing' they could fashion into a bivouac at the faintest sign of trouble, who jingle and clack with the noise of various clasps and clip-ons as they walk? I like my adventurers to look like Beth. Scrub-faced, crop-haired, strong-bodied, smiling. A woman who let go of the need for a lane rope, let go of anything that might stop her. Amazing woman. Inspiring role model. Adventurer. The 'ordinary' Beth French.

The older I get, the more I am convinced that the phrase should be 'behind every great woman is another great woman'. The original, 'behind every great man is a great woman', is outdated, we've moved way beyond being a ghostly troupe of invisible helpers. Anyway, the notion that women were the 'real power' was a myth. It was a sop. It might have pretended it was about celebrating our nurturing role, but actually it perpetuated the idea that women are nurturers by default, that it's all we are. That while they rampaged, we nursed, while they noisily hunted, we sat by the fire ready to greet them on their return with 'thank you so much for your great hunting, dude' and other kindly encouragements that would push them on to greater things, bigger beasts, the best seat by the fire. The idea that a woman's place is 'behind a man' belongs in the bin. BUT. I am conflicted. Is it OK if equality has brought us to a point where instead of standing behind a great man, we stand behind a great woman? Is that any better, when the view is still over someone's shoulder, still more or less the same? Is this how mature society works? Because not every great woman in the swimming world is on the podium. Some of the exceptional ones stand behind, as nurturers, enablers, teachers. And they do it bloody well, the women like Freda Streeter and Charlotte Epstein. So I say yes, it is OK to take a nurturing role, when it's a choice and not a prescription. If you make that choice to use your skills for the ostensible benefit of others, you need a very keen sense of what your skills actually are, and the desire to share them. It's an awesome combination, the very essence of generosity. There are some great women 'standing behind', so let's revel in this being their choice, revel in the fact that equality has got us this far, and listen to what they've got to say. Maybe they can teach us something.

One great woman I'm choosing to listen to is Becky Sindall, the first female instructor to go to Sudan with Nile Swimmers, a UK charity that works to prevent drowning by teaching communities there how to stay safe around water. This is not about swimming as a leisure activity. This is about basic survival skills where drowning is a leading cause of childhood death. 'At the most basic level, the vast majority of people who drown are people from low- and middle-income countries and it's because they end up in the water unintentionally and they don't have any way to get themselves out again,' Becky tells me. 'You ask a room full of people [in Sudan] "How many of you know someone who's drowned?" and probably two-thirds of them will put their hands up.' It's a brutal anecdote borne out by statistics. 'These are people who maybe went down to the beach for a picnic, decided to go in for a paddle, they got too deep and lost their footing and there was no one around who could help them because everyone was in the same position: none of them can swim.' Our own history of swimming has drowning statistics at its beginnings too, but while we can splash around merrily linking swimming to suffrage in the Western world, it links more fundamentally to life and death in low-income countries. The ability to keep yourself safe becomes less about equality of the sexes, and more about rights to survival.

It is still about equality of the sexes though. When Nile Swimmers began in 2007, it was only working with men; Sudan is a conservative Muslim country, and 'the idea of having men and women in the same place for something like swimming was inconceivable, not a possibility. Even the idea of having women swimming ... it's almost taboo,' Becky explains. So how do you even begin to help women, who are, after all, the ones whose daily lives, and all the concomitant duties, put them at risk? 'We had a women's course in 2015 because one of our local partners – the Sea Scouts – had a couple of very strong female leaders who had been pushing for more gender equality in the activities that the women were offered,' Becky says. These women are Mai Elemin and Beena Kashif, and they sound most excellent. 'They argued and argued and argued and argued and argued ... and eventually they were told fine, we'll do something in the classroom for the women,' but it had to be land-based. So Becky ran a drowning prevention programme entirely in the classroom. But once barriers started falling, pushed rigorously by Mai and Beena, they fell quickly. 'We were running a pilot pool lifeguard programme for men and straight away Mai's response was "Why aren't you running one for women?" So we said, "OK, we can run one for women."' Mai pushed again – they ran two. Becky recalls handing out certificates at the end of the first course, how one woman burst into tears 'and gave me this huge hug and said, "I never thought this would be possible for me, and look what I'm doing. I can take the certificate and go and get myself a job as a lifeguard."' This was really making a difference to these women's lives.

Mai kept pushing, the barriers kept falling. And just because this is not frivolous doesn't mean it's not fun. Becky was eventually allowed to take some women on a beach trip to practise their burgeoning rescue skills, along with two men to protect them and ensure they remained unseen. The party took a boat downriver to a really secluded beach, Becky and 'about nineteen women who were dressed in the most inappropriate swimwear I've ever seen. We're talking about loose jogging trousers. Then, a long-sleeve, high-neck T-shirt. Maybe a summer dress over the top to hide your shape. Then a hood, or a swimming hat, or a scarf over the top. It must have been ridiculously heavy. But they loved it, they thought it was brilliant.' It sounds like a riot, but pushing boundaries, little by little, is not without risks. 'If national security would have shown up at that beach and said "you can't have women in the water" then Sea Scouts, as our local partner, could have got themselves in a huge amount of trouble and they could have deported or jailed me,' Becky says. It certainly adds perspective – where our swimming suffragettes fought laws and attitudes and social mores, these women are swimming pioneers, and their fear is real enough.

I'm not a fan of the word 'empowerment', it's become tarnished by overuse. When it's used to sell high heels, it's time to retire the concept. But it's impossible to describe what Becky does in any other light. It's empowering. Becky is clear that it doesn't come from her or other international trainers. 'I think that comes from the people in Sudan,' she says, 'who come on the courses and ask for the course. They're saying "this is what we want, this is what we need" and we're going "OK, we can provide that". So we can step in and do that thing, and they can take it and build on it and grow it and do it their own way.' They're empowering themselves, I say, which gives it so much more meaning, more sticking power. 'It's also really, really good fun,' Becky reminds me, pulling me back from getting too hyperbolic.

I'm changing the phrase again. 'In front of every great woman is another great woman.' In front of Becky Sindall stand Mai Elemin and Beena Kashif. In front of them – women unknown. Women whose lives will change. Women who will take this story, make it their story and push it on to its next stages.

Chapter 15

Why Do Women Swim?

Why do women swim? Hell, as soon as waterproof mascara was invented in the 1940s, why would we not? Once we knew we could get in and our eyes could still be entrancing, there was really nothing to stop us.

Why do women swim? Maybe Annette Kellerman can give us the answer. 'I believe swimming is the best sport in the world for women,' she wrote in *How To Swim* in 1918. 'I am not trying to shut men out of swimming. There is enough water in the world for all of us. But as men can indulge in so many other sports where women make a poor showing or cannot compete at all, swimming may well be called the woman's sport.'

The reason she particularly wanted to encourage women into the water was not, however, about encouraging power or strength. The idea that women should compete with men, or 'try to ape men in athletic affairs', was, to her, a terrible proposition. A woman 'makes herself ridiculous when she attempts to compete man-fashion in man's sports'. Instead, her views are strongly aligned with the Pierre de Coubertin, 'aaargh women doing sports pull ugly faces shield me shield me' school of thought.

'To me,' Kellerman wrote, 'swimming is the one sport that can be absolutely "feminine" and yet be efficient,' and 'a woman has the chance to appear in all her gracefulness in swimming'. Her beliefs are predicated on the notion that the only ideal for women is the feminine ideal. 'The world cares very little about the beauty of its men,' she says – which is a) not true, cf. all Greek and Roman statues, and b) makes me feel a bit sorry for the better-looking man hopeful that his looks confer some status – 'and hence this advantage of swimming over other sports does not apply to the male half of humanity.' Swimming, for Kellerman, has everything to do with elegance and grace, with fine balance and poise, requiring the same skills at a top level as the expert piano player. 'Diving is a beautiful art for women,' she says, 'if a woman will … handle herself when coming up out of the water. Many women divers fail here; they make a fine dive and then come up choking and fuming and kill the beauty of the sport.'

Bloody spluttering women, ruining everything. They should do us the courtesy of drowning sooner than look imperfect or cross. Kellerman would surely have fallen on a waterproof mascara quick as a teenage boy on a fried chicken wing.

But are women swimming because actually, unknowingly, we're subconsciously expressing our innate 'femininity'? No. That's a no. And again, no. Kellerman supposes we're not competitive or aggressive, that we care more about grace than winning, that how we look is more important than a sense of achievement. But surely we now see femininity as one of the ways, not *the* way, people express their womanhood. A hundred years ago, Kellerman's views excluded the possibility that there might be an unfeminine woman. I think I might be saying 'Kellerman's views exclude ME'.

Of course, now that women can do all sports, her reasoning – that men get everything and they should leave one nice thing for the ladies cos we do it prettier – doesn't work. So why do women swim? Maybe there's some kind of magic at work. Maybe we have no choice, it's an urge beyond our control. It's all writ in the heavens. Some like to believe that the whole 28-day cycle to women's lives links us ineffably to the tidal pull of the moon, that it is in some unknowable way connected to our uteri, tugging us into the deeps where we … become as one with the water? Return to the place we belong? And maybe dreamcatchers really do catch dreams, and sticking pins in a doll really will hurt someone. It's all a bit 'sirens of the deep' for my tastes. You may as well believe your horoscope which, if you're a Gemini like me, you'll only take half seriously. (Someone once told me that my birthdate put me in a mysterious thirteenth sign, the Arachnid, whose people have special extrasensory powers. I loved the idea I was psychic, it made me feel special and, er, spidery. It made sense: after all, my grandmother had read tea leaves so it was just part of my heritage. I'd practically set off on a tour of regional theatres before I realised it's hokery-pokery, and it turns out I can read people's minds as successfully as I can spin a web with silk thread coming from my arse.) I'm not immune to the idea that we are all 'of the earth and of the water', particularly when I'm sat on a moonlit Cornish beach and have had a cider. But the pull of the moon no more controls my unconscious than Valerie Singleton does. So that's a no, for the magic reasoning, from me.

Maybe women swim because of evolution. The Aquatic Ape hypothesis had a brief moment of popularity in the seventies, as did devilled eggs and Sweet, and it posited that our human ancestors evolved from a semi-aquatic existence rather than a land-based one. It's why, the hypothesis says, we are bipedal, have subcutaneous fat but little hair, brains that thrive on nutrients mostly found in shellfish, and dolphin tattoos on our ankles if we're posh. Anthropologists generally don't back this hypothesis but I know some swimmers who like it, it resonates, helps them understand why they feel that water is their element. And it does go some way to explain the popularity of shaving your legs and eating whelks of a Saturday night in Margate. What it doesn't do is explain why women *in particular* swim; why, as ASA statistics show us, swimming is the second most popular physical activity for women and girls, beaten only by exercising in the gym. Statistics from the Great Swim series show that more women than men take part in their open-water events around the country, most of them aged between thirty-one and forty-five. It's only 1 per cent higher (50.5 per cent women as opposed to 49.5 per cent men), but even that slight skew sets it apart from any other sport.

The breakdown for Channel swimmers is different – only 36.5 per cent women. But given there's a massive difference in undertaking an intensive, exclusive (expensive) endurance event like the Channel and an accessible, attainable one-mile event like the Great Swim I'd suggest that's not surprising. Even now, in the early twenty-first century, women are socially conditioned to take themselves less seriously, to defer, to push themselves to the fore less often, to seek to work cooperatively, as well as still often being constrained by an extra set of duties. It is shifting but the woman who challenges that set of expectations is still the exception, and probably quite tired, what with a range of mountains to climb before they've even started. It makes sense that women are more likely to choose to do relay Channel swims than solo events, when you consider that we're less conditioned to compete, get more out of the team element and have less of a need to be individually validated.

It doesn't mean women are less capable physically – in fact, long-distance swimming is one of the few places where, under equal conditions, women's records beat men's. And while I scoff at Kellerman's ferocious promotion of femininity, and disparage her pronouncements that because she couldn't do it, then no woman would ever swim the Channel, she was bang on when she talked about this back in 1918. She wrote that 'comparing the average men and women who have had an equal amount of training, I believe that the women swimmers show superior endurance'. Women know how to 'husband their strength to better advantage'. It's not about that 'brute' strength, it's about our ability to sustain, and it's borne out with more recent statistics. As reported by Melissa Dahl in *New York* magazine, exercise researcher Beat Knechtle (and oh, the sheer perfection of that name, heading straight into my Top Ten) has studied thirty years of finishing times for the 28.5-mile Manhattan Island Swim, and says that, on average, the best women are 12–14 per cent faster than the best men. Open-water swimming expert Steven Munatones studied 12–13 amateur races over three years, and his figures show that while the elite men are still faster than the elite women, the average woman, the middle-of-the-pack swimmer, is faster than the average man. Moral: if you want to beat a man, be an average, amateur woman.

In almost every other sport, it's claimed that women will never match men's achievements because men have the physiological advantage; they are stronger, taller, and so on, 'but things really start to turn around when the two genders get in the open water', the Daily News of Open Water Swimming blog says. 'It does not matter if the women are competing against men in fresh water or salt water, calm water or rough water, cold water or warm water. When the distances are at least 10 km, the tables are turned. Women may not start faster, but they are able to sustain their momentum and are faster on average than men over the long haul.' It's only partly about husbanding our strength, though. Strength can only take you so far, according to Marathon Swim Foundation's Evan Morrison. 'In swimming, even compared to running, technique is very, very important,' he says. 'And there's no sex difference in the ability to develop a good swimming technique.'

As in the Manhattan Island Swim, so in the Channel. 'This differential [in timings] is most clearly observed,' the Daily News go on, 'when comparing the average crossings of the English Channel – where women are 32 minutes on average faster than a man. That equates to nearly a mile. In other words, the average woman has dried off, taken her lanolin off, downed a cup of coffee, taken memorial photos with her support crew, and is fully dressed before the average man finishes his English Channel crossing.' Maybe she's even had time to reapply her waterproof mascara for the photos.

So while fewer women attempt the Channel, those who do are faster? Ace. Beat Knechtle reckons it's down to one specific physiological feature: body fat. He notes that female open-water ultra swimmers have a higher percentage of body fat than their male counterparts – averaging 31 per cent to 19 per cent. This fat is mostly found in the lower body, so women's buoyancy is improved, which will help position in the water.

But talk of body fat makes me anxious. Even though there's a clear difference between body image and how we're physiologically constructed, I still find myself resistant to talking about women in terms of their fat distribution because it's too closely allied to how women are judged all the time. Too redolent of the weight discussions that plague us from the moment we look at ourselves sideways in a mirror and pull our stomachs in. And it seems that every time you talk about women swimmers, everyone has a view on their bodies, and they are often ridiculous. I've mocked early physicians for talking about womanly bits giving you a greater ability to float. Thrown a muffin wrapper at Kellerman and her talk of our 'beauty curves' and their concomitant fatty tissue helping us to float. Laughed gustily when one writer in the 1890s described how 'the smaller size of her lungs gives her much less buoyancy'. Waited with my beak open for some bread after the description from the *Penny Illustrated* in 1874 of lady swimmers 'expressly made by Dame Nature as to swim like ducks. Blessed with what may be termed, without profanity we hope, natural life belts.' But are they right? What's the deal? Do we actually have tiny lungs, and are boobs and wombs actually internal airbags? I could feel my scant anatomical knowledge slipping out of my grasp with every new explanation. I was getting more confused by the day. I needed to get some help, so I called a doctor. Dr Sheetal Sharma is a wonderful pal who I met through swimming and who swims at the exact speed I do. Over the course of many sea miles Sheetal has been to my left, because it's the side I breathe on, and that way I can see her every single stroke. As soon as we drop into the water from the boat, she'll move into position; it's terrifically reassuring to be in deep water with someone who will do that for you; it reveals the kind of unspoken kinship that water engenders. I emailed her. Our conversation went like this:

Me: I've spent my whole feminist life loudly declaring that we could do ANYTHING men can do, and I've slightly climbed down from that position and do reluctantly concede that men are usually stronger, taller, faster. BUT … in the water? Are we better suited to water than men? HELP paging Dr Sharma.

She replied, with a kind of patience that almost leapt off the screen: Physiologically, there are of course differences – women generally have more body fat (which helps you float). And their fat is generally distributed around the hips/ glutes (which perhaps helps legs stay up – a bit like a pull buoy) whereas men's fat tends to be intra-abdominal (think beer belly). So theoretically we are more buoyant because of our distribution of body fat. Breasts (when fatty, which not all breasts are) also ought to help with buoyancy.

Me (sounding increasingly like a teenage boy): I'm quite intrigued by the idea of fatty boobs. Is that just … a thing?

Can you alter that? Is it that if you're really fat everywhere it'll also be on your boobs?

Her: Breasts are hugely variable. Some are completely fatty and some are very dense (full of glandular tissue which is lumpy and sensitive to hormones so can be very sore) and most are somewhere in between. We often see women who have gained or lost a lot of weight in the three years between screening mammograms and their breasts have massively increased or decreased in size in the interim. So yes, if you're really fat you will also have more fat in your boobs.

I found myself looking down at my own small empty pockets of breast tissue, almost glad to have found another pair of excuses for a lack of speed. I emailed back, with somewhat of a wistful tone, 'What about wombs?' I was drifting on a small hopeful reverie that uteri were a benefit in some way, other than growing babies, obviously.

Her: I'm not sure that having a uterus has any physiological benefit in the water – not that I can think of or find any evidence of anyway.

OK. I felt I was on safer ground. We can discount the uterus, and being fatty-boobed might minorly assist buoyancy and the ability to keep warm in cold water, but Sheetal confirmed what Beat wrote, that it's the way fat is distributed around all women's bodies, regardless of breast size, that is most relevant in swimming. The physicians of yore might have actually been on to something, damn it. Apart from the feathers, we do resemble ducks. But I'd started by asking Sheetal a more general question – why do women swim? – and she answered first as a doctor: 'There is very little concrete physiological evidence that women are more likely to swim than men.' And then as a swimmer: 'My gut response is that the reason more women swim (recreationally) than men is it's more of a mental than a physical thing. And as we know, the swimming community is welcoming, friendly and non-judgemental. All of which are great motivators for women.'

Given that another statistic (this one in an Active People survey) showed that three times more women than men gave up swimming between 2005 and 2014, with body confidence cited by Sport England as a key factor, the message that the swimming pool is a non-judgemental place has clearly failed to take hold. You can't escape talking about women's bodies when you talk about swimming, because this is where bodies are exposed, and that's a fraught area full of internalised and explicit messages, made even more complex by different religious and cultural attitudes to women's clothing when they're swimming. If we're not told to cover, we're told to bare, told what size we should be and told whenever we fail to achieve an 'ideal'. An ideal somebody else has decided, at that. But once you start asking women why they *do* swim (rather than why they don't), their replies run contrary to that statistic. Women talk of liberation, of feeling free, of being able to celebrate what they can do, rather than worry about what they can't. This is a pool, after all; Simon Cowell is not sitting on the side marking you down for having a few stray pubes sticking out your cossie. You can be out in public without the public gaze. For women who do swim, the reality is that nobody is judging, except maybe themselves. In essence, the culture of women is toxic and demands that we hate our bodies, except here, this pool, is one place where we don't have to wade through that shit. The relationship we have with our bodies can somehow be turned on its head when we're swimming. Contrary to Kellerman's thesis that women swim because they could look pretty doing so, many women are swimming for the opposite reason – because we can dump all that self-conscious performance of our bodies and just get on with enjoying what we're doing. Sometimes, if we're lucky, that positive thinking in the water can be carried out back onto land too.

(It's not always such an idyllic picture. If the shower at your pool is colonised by loud teenage girls, I can recommend no quicker way to clear the area than strip off your costume. It will be met with total silence, unsubtle tortured glances and then a group departure. You can count one, two, three, as they disappear round the corner before the horrified gasping and ohmygods start. 'This is what old bodies look like, girls,' I want to shout with great cheer. 'This is pubic hair!' Don't worry, I've never done this, it would be wrong – even I have limits.)

In swimming you expose a lot of your*self* and for women like my friend Jackie you can do it 'without needing to talk about it'. This is not a therapy centre, there's no one waiting at the end of the lane earnestly asking 'And how does this make you feel?' In fact, nobody's asking anything of you at all. In the pool, 'nobody's relying on me,' Jackie says. 'I'm not having to organise any shit.' That's a feeling I recognise, that when I'm in the middle of the pool no one can ask where their socks are (please excuse me while I put my cross down for a second, it's rubbing my shoulders). 'It's basically meditation, isn't it?' another swimming friend, Jenny F, adds. Jenny F is a formidable triathlete and fell runner, a woman absolutely packed with life. She'd thought about my question 'why do women swim' when she was out for a run one morning. 'It's like meditation because it's all about controlled breathing,' she tells me. 'From a sensory point of view, you can't see much, there's no auditory distraction apart from hearing your breathing and feeling your breathing.' And as she recounts how she chants 'this is one this is one this is two this is two', going up and down the lengths, other women round the table agree – we all do that, we just never thought to call it meditation.

Isn't that why *people* swim, I say, rather than why women do? 'I have a constant stream of internal chatter that I can't switch off or silence until I'm in the pool,' Jenny F replies. 'I just don't think men have the same thing.' Blimey, you're a massive sexist, I joke. Michael Phelps, for instance, has talked about how he feels most at home in the water. 'I disappear,' he said, which is the same thing, isn't it? I suspect, though, that men would never call their internal voice 'chatter', it would have a far more important name. So now who's the sexist? But to have that constant 'internal chatter' shut up for a while … it's no wonder that Sheetal feels swimming has mental benefits. 'When you look at a group of runners,' Jenny F goes on, 'you generally know which woman will win, without knowing much else about them. But you look at a group of swimmers and you never know who's going to be the best.' The fact that there's no perfect 'type' for swimming is beautifully inclusive. And also, in the pool 'you don't get left behind', she says, and oh, that hits a nerve. You may get lapped but you don't tend to watch the receding backs of swimmers disappearing into the distance, that sense of COME BACK! WAIT FOR ME, oh God, I'll never catch up. It's a feeling I can't imagine Jenny F is familiar with, but I am.

For Jackie, the question of why she swims is a simple equation: 'If my body is working well and I'm feeling fit, I'm really happy.' It is the act of swimming as an emotional enabler. Water helps Jackie get strong, helps her feel strong, and feeling strong leads to feeling happy. This is so straightforward it feels almost radical, and is also such a basic requirement it should be top of a national curriculum for women. And it happens in an environment that Jackie describes as 'generous, kind and safe'. Like Jackie, Alice Gartland (whose blog A Lotus Rises celebrates women who love open-water swimming) has found that swimmers are 'her people, her community'. I've met a lot of women swimmers, I say to Alice, and the one quality they share is that they all seem so damn nice. 'Yeah,' Alice agrees. 'You seem to get really smart, intuitive, kind people who swim.'

I mentally throw my arms round the shoulders of my brilliant gang. Is this some kind of magical sisterhood? I wonder aloud. For Alice, a fizz bomb of positive energy, the answer is yes, the women she's met through swimming have been unequivocally inspiring, supportive and impressive. Reflecting after our conversation, I am the Grinch compared to her as I try to unpick this sense of sisterhood. Is it possible that I might meet a swimming woman I don't actually like? Has that happened already? And it takes a while, my picky fingers meanly turning over every stone to find the negative, but the answer is yes, it has happened. In the water, we mostly share what there is to share. But on land I will not feel solidarity with every single woman. (It's not a hill I'm prepared to die on, but I support the right of women to be absolute arses. I will be on that march yelling, What do we want? Mind your own business. When do we want it? Stop pestering us with these inane questions.) I can have a feeling of sisterhood without liking every woman. It's an impossible standard, we are not some homogenous mono-being. So maybe it isn't magic, after all. Maybe we just bring a hope for friendship to the water.

Bodies are a key part of my conversation with Alice, particularly hers, and particularly what swimming has done for it. 'I'd always been a really good athlete when I was younger, and that got lost in my late twenties and working in the city and all of that,' she says. Two things brought Alice back to the water (and then some – she's a very accomplished swimmer) but you don't need to go through what she has to reach similar conclusions about body confidence. Firstly, she was in a road traffic accident – knocked off her bike by one of those big bastard lorries on her way to work. Secondly, she was ending a relationship. She needed a place to recover from both of those things, and water became it. First, Alice got into running, but swimming provided a therapeutic space in the way running couldn't. 'To me, swimming you can enjoy much more at your own pace. It's your own body doing both things, but with swimming, if you want to float, you can float, [but] if you stop running, you're just standing still.' With swimming, I say, even if you're not moving, you're still being held in some way. 'And there's no pressure,' she replies. 'If you run, you're generally running somewhere but with swimming you don't necessarily have to be swimming anywhere.' The idea of not going anywhere is particularly appealing; this is not about 'moving forward', the state we're all supposed to be permanently in, it's just about moving. Or even not. Being still has its own merits. 'It's on your terms in a way,' Alice continues, and that thought, that you have the right to do things on your own terms, can be powerful and liberating for any person who has felt hijacked by everyone else's demands. It essentially comes from the same place that Jackie's relief that in the pool 'nobody's relying on me' does. 'I just think it's more peaceful,' Alice says. She found that it was 'kind to my body' at a time her body really needed some kindness. 'And I just really enjoyed it and it did become obvious that I had an affinity with water and I was like, this

287

is really, really cool.' It is cool, Alice's dynamic enthusiasm is cool, and infectious. Her relationship had taken its toll, stamped down her self-belief, but with 'every swim I did, I reclaimed my body, I reclaimed faith in my body. It was reconnecting with my body but it was reclaiming myself and swimming, that process of training and building my confidence and discovering … it just seemed incredible to me that I could do that.'

A relationship with her body is at the heart of Tanya Shadrick's feelings about swimming too. Tanya spent the summer of 2016 as the writer in residence at one of my favourite lidos, Pells Pool in Lewes. (File under 'dream job'.) She'd set up her stall under a tree using an old coffee table that had belonged to her grandad, adapted to hold the scroll of paper she was writing on; sat in a fixed spot like an ancient wise woman, a matriarch. Tanya began writing and returned to swimming at the same time, seeing the energies as similar. For her, both are about 'learning to be in your skin' as well as being, paradoxically, 'a way to slip the confines of my own skin'. Being at once more comfortable within it, and able to dip out of its restrictions. 'If you want to be a swimmer,' she says, 'you have to be able to swim in front of other people,' which is 'the same as writing'. A sudden near-death experience after the birth of her first child had propelled her both to write and to get back into the water. 'Like a surfer watching the sea for swell, I waited for my children to start school. Then I launched myself into the nearest outdoor water and began to keep the promise I'd made to myself: To live more vividly in my skin; to swim back to my young self who battled waves on a Cornish beach, using her home-made surfboard as a shield.'

Tanya writes eloquently about that 'young self', a nine-year-old enjoying the freedoms of a long country summer, her flip-flop-tanned feet, her status-symbol bruises, and how 'the coast and its cold water was the site from which my glorious girlhood sense of self-sovereignty sprang'. Sovereignty is usually a word we hear in the context of frothing about Europe or gaw' bless ya ma'am deference to the Queen (often from the same crowd). Tanya's use of the prefix 'self' puts it in opposition to Elizabeth Blackwell's earlier use of it, when she decreed that women's health is entirely in service to the higher purpose of motherhood. In Tanya's words one can feel the sense of personal ownership and self-sufficiency that resided, unexamined, in her young body. Nobody rules you, nothing has ruined you, you are gleefully, determinedly, yourself. That sovereignty was returning to Tanya thirty-three years later via Pells, 'the spring-fed pool in my small Sussex town'. Writing there, swimming there, brought it back to her. 'I'm kneeling here,' she writes, 'with the calloused feet of all but the most careful middle-aged women, have green and ropey varicose veins on the calf of my left leg (legacy of pregnancy), & the skin on the back of my hand stays raised and wrinkled long after I pinch it. And yet.'

And yet.

If we can't escape talking about bodies, we also can't avoid talking about age. Swimming is a sport that doesn't require you to be youthful. In fact, the opposite is true: water is great for old bones. Kind to bodies that need some care after a lifetime of active duty. Water softly holds the joints that make you go 'oof' when you stand up, buoys the bits that might otherwise be sliding towards the floor. Go to any swimming place and you'll find older women, the 'English matriarchs' as Caitlin Moran describes them, women with 'the kind of female bodies that speak of strength, life, happiness and not giving a fuck', women over fifty who are 'strong, calm, happy to be away from duty, and gravity'. Yes, 46 per cent of the participants in the Great Swim series are in the 31–45 age category, but there are twice as many women in the over-45 category than there are in the 16–30 category. Diane Nyad was sixty-four when she finally completed her historic Cuba to Florida swim. Irene Keel was seventy-three when she attempted the Channel. Mieko Nagaoka was the first hundred-year-old to complete a 1,500m freestyle swim – and she only took up swimming aged eighty-two as therapy for her knees. See? It's kind to old bodies, but dear God let us never underestimate what these old bodies can do. Just know you're never too old to swim.

As I listen to individual women talk about their reasons for swimming, another theme begins to emerge – that of grief. The idea that water is the safest place to express dark feelings that are too difficult to release on land. A place to mourn, where you can suspend the noise of life and dive into somewhere that can hold you in your deepest sadness. 'I was introduced to the [Hampstead] Ladies' Pond by my new partner who took me there on about the third day after I arrived in London,' a woman said, stopping me in my tracks as I heard her recount it on the radio. 'My partner had terminal breast cancer and she was always looking for somewhere to take her stress of being ill and the knowledge that life was going to end. She would just come here, and in these brown silky waters, would float and look up at the sky and I suppose it becomes like a feeling of ... forever.' During the illness, the ponds were a place of respite, and then her partner died and 'I came here to grieve. I learned to swim as a treat to cancel out the grief, or to wash it away. On the day I was at my lowest ebb, I came here and swam underwater into this fantastic green colour I've never experienced anywhere else. And the pond sort of lifted me to a point where I was floating and looking up at the sky and it felt like it was literally holding me in its arms. A very wise swimmer told me that water represents feeling and it will take whatever feeling you have and give you back a good one. And it's true, it does. I tested it out over years. I'm still testing it out, seven years on.'

After grief comes healing and recovery. Water helped heal Alice and Tanya. I am certain that Lynne Roper would encourage her friends into the water as a way of healing from their loss, to celebrate her life. The Venn diagram of my swimming friendships is a complex set of circles, and Lynne was at the centre of many of them. 'It's to do with tribes,' she said, echoing Jackie's and Alice's views on the strength of this community. Hers was the wild-swimming tribe; it was an integral part of who she was. Described by the Outdoor Swimming Society founder Kate Rew as an 'amazing, vibrant, clever, funny, forthright woman', she epitomised the sense of adventure and freedom that 'wild swimming' implies – her Twitter name was @wildwomanswims1 which speaks to her character. It was a passion she was knowledgeable about and that she absolutely revelled in sharing. Her obituary talks of how 'for her, wild swimming was never about how far or fast you swam, or how cold the water. It was always about the experience itself, and the connection with the environment.'

The desire to get in and swim was strong with Lynne to the end. I talked to her while she rested in a hospice in the last days of her terminal brain cancer. She had been swimming as far into her illness as she could, describing 'doddering down to the water' by her Devon home, but at the points in her treatment when she was stuck in hospital Lynne spoke of feeling 'desiccated', dried out, as if her very existence was sustained by immersion. 'The thing that's pulled me always is the water,' Lynne said. 'I felt trapped by this lack of life.' As if she was, in some way, a woman born to swim. Water was where Lynne could feel most fully like herself. Water equalled life.

This being Lynne, when we spoke she was making plans for a full-moon swim at her favourite spots of Mothecombe Beach and Bugle Hole, the kind of experience she had lived for, out in the wilds, taking risks, 'being adventurous'. She knew that were it to happen, it would involve loyal friends and paramedics, hoists and tows, a whole raft of paraphernalia that in the past she would have eschewed. But still she planned, full of enthusiasm, to get in. She didn't make that swim, but did get to a hydrotherapy pool where she was held in her element by friends. It was 'a party from which she didn't really wake up', Kate Rew said, and Lynne died a few days later. I'd talked to Lynne about how inspiring she was to a multitude of swimmers but 'we get so many good things from each other', she'd replied. 'It's to do with tribes, and passing it down the line.' After grief comes healing, and then grief again. For Lynne, passing it down the line didn't need to end at her death. 'People can swim and take me with them,' she said. 'Take my spirit with them.' This idea of a continuum, of teaching the ones coming after us, giving them skills, leading them towards possibilities – it's like we're a family. So yes, I'll take Lynne's spirit with every splash of salt water on my face, take it and pass it down the line.

Sometimes, the question 'why do women swim?' is answered when they describe *how* they swim. Comedian Josie Long talked of what she does, on getting in the water: 'Whenever I get into the sea or a lake or the river I do the same thing. I lie flat on my back and with my head in the water I take a few breaths that are always a little bit stressed. And I just take in the sky above me and the water around me. It's a moment where you're completely taken out of yourself and I have to do it every time. Every moment is that. Every moment is that.' This idea of 'being taken out of yourself' is one I recognise. It's about shedding all the baggage that makes you drag your feet on land and keeps your eyes looking down. About being a version of yourself outside all the noise of Smile! Cheer up! Hey, lady, over here! But if we need to lose ourselves in water, are our land-borne lives really so hard to bear? Are we saying we're not privileged? Because as I stand here in my meagre covering, toes curling over the edge of the pool, acknowledging that the hard work of my foremothers brought me to this freedom, I also see that they brought me to a position of privilege. This is privilege. It might not always feel like it on land, when women are sexually harassed or assaulted, paid less for their labours, dismissed as harpies if they argue or cunts if they refuse a man, where they can't even campaign to be president of the United States without being called shrews and much worse. It might not feel like privilege then. But if you can put on a costume – and maybe it only cost 29p from a charity shop – get into a pool without question, you're privileged. I am privileged.

Not every woman wants to swim – as Becky Sindall reminded me, people have other, more pressing issues to face. But take another look – the map is not always drawn as precisely as you might think. Divides are there where you might not want to see them. The ASA statistics show us that swimming participation is highest for British white women, and lowest for black and Asian women. Broadcaster Andy Akinwolere writes of how it's a ridiculous (and racist) stereotype, a misconception that black people can't swim, but it is often true that black people *don't* swim. Ethnic minorities in Britain are three times less likely than white people to know how, and he outlines cultural, social and economic reasons why that statistic stands.

Then there's French beaches in the summer of 2016, the ones that implemented a ban on the burkini on the beach, meaning that a small proportion of women were essentially forbidden from accessing a free public space. The message this ban imparted was wrong, because burkinis are not intended for terrorism, they're intended for swimming. A garment designed to give women more freedom became the very thing that took that freedom away, at police gunpoint in one instance. I don't support women being forced into any item of clothing, but neither do I support forcing it off them. A secularism riven with racism and misogyny is not one that I want any part of.

Then look at the 'what about the menz' hoo-ha if any pool offers women-only swimming. And in the United States, where public pools were racially desegregated in the sixties, but black kids still get trouble in white kids' pools. That is not my story to tell. It is the story of people like writer and swimmer Dionne Irving. 'Water is loaded for African Americans,' she writes in 'Living with Racial Battle Fatigue'. 'A horrible legacy surrounds water and the story of who has access to it is a story dominated by a violence that is intricately tied to the ongoing battle for civil rights and against racism in the United States. Who has access to water and who doesn't, who is allowed to swim and when and where and how that swimming takes place, connotes a privilege.'

This is not my story to tell. But this is our battle because it's no good having privilege if you only intend to keep it to yourself. Where is the value if you can't share it out? You have to be thankful first – I am thankful – and then make noise. It was not my story, but, still, I made a lot of gleeful and celebratory noise when Simone Manuel became the first African American woman to win gold in the 2016 Olympics for 100m freestyle. I did noisy dancing from my sofa because I knew that for the people whose story Simone *does* represent this was a massive thing. I made noise for the sheer delight on her face. 'I want to be an inspiration,' she said afterwards, 'but I would like there to be a day when it is not "Simone the black swimmer".' Let's make noise so that one day we'll have a multitude of Simones.

So why do women swim? Physiologically, we're good at it. It's a feminine art, even if we're not the feminine kind. It holds us, heals us if we need it, and some of us feel the moon's tidal pull. We can grieve here, get strong, meditate, take up space. Nobody asks us to fulfil another duty. We're safe. In a place with nowhere to hide, we are freed, in a way that men don't need to be freed. We can be ourselves, liberated. Every moment is that. Every moment is that. Why do women swim? Because we can.

Chapter 16

My Waterbiography (Part V)

One length becomes two. Two lengths becomes four. Four lengths becomes eight. This is one this is one this is two this is four. Before I knew it, I was swimming a kilometre every time. Then a mile. Before I knew it, I'd started going swimming quite often. I'd scan my diary, an actual book made of real paper, each week-per-page scrawled with fixtures and fittings, birthdays transcribed year to year in pen and 'lido?' in pencil on Wednesday and Friday or whenever I could fit it in. I'd write it in my diary so it became an immovable thing that no family commitment could readily budge off the page. Well, a less-movable thing. I'd go on my own, not just to be with friends. I started to think of people at the lido as my friends, even when I wasn't sure of their names.

They weren't sure of mine either, they'd approximate with any random J name which is fine because we all look a bit the same in a costume, cap and goggles. Jenny? Jackie? Judy? Jane? I was not ready to say 'I am a swimmer', I'd laugh it off with 'oh no, I'm just, you know, playing' but I was definitely a lido regular. I knew this because they'd recognise me at the gate and say hello. I had a preferred changing cubicle.

I become a member of Tooting Lido because it's much cheaper to have a year pass than shell out every day. I stopped showering at home. There was often a costume hanging on a heater to dry. I got a dedicated swimming bag, permanently ready by the front door and full of essentials that weren't really essential, like at Waitrose. My mental maths improved as I totted up how far I was swimming on any given day (eleven lengths of Tooting for a kilometre, eighteen for a mile) and how much each swim cost. The more you swim, the cheaper each one becomes. I became so casual about meeting celebrities while swimming (they love lidos) it was almost like they were people. As a for-instance, once, after a swim with some friends, we'd towelled our hair dry but none of us had a comb. At the exit, we bumped into Suggs from Madness. 'Nice hair, ladies,' he said. We shrugged, we weren't phased, it was just an everyday celebrity interaction of the kind I was getting used to. This was my life now. No biggie.

(This anecdote from my glamorous showbiz life will never win first prize in a celebrities-in-pools competition. That goes to my friend Sheetal, who went to Iceland to run a half-marathon. She was relaxing in a hot tub post-run and who was in it with her? Björk. It's almost unfathomable but there she was, in a hot tub. And when Björk went for a swim, Sheetal followed, a bit like a stalker might. What Sheetal did next might surprise you. She got in the next lane to Björk … and raced her. Without Björk knowing, of course, because saying 'Shall we have a race?' to Björk would be distinctly peculiar behaviour. They were both swimming breaststroke, and Sheetal won. I too would have raced Björk given the chance, and I was full of pride for my friend both in the idea and the execution. And yes, I did want to know what Björk was wearing. I was expecting fancy twirls of boiled felt springing off her shoulders or shoulder pads made of dead puffins at the very least. She wore a navy high-necked costume with a white accent stripe. Quite stylish apparently, but still disappointing.)

Then something happened. I started to take it … not seriously, that's not it, there was nothing serious in this. To be 'serious' suggests you see some higher purpose in it when I wanted to keep it light, not to think, not to analyse it in case it proved to be as delicate as a puffball: one small step and the whole shebang might go off. So I avoided thinking. But it started to become part of the fabric of my week. Without it, I didn't feel quite right. Two days could pass but by the third day my body just wanted to be in the water; I'd visualise it, get a bit antsy. I started seeing possibilities where none existed; we visited the V&A and I was tempted to strip off and swim across the tiny ornamental lake in their courtyard (don't bother, it's too shallow). 'Mummy needs to go to the lido,' I'd say by way of apology to anyone that I snapped at, including the postman. Writer Nell Frizzell calls it a 'swimmers' equivalent to thirst – a scratchy, headache need to get in the water' and a 'waterlorn feeling'. It sounds a bit like addiction, and it felt like the beginnings of one. Like it was ceasing to be a choice and starting to become a necessity. I started to swim a bit longer, more often, sometimes slowly, other times I could do a sprint. I didn't always feel like a fraud. I started to get confident. I thought blimey, I've changed, and I'd think back to PE at school and Mrs Hassle pipping her whistle and afford myself a little chuckle, flinging imaginary Vs at her when I'd jump in. I started to feel a different kind of happy.

Swimming had crept up on me, it was becoming part of my identity. Part of who I am. So I kept going. I was ambidextrous: where some lido-goers are purists and would sooner snip off their own hair than go to an indoor pool, sometimes I'd swim indoors. Then Crystal Palace was my favourite pool, for its length and expanses of glass and concrete and brutal beauty, even as it gets tired through age. Or maybe especially as it gets tired. But even here it felt mainly like exercise, whereas in a lido that was the last thing it felt. I've said before that the lure of a lido is qualitatively superior to an indoor pool, and we know this because every summer a glut of media articles appear about where to swim outdoors, particularly in London. It's as reliable in the schedules as a failing fondant is on *MasterChef*.

Outdoor pools were where I most felt at home, and while I had a growing loyalty to Tooting Lido in the way that other people have loyalty to football clubs, it wasn't an exclusive relationship. I saw other lidos wherever I went. Each was different – they were heated or not, salty or fresh, open all year or not, long and short, new or dilapidated. But I found some things to be consistent. They were all loved by a wide variety of people. As they were in the 1920s and 30s so they still are – the antithesis of elite. Ordinary but magical places of timeless mystery and romance and liberty and equality and fraternity and good lord before you know it we're all French and the living embodiment of Nigel Farage's worst nightmare. *Salut!*

Feelings cannot always be quantified. Not all the lido swimming happiness indices are measureable, some are intangible. The value added is not always the kind of thing you can put on a spreadsheet. There's more to it than clouds, and at the same time it's exactly as simple as that.

The mental health benefits of any kind of swimming anywhere are undoubtable. The chance to stretch out and get some semblance of freedom, to escape from the clatter-clatter of your mind into something approaching peace. The chance to fall, slowly and then twist and push off and sail through the water, the opportunity to hit that sweet spot where you can disappear momentarily. All that can happen in any kind of pool. Outside, without even trying, every swim is different. But inside, people work hard to try and make every swim the same. The lighting is controlled, temperature is controlled – indeed, pools shut down if boilers break and they fall below a prescribed level, even though that might be way above what some of us find comfortable. Some lidos have lanes, but they never seem as mean as the ones indoors that designate how fast we'll swim. Many of us will have experienced lane rage when people align themselves with the wrong one. If there was ever a job creation scheme waiting to happen, it is Lane Monitor in swimming pools. One day I'll be in charge and my fascist regime will employ thousands of these Lane Monitors parading up and down every poolside, their beady eyes and ready whistles looking for every slow person in the fast lane, or equally annoying fast swimmers in the slow. (In the evenings, these monitors will then be employed as Audience Height Regulators in theatres and cinemas. Tall people to the back, short people at the front. You're in a mixed-height couple? Tough. You can compare notes in the interval.) You see how this works? Inside I turn into a fascist dictator, while outside I'm so laid-back I'm practically horizontal.

Lidos might be basically the same as they've always been, but some of their benefits feel very pertinent to how we live now. We're constantly heated or cooled, our air is conditioned or treated, our communication is packaged, our feelings judged, our responses careful and monitored. We're protected from experiencing things elemental. We're wrapped in cotton wool, we're risk-evaluated, we're cossetted. We're health and safety-ed to the hilt. Swimming outdoors takes us firmly out of all that. Weather has remained the same, but our experience of it has been entirely moderated; we can shield ourselves or be shielded from it at almost every turn. We run from our cars to the shop; we turn the heating on the minute it gets chilly, we have different coats for every possibility (though we usually forget to bring them with us). In the lido, we start to experience the weather in all its eternal simplicity, in the way it has always been. Just for a flash of time, we take ourselves out of a controlled environment, and put ourselves right at the heart of the day, whatever it is flinging at us. It puts us back to our basic selves, where we can access things we've put away. The freedom of children before they know what's what. But this is not an unfettered freedom. There are literal boundaries. The level of bravery it requires is totally accessible even to a natural coward, not like in the scary sea. That's the liberty part.

And this all happens in quintessentially ordinary spaces. In a country absolutely riven with class and all its privilege, it's rare to find a place where what you do is the least relevant thing. Or who you are, beyond your corporeal self. You could arrive on a rackety bike or in an enormous Car of the Selfish, it's not relevant. You could be any rank or profession, a postie or a politician (though you might keep that quiet), it's not relevant. Nobody is better or worse, less or more valid, has fewer or more rights. I rarely have any idea of how my fellow swimmers live, who or what they sleep with, what they earn, any social signifiers at all because we're stripped of it; your baggage remains in the cubicle. And because our needs in this place are relatively few, and relatively cheap, it's hard to outstrip someone in terms of what you have, or to glean much about them based on the quality of it. Nobody has gold-plated goggles, or a swimming costume that costs thousands and makes the rest of us feel inadequate. I know who has an allotment because sometimes they'll bring surplus veg for anyone to take, but that doesn't say much about them beyond 'likes growing stuff'. There is no judgement in any part of it. Some people swim better, but that doesn't matter when nobody is saying 'you stay in the shallow end, this is not for you'. Of course some people cannot escape their innate twattishness; there is occasionally a Dick looking to grab your leg. But mostly this is an entirely level playing field. That's the equality part.

The fraternity part – perhaps better defined as 'community' – is as described by Lynne Roper and Alice and my friend Jackie. You meet people in lidos, you meet your extended tribe. Yes, those same people are also in indoor pools but a lido is a space specifically designed to encourage hanging out, whereas nobody would actively seek to spend a minute longer in Balham Leisure Centre than is absolutely necessary. It works – lidos are designed to create community, and they do. This is a testable theory – just rest a moment at the end of a lido length and somebody will chat to you. (It's often me. Hello.) On a trip to Haltwhistle pool with friends, I stopped and pushed my face to the sun for a second and a stranger next to me struck up conversation – she was inquisitive, we were new, we'd landed in her place and why not ask 'What brings you here?' It's a space where it's OK to do that. It was convivial, we shared stories of other pools we loved, of this one – she was keen to talk about what it meant to her. People are always keen to share their history of a place. I looked around and commented that it was all women in the water. Is that usual? I asked her. 'There's sometimes one or two men in,' she replied, 'but this is nice.' Let's call it accidental sorority.

We share this thing, this bond. The same sorority exists under the shower afterwards, where again the chances are high that somebody will chat to you. (It's often me here too. Hello.) There's an immediate but boundaried intimacy – it seems that lidos are as much about the boundaries as the freedom. In the shower I've admired tattoos and been impressed by luxury products, I've borrowed shampoo from strangers, and given it, I've chatted meaninglessly about nothing and had deep conversations about death and cancer and scars until the water's run cold. (There are few other situations where your first introduction to someone is naked in a shower after a shared experience. I say 'few', clearly I've taken that under advisement. But imagine if that was the way you met new colleagues at work. Imagine how the dynamics would shift, what this form of intimacy might bring. No, cancel that. Do not imagine it, it's a terrible idea and I apologise for it. I was momentarily made giddy by the fact I work alone.)

Beyond those three tenets of freedom, equality and community, there's the act of swimming itself. Obviously, this is where the differences in being indoors and outdoors are most apparent. In both spaces the arms swing over and the body rolls and reaches and the breath comes out underneath in a flotilla of bubbles. But outside, those bubbles might glimmer, take on a sharp clean outline via the glint of the sun, or appear like a transparent jellyfish under your hand, bringing you slamming into the moment. And as your head turns to take the breath in – outside, that becomes a variable too. It may be crisp with a tang of autumn air, or snatched out of the wind, or warm, too warm. The skin on your arm might shine as it's sunlit or goose-pimple in the cold. You might notice that a cloud has come over and dulled the clean reflections that batik and sparkle the bottom of the pool; you might only spot another swimmer by seeing their hulking shadow blurring those patterns. Inside or out, your hand could catch a malevolent clump of loose black hair or the plastic gusset-protector off a new costume as it twirls down through the water like a dropped sycamore seed. But outside, it also might catch a struggling bug or a leaf from a nearby tree that makes you realise it's autumn already. It might be the one point in your day that you fully notice the colour of the sky, or that raindrops delicately go tink-tink as they animate the surface like a thousand dancing Disney sprites. You'll also notice how hail stings hitting your back, or the day of the year that the sun has become high enough to be warm. You'll notice when the wind is hard and mean or when it feels like a fat gust pushing you along. You'll notice if there's been a lot of swimmers in the water on a hot day because it feels creamy and cloying. Sometimes the surface will look grey and dark, sometimes it's so bright you need shaded goggles. You'll know if there's thunder because they'll blast a siren to get you out of the pool and for a second you'll get an image of yourself getting fried by a bolt, cartoon-style. Sometimes even that simple thing will create memories – I'll never forget my fiftieth birthday when I raced to the lido for a swim in the hour that my son was in surgery for a mashed-up thumb and the thunder came when I'd only done two lengths and I had to get out. Damn it.

And finally it's exercise, which is, after all the rest, good for you.

So I kept going. Kept slinging my towel over the door of my preferred cubicle, doing my lengths, sometimes stopping for coffee and sometimes scuttling in and out not wanting interaction with a human. Even at the end of a summer, as the light hung lower in the sky every day and the front of my costume became a leaf-collecting scoop, I kept going. The days shortened and the temperature dropped, the water got colder. And colder. Then one day there was ice. Then one day it snowed. And I just kept going. Swimming outdoors. In my normal costume. In the snow. Without making any kind of a plan, I'd become a cold-water swimmer, and it was ace.

As the water got colder, my swims got shorter. Eight lengths became four. Four lengths became two. Two lengths became one and then I was down to widths. I started listening to my body like never before. I knew, for instance, that when I suddenly felt giddy with hunger even after a very short swim, I wasn't necessarily giddy with hunger, but maybe my blood was racing to my core to protect it from the cold and it was time to get out. I knew that after 200 metres in 8-degree water, or 30 metres in 2-degree water, my fingers would feel like sausages in a hot pan just before they burst. I stopped asking other people how far they had swum and judging myself against them because we're not the same. I did what I could do; other people did more, and less. I focused just on the very immediate and intense feelings.

How did I get in on an ice-air day? How do I? Stripping off your clothes is the hardest bit, but still, walking down the steps is hard. The key thing is not to think, and not to gasp at the shock of the cold although that's your instinct. Breathe. Breathe. Control. Sometimes I sing, a little operatically perhaps, because the cold is forcing the air out and there's space here for my voice to be loud if I want and nobody will care. I drop my knees to get my shoulders under – don't think – then start to swim, dipping my head like a reluctant bird, my face going further into the water with each stroke until I feel ready to put it right into the sharp cold. On the most frozen of days, the lifeguards push the ice away from the shallow end so we can swim across. Don't think. Then when my head is under I can hear the way the ice sings, creaking and sweet, and see flecks of it suspended in the blue thick water and it's like being in a weird indie film with a soundtrack by the Cocteau Twins. And the water will pinch my skin and slap slap slap sting me even though it's thick like treacle, but I swim across one side to the other, maybe also swim back if I can, and now my fingers are going to burst and my knees (no, I don't know why) are hot like boiling cakes and I'm smiling so hard my face might actually have frozen and that's enough. I grab the ice-clad steps to haul myself out, I look like a steaming lobster pulled out of the pan. And I realise that none of this makes it sound tempting at all but then I skitter to the sauna and maybe I laugh a bit out loud to nobody and I think, for the tiniest time, that I might be a goddess or an Amazon or a fantastic woman at least, and I feel very alive, totally alive, like I've never really felt alive before.

Feeling temporarily like a goddess must be addictive. Because as swimming became an addiction, so swimming in cold water did too. I started chasing the snap, the brisk yowch, the brain freeze, the way my fillings hurt. And the hunger. It makes you so hungry. And that inconsequential part of it can in itself be liberating in a life spent trying not to listen to hunger. I would sit in the sauna, a place for gentle contemplation and meaningful conversation, planning a meal disproportionate to the amount of 'exercise' I'd done.

If people find out you swim all year in an unheated lido, their reactions are predictable. 'You must be mad' is the most common – and what if I was actually 'mad'? What if I said yes, I have a mental health issue, thank you for noticing. Would that be satisfactory for them? I concede that setting out to become a cold-water swimmer would be the strangest of goals, but it was not something I decided to be. In reality, I think continuing to swim outside year round is a contributor to good mental health, not a sign that it's poor. It has physical health benefits too, like improved circulation and an activated immune system, things you might not notice but there they are. Nonetheless, thoughts of being mad do undoubtedly creep in, on the days when the rain pelts down and my parka is snug and I am about to strip to nothing and let all the warm out and submerge my silly self in freezing water. Then I do wonder why I'm doing it. But it's best not to dwell on the 'why' because that stops you doing things. And I don't want to stop myself doing this because I know, every time, that I'll feel so incredibly alive any minute now.

After 'you must be mad', then people say 'you swim in a wetsuit, of course', and again, the answer is (usually) no because to insulate myself is to precisely miss the point of being out there in the day feeling it to my literal core. If you want to stop yourself from feeling the very things that cold-water swimming makes you feel, swim indoors! And anyway, putting on a wetsuit would take longer than getting in, swimming, and getting out again. It's a bore. Then there's 'you're hardier than me', which is likely true, I am hardy. I was raised on English summer holidays huddled under a towel shared between four and storage heaters that came on at night and 'just put an extra pair of tights on' and did I mention I'm from the Midlands? But resistance to the cold isn't only available to a select group born within the sounds of the M6. Anyone can gain access to this club. It requires practice, it gets easier over time, but it won't happen if you don't start. And you need to plan ahead a bit. For instance, it's best not to start cold-water swimming in November. November is a tricky month, as is February when the temperature just never shifts, weeks on end stuck at 3. But March can be nice. In April you can see the thermometer creep up, there's often a cheeky hot week in April. May can be nice. June is nice. June, actually, is great. September is my favourite – schools go back. And October. December there's always a frisson. January full of good intentions. Oh, face it, it's all pretty good (apart from November and February maybe). The best way to do it is to start when it's nice, when it's not actually that cold, and just keep going.

Even temporary goddesses need to keep learning. There was something missing from my growing lexicon of swimming skills, one that some people have been able to do since they were seven. I learned to dive. If you've been diving since you were seven, you have no idea of what it holds for a woman in her middle age. There is so much potential for wrong, pain, humiliation and fear. Actual physical pain, not just the mental anguish of feeling inferior because a seemingly simple activity was totally beyond your uncooperative limbs. Not for me the casual running up to a pool with a tinkling laugh and throwing myself in in one elegant swoop. I was more in the 'casual running up to the pool, my brain yelling no, no, you can't, stopping right on the edge, teetering and falling clumsily in by the sheer force of forward movement' school. I was on a swimming holiday in Majorca, and people were practising their tumble turns. I was really giving it some, focusing dead hard on the task, but every time it went wrong. I couldn't tell which way was up, my limbs would all go in a bundle and be as good as liquorice boot laces. I'd squirm round once my feet had made contact with the pool wall (*if* my feet made contact with the wall) and for a second my world would be a blue and bubbly mess. I'd surface in a random direction with an enquiring grin in a face of pain, no idea of what I'd done. Was I even close? How about this time?

So when teachers Mike and Sarah suggested that we did some diving, I had to say 'I can't'. When you've spent years saying that, it's firmly ingrained in your psyche. And if you never try, then you never fail. But I thought, oh Christ, let's give it a go, it has to be better than my tumble turn, yes? So I clambered to the side and stood, my toes curling over the edge, as instructed, my head down between the arrow of my arms, legs bent, jelly legs and jelly stomach, flipping with nerves. I tried not to listen to the voice in my head saying I can't, I tried to get into character. The character of a woman who can, who has physical confidence, whose arms and legs behave in the right way. On the count of three I pushed off, flew through the air and hit the water. It didn't feel awful.

It could have been all right. I surfaced with an inquisitive look – was that it? That was it. I'd done it! I felt amazing, buoyed, a success. Sarah showed me the photo and I could see this character doing a perfect dive, like she'd been doing it all her life. This successful woman was me, and I was thrilled. What the hell had been wrong with me, all those years? Idiot.

I can dive! Elated, I tried it again. Horrible stinging belly flop, my goggles forced wonky on my face. Idiot. Happy idiot. One photo to cherish, looking for all the world not an idiot at all. And at least now I know that if I was in a life-or-death chase with Nazi storm troopers and I had to dive off rocks into the water to escape, there's a chance I could do it. A chance they might even be impressed.

Once you can dive, and you've become accustomed to swimming in freezing water, and you've done a 3.8k swim in the Thames and a 5k crossing between Greek islands, what comes next? The Dart 10k, the swimming marathon. One late-summer euphoric evening a bunch of us decided we'd do it together, yeaaaaah, and drunk-group-think translated into me sat in front of my computer very early one horrible February morning, manically refreshing the Outdoor Swimming Society's race entry page while simultaneously texting Sheetal in Newcastle who was doing the same thing. After a frenetic half an hour of sites crashing and credit cards not working and dogs barking and texts overlapping and what if everyone else gets a place and I don't … Success. We all got in. Now all we had to do was nothing, for a while.

It was a couple of months before I could face opening the email with the training schedule, and began complex negotiations with myself about how much I'd actually do. My inner grumpy teenager began discussions with my inner anxious swot. And when self-doubt and fear slightly subsided, I thought I should crack on with more prevarication, the sorting out of a schedule with my friend Jackie. It's good to train with a person, it stops that inner grumpy teenager getting the upper hand. Four months of training followed, some of it hard, mostly in a lake in Kent. Long swims, going round the lake once more each time. Getting out covered in ducky slime and rinsing my face off under a measly tap but still smiling. Absolutely cherishing the coffee from a flask on a bench afterwards. Sometimes I'd be right at the far end of the lake, away from the small jetty where the rescue kayak was moored, and I'd think, 'No one can see me. What if I just let go now and sink to the bottom? How long before my body would be found?' and other such cheering thoughts. I think my inner grumpy teenager might be a goth.

I smelled permanently of water that had stood too long. I had sore shoulders, a tired body, so hungry. I ate industrial vats of home-made fudge that I insisted my daughter make, practically pushing her into the kitchen so she could 'feel involved'. COME ON, FEEL INVOLVED. Texts would fly between us all – how much have you done? Have we done enough? Can I do less or more? I felt anxious as the bigger swims approached, the first time I'd swim 6k. 7k. 9k round and round a lake. Mind-numbing. I got given an underwater iPod, wore it to make the lake less boring and jumped right out of my stroke listening to a friend's podcast as her raucous laugh broke through, right into my head. I became something of a snack expert, my *Mastermind* specialist subject. 'You have two minutes on swimming snacks starting ... NOW.' I ate a lot of peanut butter and found ways to incorporate it into every meal. I lay awake dealing with The Worries. I might be last. (So what? Someone has to be.) I might not be able to keep going. (Does that really matter?) (Yes, a bit, but it won't last.) I might drown. (I won't. And if I do, I will get that statue at Gracefield Shopping Centre with a commemorative plaque saying 'She made a lot of fuss but at least she tried. How about YOU?')

Then flash, the day was done, the swim was swum and I had learned things. That it's much better to be in a long swim than to be training for one. That when you're 7k along and feeling a bit 'that's enough', seeing your friends' lovely goggled faces will propel you to the end. Not to listen to other people's anxieties beforehand because they might rub off. That the hot chocolate at the end will be the best hot chocolate you'll ever drink in your life. That I can actually swim 10k in 13-degree water, and that I'll even enjoy wearing the mandatory wetsuit. Because once you've put in the work, once you're in the water, what are you going to do? Just keep going. 'The thing I enjoyed most was walking down through the crowd,' says Jackie, recalling the bit where we became part of something, we swimmers heading to the river, snapping on our hats and fiddling with our goggles, our kinfolk waving and wishing us luck. Squash the flips of anxiety down: breathe. Breathe. Control. Keep walking – and we were in the water, we were off and that was it. We were part of something.

'The swim is the least interesting bit. It's all the rest,' Jackie says. The swim as an enabler. That is, in the end, the point of it all. Not just the thing itself, the act of moving my arms and kicking my feet. All the rest. Indoors and out, lake or river or sea, fresh water or salt, all the things that swimming has gently handed me, and I've snatched from it like a greedy child. I swim for the healing, the health, the confidence. The adventures, the risks, the fun. The way it feeds me, and at the same time clears my head and fills it with a cloudy bit of peace. The enrichment, and the escape. The community, the friendship, the camaraderie. Paradoxically, being alone. This has only ever been about me, all any one of us ever brings to the pool is ourselves, alone. To focus on my brain and body, my thoughts and feelings, is that not incredibly self-centred, Jennifer? How dare I? I dare. Watch me. I dare.

I swim because it's part of my identity now. I swim for the feeling of freedom in my own body, for that self-sovereignty Tanya Shadrick describes, all the better because I can get it without having to change my body a jot. I can be imperfect in here, and that's bliss. I swim to be nourished. I swim for the chance to travel somewhere different every time and yet be ten minutes from home. I swim to be stripped right back, cleared out of all the extraneous life bobbins but never left feeling empty, no. I swim as myself. I feel pleasure in that. I feel pleasure in my physical abilities, though they're not that much and I'm constantly learning. I feel able to say 'look at me!' which is actually not easy at all. I try not to feel stymied by what I can't do, but I'm not always successful in that. I try to feel positive but sometimes I'm full of envy and spite. I celebrate what other people can do, whether it's Hilary Jennings ruling the plunge or Jackie Cobell in the Channel. I swim for a sense of possibilities. It's possible one day I'll be able to undulate and do butterfly. It's possible one day I'll tumble and turn. Beyond it all, though, I'm glad I swim because it's made me some absolutely bostin' friends. I think that's the most important thing.

I've kept all my Tooting Lido annual passes and on my work wall there is a row of them, each year a different colour and a new photo. It's a memento to haircuts and of how things change. At the start, there were three passes each year (one for me and one for each of my two children), then there were two as the older one peeled away. Now it's just me and that's fine. Sometimes I'll go because I need a shower. Sometimes in summer I long for it to rain so the pool will empty. Sometimes I wish Björk was there so I could secretly race her. I have never regretted a swim. I've gone there furious and I've cried in my goggles, but I've never got out feeling worse. Always better. Swimming has made me happy.

So for that happiness I'll stand on the side of whatever body of water is in front of me, and thank the women who came before. I'll thank every single swimming suffragette who fought on my behalf, every swimming pioneer who broke the mould and broke the ice and stuck it to the man. I'll thank Annette Kellerman for being daring with her costume and Jemma Golby for her knitting skills. I'll thank Elizabeth Eiloart and Miss Emma Dobbie and Aunty Mary. I'll swim with the stories of Hilda James and Fearne Sparke and Beth French. I'll relish the friendships and enthusiasms of all the women that swimming has brought into my life. I'll take the spirit of Lynne Roper into the water with me. And I'm ready to say it. My name is Jenny, and I am a swimmer.

Bibliography

Ayriss, Chris, *Hung Out to Dry: Swimming and British Culture* (Lulu.com, 2013)

Bier, Lisa, *Fighting the Current: The Rise of American Women's Swimming, 1870–1926* (McFarland & Co., 2011)

Carter, Neil, ed., *Coaching Cultures* (Routledge, 2011)

Daniels, Stephanie, & Tedder, Anita, *A Proper Spectacle: Women Olympians 1900–1936* (ZeNaNa Press, 2000)

Davies, Caitlin, *Downstream: A History and Celebration of Swimming the River Thames* (Aurum Press, 2015)

Davies, Caitlin, *Taking the Waters: A Swim Around Hampstead Heath* (Frances Lincoln, 2012)

Gibson, Emily, *The Original Million Dollar Mermaid* (Allen & Unwin, 2005)

Gordon, Dr Ian, & Inglis, Simon, *Great Lengths: The Historic Indoor Swimming Pools of Britain* (English Heritage, 2009)

Hargreaves, Jennifer, *Sporting Females* (Routledge, 1994)

Hobsbawm, Eric, ed., *The Invention of Tradition* (Cambridge University Press, 1983)

Holt, Richard, *Sport and the British* (Clarendon Press, 1989)

Kellerman, Annette, *How To Swim* (George H. Doran Company, 1918)

Krasnick Warsh, Cheryl, & Malleck, Dan, eds., *Consuming Modernity* (UBC Press, 2014)

Love, Christopher, *A Social History of Swimming in England, 1800–1918* (Routledge, 2008)

McAllister, Ian, *Lost Olympics: The Hilda James Story* (Amazon, 2012)

McCrone, Kathleen E., *Playing the Game: Sport and the Physical Emancipation of Women, 1870–1914* (Routledge, 1988)

Parr, Susie, *The Story of Swimming* (Dewi Lewis Media, 2011)

Smith, Janet, *Liquid Assets: The Lidos and Open Air Swimming Pools of Britain* (English Heritage, 2005)

Sprawson, Charles, *Haunts of the Black Masseur* (Vintage, 1993)

Vertinsky, Patricia A., *The Eternally Wounded Woman* (University of Illinois Press, 1994)

Walton, John K., *The British Seaside: Holidays and Resorts in the Twentieth Century* (Manchester University Press, 2000)

Williams, Jean, *A Contemporary History of Women's Sport,* Part One (Routledge, 2014)

Woolum, Janet, *Outstanding Women Athletes* (Oryx Press, 1998)

Worpole, Ken, *Here Comes the Sun* (Reaktion Books, 2000)

The Gentlewoman's Book of Sport (Pushkin Press with the London Library, 2016)

Online articles and blogs that I found useful:

Dahl, Melissa, 'The Obscure Endurance Sport Women Are Quietly Dominating', *New York* magazine, September 2016

Day, Dave, 'A Modern Naiad, Nineteenth century Female Professional Natationists', 2008

Day, Dave, 'Kinship and Community in Victorian London', History Workshop Journal, 2011

Day, Dave, 'What Girl Will Now Remain Ignorant of Swimming', Women's History Review, 2012

Fletcher, Jennie, 'Aquadynamics and the Athletocracy', Costume Journal, 2012

Irving, Dionne, 'Living with Racial Battle Fatigue', lithub.com, July 2016

Nevinson, Margaret, 'Women free to swim without fear of arrest', *Guardian* archive, July 1930 (the article that set this whole book off)

Consumingcultures.net

The Daily News of Open Water Swimming

Alice Gartland's blog: A Lotus Rises

Keith Myerscough's blog: Sportinglives.blogspot.co.uk

Tanya Shadrick's writing is at TanyaShadrick.com

Acknowledgements

I spent too long in church as a child to be comfortable around the word 'blessed'. I choose, instead, to say that I'm lucky. I'm lucky to have been generously supported by family and friends and some complete strangers in the writing of this book and I owe some thanks.

So thank you, to Dave Day for kindly giving me access to his work, Eleanor McDowall and Josie Long for their help with 'Field Guides' (Radio 4), and to Margaret Simmonds, Liz Street and Mark Street for help with records. Thanks to Rose Collis, Tracy King, Sarah Ditum, Sian Norris, Hilary Jennings, Jenny Featherstone, Helen Gilburt, Tara Duffy, Kate Rew, Nando Farah, Caitlin Davies, Carl Reynolds and Catrin Rowlands. To everyone who gave their time for interviews or offered contacts, advice and wise words, particularly Tanya Shadrick and Alice Gartland.

Thanks to Lucy Petrie for doing Dover with me, and to Becky Milligan for the Serpentine jaunt. To Sheetal Sharma for excellent breast contributions and for swimming on my left. To Mike and Sarah Johnstone of Streamline Swims for eventually getting me to dive. To Jemma Golby for my utterly fantastic knitted swimsuit that I shall treasure forever.

When I disappeared into this project, I really appreciated friends who popped in every now and again to check up on me. Thank you Shelley Silas, for sending me a positive message every single Monday. Thanks to Nina Davies, Wendy Lee, Rachel McCormack, Justin Lewis and Dayna Winer. Thank you all of DT. Thank you to John O'Farrell for the conversations and Lee Randall for the links.

I am lucky to have a great agent, Becky Thomas of Johnson & Alcock, and a fantastic editor, Charlotte Atyeo at Bloomsbury. I owe special thanks to Jackie O'Farrell for her enthusiastic support, advice and always being up for a swim. Finally, thanks to Mark for being Mr Landreth, and to Charlie and Izzy for being such superb cheerleaders.

Index